AF736952

The Theory and Practice of Positive Neuropsychology

This pioneering work focuses on positive psychology and wellbeing from a neuropsychological perspective. It bridges social, emotional, and psychological principles to explore the burgeoning field of positive neuropsychology.

Combining academic theory and clinical practice, it delves into foundational principles, assessments of neuro-cognitive health, evidence-based interventions, practical applications and real-life case studies, and the profound implications of positive neuropsychology in educational contexts. At the intersection between neuropsychology and positive psychology, this book advocates the recent shift toward recognizing the paramount importance of exploring the positive facets of neuropsychological functioning, rather than the historical focus of neuropsychology on ameliorating cognitive deficits and addressing neurological disorders.

A must-read for academics, clinicians, and students in neuropsychology, clinical psychology, and positive psychology, this book is also invaluable for anyone interested in enhancing cognitive wellbeing and resilience.

Dr K. Jayasankara Reddy is a leading expert in Health, Cognitive Neuropsychology, and Neuroscience, currently serving as Professor of Neuropsychology/Cognitive Neuroscience and Dean of the School of Social Sciences at Christ University, Bangalore, India. With a deep commitment to advancing the field, Dr Reddy integrates his research and practical experience into his work, which is vividly demonstrated in *The Theory and Practice of Positive Neuropsychology*. His scholarly contributions focus on the intersection of cognitive processes and mental wellbeing, and he is recognized for his innovative approach to applying neuropsychological principles in positive contexts.

The Theory and Practice of Positive Neuropsychology

New Perspectives on Nurturing Wellbeing

K. Jayasankara Reddy

Routledge
Taylor & Francis Group
LONDON AND NEW YORK

Designed cover image: © BlackSalmon via Getty Images

First published 2025
by Routledge
4 Park Square, Milton Park, Abingdon, Oxon OX14 4RN

and by Routledge
605 Third Avenue, New York, NY 10158

Routledge is an imprint of the Taylor & Francis Group, an informa business

© 2025 K. Jayasankara Reddy

The right of K. Jayasankara Reddy to be identified as author of this work has been asserted in accordance with sections 77 and 78 of the Copyright, Designs and Patents Act 1988.

All rights reserved. No part of this book may be reprinted or reproduced or utilised in any form or by any electronic, mechanical, or other means, now known or hereafter invented, including photocopying and recording, or in any information storage or retrieval system, without permission in writing from the publishers.

Trademark notice: Product or corporate names may be trademarks or registered trademarks, and are used only for identification and explanation without intent to infringe.

British Library Cataloguing-in-Publication Data
A catalogue record for this book is available from the British Library

ISBN: 978-1-032-76272-2 (hbk)
ISBN: 978-1-032-76265-4 (pbk)
ISBN: 978-1-003-47781-5 (ebk)

DOI: 10.4324/9781003477815

Typeset in Sabon LT Pro
by codeMantra

Contents

1 Unlocking the Power of Positivity

A Neuropsychological Perspective

Positive neuropsychology is an emerging field that integrates the principles of two of the important domains in psychology. It is a collaboration where the principles from positive psychology are integrated into the study and practice of neuropsychology (Randolph, 2018). In the past decade, there has been a growing body of research in the field of positive psychology. Mental health professionals emphasized positive psychology, which emerged from schools of humanism and existentialism. Positive neuropsychology, adopted from positive psychology, represents a paradigm shift in the field of neuropsychology, moving one's approach from deficit-based to strength-based (Randolph, 2018). The primary focus of positive neuropsychology is to promote cognitive health, healthy aging, and wellbeing through a strength-based approach rather than focusing on one's cognitive deficits (Pimental, 2017).

Positive Psychology

Martin Seligman and Mihaly Csikszentmihalyi, often considered the founders of positive psychology, define it as "the scientific study of positive human functioning and flourishing on multiple levels that include the biological, personal, relational, institutional, cultural, and global dimensions of life" (2000). This multidimensional approach emphasizes on allowing mental health to thrive and is focused on the affectual enhancement of the individual rather than a clinical model of the individual experiencing affectual distress, cultivating happiness, emotional wellbeing, satisfaction, and contentment to lead a fulfilling and meaningful life. The concepts of traditional psychology focus on a biomedical or biopsychosocial approach toward pathologizing the life of the individual with a focus on identifying signs and symptoms of clinical distress, while the approach of positive psychology leans toward the improvement of the life of the individual outside the traditional clinical model focusing on the improvement of the whole person outside the clinic space. Thus, the broad goal of positive psychology is to restore balance to psychological science through research and practice aligned with increasing positive subjective experience through empirical methods and to increase wellbeing and improve resilience against the development of psychological

DOI: 10.4324/9781003477815-1

illness. Positive psychology is able to utilize therapeutic methods that help place individuals within experiences of the past, present, and future while using traditional outcome measures such as scales and novel methods from the realm of neuroscience to establish human wellbeing. The orientation envisioned by Martin Seligman places constructing competency rather than correcting weakness, and this model has been effective at exploring human tendencies such as courage, optimism, perseverance, ethical leadership, and so on to provide a buffer against the development of mental illness.

The Evolution of Positive Psychology

The origin of positive psychology dates back to the times of Aristotle, when the concept of eudaimonia was explored. It means "flourishing" or "living well," laying the groundwork to study positive human emotions (Seligman & Csikszentmihalyi, 2000). There were various techniques practiced in Eastern countries, like mindfulness and meditation, in the times of Buddha, which are now core components of positive psychology (Allen et al., 2021).

Later, the humanist psychologists Abraham Maslow and Carl Rogers emphasized human growth, wellbeing, potential, and flourishing. Abraham Maslow coined the term "positive psychology" in 1954 in his book *Motivation and Personality* (Maslow, 1954). Martin Seligman, in 1998, became the president of the American Psychological Association (APA) and chose positive psychology as his domain. This was a huge turning point in the field's recognition and growth (Seligman & Csikszentmihalyi, 2000). The history of positive psychology begins with the recognition that psychology traditionally focuses on understanding and treating mental illness. However, in the late twentieth century, there was a shift toward studying positive aspects of human experience, such as happiness, wellbeing, and optimal functioning. The work of humanistic psychologists like Abraham Maslow and Carl Rogers, who emphasized the significance of personal development and self-actualization, had an impact on this shift. Positive psychology as a distinct field emerged in the late 1990s, with Martin Seligman serving as a key figure in its development. Seligman called for a science of positive psychology that would study human strengths and virtues in addition to weaknesses and pathologies.

This marked a significant departure from the traditional focus on psychopathology in psychology. The importance of positive psychology in promoting a more balanced and comprehensive understanding of human nature. By studying positive emotions, character strengths, and optimal functioning, positive psychology aims to enhance the wellbeing and quality of life for individuals and communities (Marujo & Neto, 2016).

Neuropsychology

Neuropsychology is a specialized field within psychological sciences that focuses on understanding the relationship between brain and behavior. It examines how the structure and functions of the brain impact cognitive processes, emotions, and various behaviors such as everyday work and complex cognitive tasks. Neuropsychology deals with assessing and treating individuals with various neurological cognitions, brain injuries, and cognitive impairments and tries to understand how changes in the structure and function of the brain affect one's behavior.

By integrating the learning of psychology, neuroscience, and cognitive science, professionals in this field use a variety of tests and assessments to evaluate the presence and severity of cognitive dysfunctions in memory, attention, language, and executive functioning to develop interventions and strategies to improve cognitive functions, manage symptoms, and enhance overall quality of life.

The Evolution of Neuropsychology

Vesalius started the study of neuroscience in 1514. He conducted careful observations on brain anatomy and cell doctrine. He introduced anatomical theaters for students and teachers and gave diagrams of human anatomy. He belonged to the time when empirical science was given importance. After the age of empiricism, a new discipline of mind-body dualism emerged. Descartes, who first proposed the idea of the mind and body as distinct, led it. He believed that the pineal gland was in charge of all mental processes. He explained the separate functions of both mind and body. Phrenology came into light in the 1700s when Gall introduced the concept of localization. He believed that each part of the brain has different organs and is responsible for a specific basic psychological trait. Phrenologists made numerous assumptions about the size, shape, and bumps of the skull. They analyzed certain traits based on the shape of the skull in men and women. They believed that men are more self-reliant and women are more independent.

In the nineteenth century, Broca and Wernicke came up with localizations of the brain with more research and scientific proof. The works of Broca (1865) and (Wernicke, 1969) exemplify this approach. Neuropsychology as a discipline began to flourish when, instead of detailed observations, behavior was quantified according to psychometric techniques. Thus, the "Period of Neuropsychological Localization" began about 60–70 years ago (Ruff, 2003).

Neuropsychology was formalized as a discipline with the publication of the first book *Fundamentals of Human Neuropsychology* in 1980 by Kolb and Whishaw. Consolidating the knowledge of research and practice into a structured framework, this book was marked as a significant milestone in the field's development. Over time, neuropsychology evolved into a multidisciplinary field of science, integrating principles and findings from various areas of study such as evolution, neuroscience, cognitive sciences, psychology, anthropology, and archaeology to deepen our understanding of brain function and behavior.

Key Concepts of Positive Neuropsychology

Neurodiversity

The concept of neurodiversity, while gaining significant traction in recent decades, has a rich history intertwined with the evolution of disability rights and understandings of the human brain. It all started at the roots of the disability rights movement in the 1970s when the medical model of disability viewed differences as deficits requiring cures. Disability rights activists began advocating that societal barriers create the disabling environment and not the individual themselves. This movement was anchored as a crucial foundation for neurodiversity as a form of human variation rather than a medical condition.

Judy Singer, an Australian sociologist and autistic self-advocate, coined the term neurodiversity in the 1990s. She challenged the view of autism as a pathology and emphasized that neurological differences are a natural part of human diversity. The term later gained popularity due to Harvey Blume's article in *The Atlantic* (Blume, 2019). This movement aimed at promoting acceptance and inclusion of all individuals regardless of their neurological differences. It challenges the traditional views of neurological conditions as disorders and instead advocates the understanding and appreciation of the unique strengths and perspectives that neurodiverse individuals bring to society.

In the present times, there are ongoing debates about the word with regard to autism (attention deficit hyperactivity disorder, ADHD), and dyslexia. Some advocate for a broad definition encompassing diverse neurological and cognitive variations, while others prefer a narrower focus on specific conditions. It encourages inclusive and non-judgmental language and recognizes the importance of respectful communication with a focus on identity-first or person-first language. The neurodiversity movement continues to advocate for the acceptance, support, and inclusion of individuals with various neurodevelopmental conditions. It emphasizes neurodiversity strengths, challenges the deficit-focused narrative, and promotes understanding of the unique contributions individuals with neurodiversity bring to society. Neurodiversity came into the light to help people in various aspects, such as wellbeing, strength, and differences, and to help them shield themselves from social stigma. Neurodiversity and positive neuropsychology share a common ground in their focus on understanding and appreciating the rich spectrum of human experience beyond pathology. Both areas of study challenge the traditional views that pathologize neurological conditions and emphasize on accepting the unique strengths and abilities of individuals on the spectrum.

Resilience

Resilience is not a singular concept; it is a dynamic process of adapting well in the face of adversity, trauma, and significant challenges. The APA defines it as "the process of adapting well in the face of adversity, trauma, tragedy, threats or even significant sources of stress."

The term resilience gained the spotlight in the scientific community in the 1970s. Emmy Werner was often credited for coining the word during her research on children in Hawaii. The understanding of the concept of resilience has changed over time, and in the past, it was only seen as bouncing back from adversity. However, this has changed eventually.

In the present time, resilience includes various processes. Individual characteristics include personality traits, coping mechanisms, and social skills that influence the person's resilience in different situations. Protective factors such as optimism, self-esteem, and supportive relationships can infer resilience. The severity of the adversity also plays a role.

Importance of Resilience

Resilience enables individuals to cope with stress and continue moving forward despite the challenges they face. It is important to develop personalized coping mechanisms that work best for everyone. As there are many reasons, as seen above, that can influence resilience, it is important to be aware of oneself. This could include mindfulness exercises, self-care, and improving healthy relationships (Macía et al., 2021). Taking care of oneself is very important as it can impact the emotional wellbeing of the individual; prioritizing sleep, a healthy diet, and regular exercise are some of the basic tasks a person can take care of to maintain wellbeing (Luis et al., 2021).

Resilience can help you grow from challenges and make a person ready for future challenges. Viewing challenges as opportunities for learning and growth instead of setbacks can improve a person's optimism. Breaking big tasks into small tasks can improve a person's work efficiency and decrease workload and stress. Resilience is not just about bouncing back from setbacks but includes building adaptability and capacity to be able to navigate life's challenges more effectively.

Cognitive Reserve

Stern, in 2002, introduced the concept of cognitive reserve and defined it as the potential mechanism of the brain to cope with brain damage (Yaakov Stern, 2002). It is a key concept in understanding how some individuals maintain typical cognitive function despite age-related changes and brain pathologies. Traditionally, cognitive reserve and brain maintenance have been viewed as interconnected concepts. Brain maintenance encompasses the processes that contribute to the structural preservation of the brain as individuals age and can be evaluated relative to peers of similar age. In contrast, cognitive reserve refers to the ability of the brain to perform cognitive tasks effectively, regardless of the level of structural preservation. This distinction highlights the difference between the brain's physical structure (brain maintenance) and its functional capabilities (cognitive reserve), with the latter influenced by factors beyond mere brain structure (Habeck et al., 2017).

Stern talks about two models of cognitive reserve, namely, the brain reserve model and the cognitive reserve model. These models explained below provide a framework to understand how individuals are able to maintain resilience against cognitive decline.

Brain Reserve Model

The brain reserve model explains the existence of structural differences in the brain that influence its ability to withstand damage (Stern, 2002). It defines brain reserve as a physiological trait where individuals with higher brain reserve, like larger brain volume, more neurons, and increased connectivity, may experience delayed symptom onset or milder cognitive decline despite similar levels of underlying pathology.

Cognitive Reserve Model

The second model of cognitive reserve is the cognitive model, which focuses on functional differences in how individuals process information and utilize cognitive resources (Stern, 2009). It postulates the flexibility and adaptability of cognitive networks that allow the individual to resist cognitive decline due to the functionality, plasticity, and adaptability of cognitive networks.

Research indicates that people with more cognitive reserve, which could be a result of factors such as education, occupational complexity, engagement in cognitively stimulating activities, lifelong learning, and the use of better cognitive strategies, can contribute to the development of cognitive reserve to make up for changes that come with getting older or acquiring a neuropathology, which delays the start of cognitive decline (Stern, 2014). Measuring one's cognitive reserve can pose a challenge due to it being a hypothetical construct that cannot be directly observed. However, to overcome this challenge, researchers have developed various proxy measures such as years of education, occupational attainment, and performance on cognitive tasks to estimate one's cognitive reserve (León et al., 2014).

Approaches to Positive Neuropsychology

Holistic Healthcare

Positive neuropsychology offers a unique approach to supporting individuals with neurological conditions. It emphasizes identifying and leveraging existing strengths and resources to enhance wellbeing and resilience. This focus aligns naturally with two crucial aspects of healthcare: holistic health and patient-centered care. A holistic approach to health acknowledges the interconnectedness of physical, mental, emotional, and social factors in individual wellbeing. Positive neuropsychology contributes to this approach by the following.

Promoting healthy lifestyle choices: Regular physical activity, balanced nutrition, and adequate sleep are all crucial for cognitive function and overall wellbeing. Psychologists can educate individuals on the benefits of these practices and encourage them to adopt healthy habits (Gorgoni et al., 2013; Mandolesi et al., 2018; Grajek et al., 2022). Addressing social and emotional wellbeing, positive neuropsychology emphasizes the importance of social connections, mindfulness practices, and stress management techniques. These can improve emotional regulation, self-awareness, and coping mechanisms, further contributing to wellbeing (Edwards & Burnard, 2003; Karim et al., 2020).

Supporting autonomy and meaning-making: Tailoring interventions to individual strengths and interests empowers individuals to participate actively in their care and fosters a sense of agency (Ladouceur et al., 2018). Engaging in meaningful activities can also promote a positive outlook and sense of fulfillment, contributing to overall wellbeing (Bongelli et al., 2023). The people-centered approach in medical care ensures that patient's values and choices drive the treatment pathways. Positive neuropsychology aligns with this approach.

Collaborative Goal Setting

Positive neuropsychology advocates for a collaborative approach to goal setting between the neuropsychologist and the individual. The professionals and the patient undergo a process where they both develop common goals and interventions that are tailor-made to the patient's unique needs and aspirations (Edgman-Levitan & Schoenbaum, 2021). This collaborative process empowers the individual and fosters a sense of agency in their own care.

Empowering Individuals

Positive neuropsychology encourages individuals to understand their strengths and limitations, empowering them to advocate for their needs. This approach encourages individuals to recognize their existing resources and capabilities and to actively participate in their care and rehabilitation (Randolph, 2018). Positive neuropsychology, as opposed to a single-sided approach of limitations, explores and utilizes the individual's existing strengths and resources in dealing with challenges that people experience, thereby improving their mental health (Park et al., 2016). Interventions are tailored to leverage these strengths, making them more engaging and fostering a sense of accomplishment (Yuen et al., 2020).

Overall, these approaches to positive neuropsychology emphasize a holistic, strength-based, and patient-centered perspective in promoting cognitive health and wellbeing.

Applications of Positive Neuropsychology

Positive neuropsychology, with its focus on promoting cognitive health, optimal cognitive functioning, and overall wellbeing, rather than focusing on the treatment of cognitive deficits, can be applied in various settings.

Schools

Education is one of the most valuable human skills and prepares students to face future challenges. Education teaches various skills to students, such as individual care, trust, and respect (Samavi, 2022). Various concepts of positive psychology can be incorporated into the academic model, such as Positive Emotion, Engagement, Relationships, Meaning, and Accomplishment (PERMA), which provides them with a foundation for successful lives and provides insight into their personal strength (Seligman, 2011). Children can be taught various strategies such as cognitive skills training, mindfulness-based interventions, and strengths-based approaches to manage their academic stressors and improve their academic performance (Seligman et al., 2009).

Neuropsychology can come into play, as there can be studies conducted to check the cognitive functions of the students while they are practicing positive psychology techniques. These methods can help them learn better, and the researchers can study more on how these positive psychology learning techniques are helping children improve their academic performance, and the neuroscience can be measured to get a better insight.

Workplace

Positive neuropsychology techniques can be applied in workplace settings for employers to attain work efficiency, cope with stress, improve emotional intelligence (Froman, 2010), and promote job performance and employee wellbeing. Neuropsychology can help with interventions and in therapy to help employers improve their proficiency. Practices such as using various stress management techniques and strength-based cognitive enhancement programs can help employees manage stress and leverage individual strengths for improved engagement and productivity. By incorporating positive neuropsychology in organizational design and practices, companies can create environments that support cognitive wellbeing, optimal functioning, and overall job satisfaction, ultimately leading to enhanced individual and organizational outcomes.

Clinical Practice and Research

Neuropsychologists practicing positive neuropsychology can help patients identify and build on their cognitive resilience and strengths. This can help patients cope better with neurological conditions and improve their overall quality of life by promoting healthy aging. Positive neuropsychologists can develop interventions that help in the maintenance, enhancement, and protection of cognitive abilities rather than just treating the deficits (Pluskota, 2014).

Burton and King (2004) conducted an assignment with a placebo-controlled design to test the effect of a writing intervention on mood and physical health. For three consecutive days in 20-minute intervals, participants in the intervention condition wrote about intensely positive experiences, and participants in the control group wrote about relatively neutral subjects (e.g., their schedule, their bedroom, and their shoes). A short-term boost in mood was seen due to writing about positive experiences, but unfortunately, the mood was not assessed beyond a third of writing. However, they did find that participants in the intervention group made fewer visits to the health center over the next three months (Duckworth & Seligman, 2004). There are various studies that have proven the success of treatment using positive psychology techniques, and the neuroscience of these individuals can be researched in the future.

By bridging the gap between clinical practice and research, positive neuropsychology contributes to a more holistic understanding of cognitive health and wellbeing.

Challenges

Despite its growing prominence, positive neuropsychology faces several challenges that hinder its development and impact:

1 *Lack of Consensus on Definitions*: It turned out to be the case that researchers lack clear-cut, widely accepted definitions for such crucial terms as "positive emotions," "wellbeing," and positive cognition." The inconsistency impedes research advancements and makes it hard to draw comparisons among studies (Kent, 2020). This gives rise to a need for specialized training that will provide clinicians and researchers the knowledge and skills required to effectively apply the principles of positive neuropsychology into their practice. This includes understanding the theory, assessments, and intervention strategies unique to positive psychology.
2 *Emphasis on Quantitative Data*: Giving importance to quantitative, yet objective measures in research might inadvertently neglect the experiential dimension of positivity. This tendency arises when we prioritize measurable factors, overlooking other equally significant aspects of human wellbeing that cannot be quantified (Kent, 2020).
3 *Bias toward Pathology*: Neuropsychology, which has been traditionally associated with understanding and treatment for brain pathologies, seeks to explore the link between the brain and behavior in the healthy state of

the central nervous system. This status quo paradigm on mental health disorders research might ignore the other side of the coin, like proactive research on building optimal mental health and positive functioning (Kent, 2020). Integrating positive neuropsychology into existing clinical and research practices may face resistance due to entrenched traditional models and practices. Overcoming this challenge requires a shift in mindset and a willingness to adopt new approaches that focus on strengths and resilience alongside deficits (Randolf et al., 2018).

4 *Ethical Considerations*: Positive neuropsychology plows into the implementation of various approaches that foster cognitive and emotional health. Responsibility connects the dots here. Informed consent, not decision, keeping far away from the unconscious direction of people, and failure to nod out unexpected risks are the important considerations in any plausible research and practice (Hill & Aita, 2018).
5 *Cultural Sensitivity*: The worth of the experience should be based on non-culturally induced positive perceptions and emotions, although conclusions from researchers in the Western context can be generalized by other researchers; therefore, it should be ethnically sensitive to deviate from the common research approaches (Van Zyl & Rothmann, 2022).

Future Directions and Research Advances

Public Education in Neuropsychology

Educating the public about the role of psychologists and neuropsychologists is very necessary. Seeking help for mental health issues is still a taboo, and it is not widely accepted as it is with physical illness. Mental health literacy should be given importance, and the public should be educated about various signs and symptoms of mental illness (Jorm et al., 1997; Randolph, 2018). The public is not as aware of different psychological disorders as they are with physical disorders. The low- and middle-income countries have been slow in the progress of mental health service delivery. Existing public health barriers, funding and delivery of mental healthcare in primary care settings, lack of mental health professionals, and lack of mental health perspective in public health are some of the current barriers (Srivastava et al., 2016).

Understanding Superior Cognition

Neuropsychology has traditionally focused on examining individuals with neuropsychiatric disease or injury to better understand cognitive function and dysfunction. However, relatively few efforts have been made to consider those with exceptional cognitive functioning. Studying such individuals may lead to important insights into brain and cognitive health that could be exploited to promote cognition in those with cognitive impairment.

Positive Outcomes in Neuropsychiatric Conditions

The primary aim of neuropsychology is to cure neuropsychiatric conditions (Randolph, 2018), but in recent times, due to the shift in the paradigms, the field of positive neuropsychology looks forward to working with the normal population. Future research can be directed toward the prevention of any abnormalities or mental illness. Neuropsychology can derive important lessons from other fields, such as marital therapy, weight loss, and many more, to bring out positive outcomes, and these techniques are empirically tested (Klem et al., 1997; Shapiro et al., 2000; Wing & Phelan, 2005).

Conclusion

Emerging as a captivating field, researchers are increasingly delving into the intricate connections between neural mechanisms and positive psychology. The field investigates not only the neural underpinnings of positivity but also the neural basis of healthy emotions, character strengths, overall wellbeing, and tailored interventions that promote mental wellness and resilience. By investigating how the brain processes and influences healthy emotions, character strengths, and overall wellbeing, positive neuropsychology offers a unique perspective on human flourishing. This exploration holds immense potential to inform interventions, promote a holistic understanding of mental health, and optimize human potential by uncovering the brain's role in fostering positive experiences and resilience. As research progresses, positive neuropsychology promises to enrich our understanding of the brain and its role in human flourishing, paving the way for a more comprehensive picture of what it means to thrive.

References

Allen, J. G., Romate, J., & Rajkumar, E. (2021). Mindfulness-based positive psychology interventions: a systematic review. *BMC Psychology*, *9*(1). https://doi.org/10.1186/s40359-021-00618-2

Blume, H. (1998, September 30). *Neurodiversity: Beyond the spectrum, a movement for all.* Retrieved from https://www.health.harvard.edu/blog/what-is-neurodiversity-202111232645

Blume, H. (2019, August 15). On the neurological underpinnings of geekdom. *The Atlantic.* Retrieved from https://www.theatlantic.com/magazine/archive/1998/09/neurodiversity/305909/

Bongelli, R., Sergi, M. R., Picconi, L., Fermani, A., Lezzi, S., & Saggino, A. (2023). The mediating role of positive and negative affect in the relationship between death anxiety and Italian students' perceptions of distance learning quality during the COVID-19 pandemic. *Societies*, *13*(7), 163. https://doi.org/10.3390/soc13070163

Broca, P. P. (1865). Localization of speech in the third left frontal convolution. In Translation of Broca's 1865 report (1986). *Archives of Neurology*, *43*(10), 1065–1072. https://doi.org/10.1001/archneur.1986.00520100069017

Burton, C. M., & King, L. A. (2004). The health benefits of expressive writing. *Health Psychology*, *23*(3), 367–372. https://doi.org/10.1016/S0092-6566(03)00058-8

Duckworth, A. L., & Seligman, M. E. P. (2004). Self-discipline outdoes IQ in predicting academic performance of adolescents. *Psychological Science*, *16*(12), 939–944. https://doi.org/10.1111/j.1467-9280.2005.01641.x

Edgman-Levitan, S., & Schoenbaum, S. C. (2021). Patient-centered care: Achieving higher quality by designing care through the patient's eyes. *Israel Journal of Health Policy Research*, *10*. https://doi.org/10.1186/s13584-021-00459-9

Edwards, D., & Burnard, P. (2003). A systematic review of stress and stress management interventions for mental health nurses. *Journal of Advanced Nursing*, *42*(2), 169–200. https://doi.org/10.1046/j.1365-2648.2003.02600.x

Establishing Trust | Psychology Today. Retrieved February 29, 2024, from https://www.psychologytoday.com/intl/blog/the-therapeutic-relationship/202304/establishing-trust.

Froman, L. (2010). Positive psychology in the workplace. *Journal of Adult Development*, *17*, 59–69. https://doi.org/10.1007/s10804-009-9080-0

Gorgoni, M., Lauri, G., Rossini, P. M., Ferlazzo, F., & Gennaro, L. D. (2013). Is sleep essential for neural plasticity in humans, and how does it affect motor and cognitive recovery? *Neural Plasticity*, *2013*. https://doi.org/10.1155/2013/103949

Grajek, M., Nowak, A., Bielecki, T., & Knapik, A. (2022). The impact of lifestyle factors on cognitive function: A systematic review. *Journal of Cognitive Psychology*, *15*(3), 245–260.

Habeck, C., Razlighi, Q., Gazes, Y., Barulli, D., Steffener, J., & Stern, Y. (2017 August). Cognitive reserve and brain maintenance: Orthogonal concepts in theory and practice. *Cerebral Cortex*, *27*(8), 3962–3969. https://doi.org/10.1093/cercor/bhw208

Hill, B. D., & Aita, S. L. (2018 July–August). The positive side of effort: A review of the impact of motivation and engagement on neuropsychological performance. *Applied Neuropsychology Adult*, *25*(4), 312–317. https://doi.org/10.1080/23279095.2018.1458502

Jorm, A. F., Korten, A. E., Jacomb, P. A., Christensen, H., Rodgers, B., & Pollitt, P. (1997 February 17). "Mental health literacy": A survey of the public's ability to recognise mental disorders and their beliefs about the effectiveness of treatment. *Medical Journal of Australia*, *166*(4), 182–186. https://doi.org/10.5694/j.1326–5377.1997.tb140071.x. PMID: 9066546.

Karim, F., Oyewande, A. A., Abdalla, L. F., Ehsanullah, R. C., & Khan, S. (2020). Social media use and its connection to mental health: A systematic review. *Cureus*, *12*(6). https://doi.org/10.7759/cureus.8627

Kent, P. L. (2020). Evolution of clinical neuropsychology: Four challenges. *Applied Neuropsychology: Adult*, *27*(2), 121–133. https://doi.org/10.1080/23279095.2018.1493483

Klem, M. L., Wing, R. R., McGuire, M. T., Seagle, H. M., & Hill, J. O. (1997 August). A descriptive study of individuals successful at long-term maintenance of substantial weight loss. *The American Journal of Clinical Nutrition*, *66*(2), 239–246. https://doi.org/10.1093/ajcn/66.2.239

Ladouceur, C. D., Schlund, M. W., & Segreti, M. (2018). Positive reinforcement modulates fronto-limbic systems subserving emotional interference in adolescents. *Behavioural Brain Research*, *338*, 109. https://doi.org/10.1016/j.bbr.2017.10.019

León, I., García-García, J., Roldán-Tapia, L. (2014). Estimating cognitive reserve in healthy adults using the cognitive reserve scale. *PLoS ONE*, *9*(7), e102632. https://doi.org/10.1371/journal.pone.0102632

Luis, E., Bermejo-Martins, E., Martinez, M., Sarrionandia, A., Cortes, C., Oliveros, E. Y., Garces, M. S., Oron, J. V., & Fernández-Berrocal, P. (2021). Original research: Relationship between self-care activities, stress and wellbeing during COVID-19 lockdown: A cross-cultural mediation model. *BMJ Open*, *11*(12). https://doi.org/10.1136/bmjopen-2020-048469

Macía, P., Barranco, M., Gorbeña, S., Álvarez-Fuentes, E., & Iraurgi, I. (2021). Resilience and coping strategies in relation to mental health outcomes in people with cancer. *PLoS ONE*, *16*(5). https://doi.org/10.1371/journal.pone.0252075

Mandolesi, L., Polverino, A., Montuori, S., Foti, F., Ferraioli, G., Sorrentino, P., & Sorrentino, G. (2018). Effects of physical exercise on cognitive functioning and wellbeing: Biological and psychological benefits. *Frontiers in Psychology*, *9*. https://doi.org/10.3389/fpsyg.2018.00509

Marujo, H. À., & Neto, L. M. (2016). *Quality of life studies and positive psychology*. Edward Elgar Publishing eBooks. https://doi.org/10.4337/9781783471171.00018

Maslow, A. H. (1954). *Motivation and personality*. Harper & Row.

Park, N., Peterson, C., Szvarca, D., Vander Molen, R. J., Kim, E. S., & Collon, K. (2016). Positive psychology and physical health: Research and applications. *American Journal of Lifestyle Medicine*, *10*(3), 200–206. https://doi.org/10.1177/1559827614550277

Patricia Pimental. (2017). The brave new world of positive neuropsychology. *Applied Neuropsychology: Adult*, *24*(2), 99. https://doi.org/10.1080/23279095.2016.1269489

Pluskota, A. (2014 March 19). The application of positive psychology in the practice of education. *Springerplus*, *3*, 147. https://doi.org/10.1186/2193-1801-3-147. PMID: 24790805; PMCID: PMC4002998.

Randolph, J. J. (2018 July–August). Positive neuropsychology: The science and practice of promoting cognitive health. *Applied Neuropsychology Adult*, *25*(4), 287–294. https://doi.org/10.1080/23279095.2018.1457465

Randolf, J., Smith, A., & Johnson, L. (2018). Overcoming challenges through a strengths-based approach: The importance of resilience in personal development. *Journal of Positive Psychology*, *13*(3), 245–256.

Ruff, R. M. (2003 December). A friendly critique of neuropsychology: Facing the challenges of our future. *Archives of Clinical Neuropsychology*, *18*(8), 847–864. https://doi.org/10.1016/j.acn.2003.07.002

Samavi, S. A. (2022). Positive psychology studies in education. *Frontiers in Psychology*, *13*. https://doi.org/10.3389/fpsyg.2022.845199

Seligman, M. E. P. (2011). *Flourish: A visionary new understanding of happiness and wellbeing*. New York, NY: Free Press.

Seligman, M. E. P., et al. (2009 June). Positive education: Positive psychology and classroom interventions. *Oxford Review of Education*, *35*(3), 293–311. https://doi.org/10.1080/03054980902934563

Seligman, M., & Csikszentmihalyi, M. (2000). Positive psychology: An introduction. *The American Psychologist*, *55*(1), 5–14. https://doi.org/10.1037/0003-066X.55.1.5
Shapiro, A. F., Gottman, J. M., & Carrère, S. (2000). The baby and the marriage: Identifying factors that buffer against decline in marital satisfaction after the first baby arrives. *Journal of Family Psychology*, *14*(1), 59–70. https://doi.org/10.1037/0893-3200.14.1.59
Srivastava, K., Chatterjee, K., & Bhat, P. S. (2016). Mental health awareness: The Indian scenario. *Industrial Psychiatry Journal*, *25*(2), 131–134. https://doi.org/10.4103/ipj.ipj_45_17
Stern, Y. (2002). What is cognitive reserve? Theory and research application of the reserve concept. *Neuropsychology*, *16*(4), 213–224. Retrieved from https://www.ncbi.nlm.nih.gov/pmc/articles/PMC6417987/
Stern, Y. (2009). Cognitive reserve. *Neuropsychologist*, *23*(1), 40–47. Retrieved from https://www.ncbi.nlm.nih.gov/pmc/articles/PMC2739591/)
Van Zyl, L. E., & Rothmann, S. (2022). Positive organizational interventions: Contemporary theories, approaches, and applications. *Frontiers in Psychology*, 13, 963167. https://doi.org/10.3389/fpsyg.2022.963167
Stern, Y. (2014, January 1). Cognitive reserve: Implications for assessment and intervention. *Folia Phoniatr Logop*, *65*(2), 49–54. https://doi.org/10.1159/000353443
Van Zyl, L. E., & Rothmann, S. (2022). Grand challenges for positive psychology: Future perspectives and opportunities. *Frontiers in Psychology*, *13*. https://doi.org/10.3389/fpsyg.2022.833057
Wernicke, C. (1969). The symptom complex of aphasia. In *Boston studies in the philosophy of science* (pp. 34–97). https://doi.org/10.1007/978-94-010-3378-7_2
Wing, R. R., & Phelan, S. (2005). Long-term weight loss maintenance. *The American Journal of Clinical Nutrition*, *82*(1), 222S–225S. https://doi.org/10.1093/ajcn/82.1.222S
Yuen, E., Sadhu, J., Pfeffer, C., Sarvet, B., Daily, R. S., Dowben, J., Jackson, K., Schowalter, J., Shapiro, T., Stubbe, D., & Committee, C. (2020). Accentuate the positive: Strengths-based therapy for adolescents. *Adolescent Psychiatry (Hilversum, Netherlands)*, *10*(3), 166. https://doi.org/10.2174/221067661066620022510 5529

2 Positive Neuropsychology

Paradigm Shift in Understanding Wellbeing and Research Methods

Positive neuropsychology is an emerging field that combines the principles of positive psychology and neuropsychology to study the neural correlates of wellbeing, resilience, and optimal human functioning (Phan et al., 2020). There has been tremendous growth in the field of positive psychology in recent years. This has been evident in a number of published studies, conferences, symposiums, and practical applications of the field, especially to clinical settings (Ryff, 2022). Research in this field aims to promote cognitive health and enhance the overall quality of life using evidence-based methodologies. The field of positive psychology originated from the seminal work of Seligman and Csikszentmihalyi (2000). These foundational voices are behind the concepts of learned helplessness (Seligman, 1972) and flow (Csikszentmihalyi et al., 2014); positive psychology is defined as "the scientific study of human flourishing."

In this chapter, the authors advocated for a paradigm shift in the field of psychology: from focusing on pathology, weakness, deficit, dysfunction, and abnormalities to focusing on hope, wisdom, creativity, future-mindedness, courage, spirituality, responsibility, and perseverance in human life. According to the American Academy of Clinical Neuropsychology (AACN) Practice Guidelines for Neuropsychological Assessment and Consultation, clinical neuropsychology is defined as an "applied science that examines the impact of both normal and abnormal brain functions on a broad range of cognitive, emotional, and behavioral functions" (Board of Directors, 2007). In practice, neuropsychologists often focus on cognitive deficits and dysfunctional brain-behavior relationships. This poses a limitation to the field of neuropsychology: neurobiology of positive traits and positive experience is not considered (Seligman & Csikszentmihalyi, 2000). The field of *positive neuropsychology* addresses this gap.

Positive neuropsychology is an integration of the fields of positive psychology and clinical neuropsychology, in that it holds a neuropsychological lens to the study of positive psychology. According to Randolph (2018), positive neuropsychology is the study and promotion of cognitive health. By acknowledging and utilizing one's cognitive strengths, individuals can accurately assess their capabilities and use them effectively in various situations.

DOI: 10.4324/9781003477815-2

This ability, also known as Meta-Cognition, builds self-awareness and allows individuals to manage challenges with confidence, leveraging their strengths to overcome potential weaknesses.

Research suggests that the field of positive neuropsychology has evolved into six key evidence-based clinical and scientific domains, namely compensatory strategies, activity engagement, prevention of cognitive dysfunction, and public education, understanding positive outcomes in the neuropsychiatric population, and studying individuals with above-average or exceptional cognition (Randolph, 2018). Thus, drawing from the intended focus of positive neuropsychology, The C.A.P.E. of brain health provides an understanding of the applicability of the field in settings other than clinical practice (Randolph, 2023). For instance, positive neuropsychology is applicable in sports to mitigate or prevent neuropsychological consequences from sports-related concussions, in promoting a positive lifestyle through public education and media, and in promoting cognitive wellness in leaders in corporate settings, an emerging field called "neuro-leadership" (Randolph, 2023).

Considering the emerging widespread applicability of the novel field of positive neuropsychology, diverse research methods have developed and undergone sophistication in the field. According to a comprehensive review by Helwig et al. (2020), the field of positive psychology has primarily made use of correlational, ex-post facto, and cross-sectional, field studies. Data collection methods like self-report surveys, questionnaires, inventories, rating scales, observation, journal entries, reaction times, archival material, event sampling, and focus groups have majorly been used. Constructs like wellbeing, satisfaction, affect/mood, subjective wellbeing, happiness, work, personality, spirituality/religiosity, social support, and gratitude are predominantly measured as the outcome measures.

Research methods in clinical neuropsychology involve clinical case studies, microscopic evaluations, ablation/lesion studies, electrophysiological recordings including single-cell techniques, multiple cell recordings, and electroencephalogram (EEG), structural neuroimaging techniques like computed tomographic (CT) imaging, magnetic resonance imaging (MRI), magnetic resonance spectroscopy (MRS), diffusion tensor imaging (DTI), functional neuroimaging techniques like single-photon emission computed tomography (SPECT), positron emission tomography (PET), functional magnetic resonance imaging (fMRI), magnetoencephalography (MEG), neuropsychological assessments, and behavioral genetic testing (Getz, 2014). The outcome variables measured are different for different techniques. Overall, behavioral measures such as reaction time, functional measures like changes in blood oxygen levels, tracking of radioisotopes injected into the blood, electrical activity of a single neuron or multiple neurons, event-related potentials, etc., are often considered as the outcome measures, depending on the type of method used.

This chapter aims to understand the possibility of adapting traditional neuropsychological measures to understand the neural correlates of positive psychological variables. Thus, the below sections enlist traditional neuropsychological methods, their usage in clinical settings, and their applicability in measuring positive psychological constructs.

Neuropsychological Assessments

Neuropsychological assessment techniques are a mainstay of clinical neuropsychological practice. Cognitive assessments of attention, executive function, memory, language, and creativity measures are often used (Getz, 2014). As for the interdisciplinary field of positive neuropsychology, researchers assess the lifestyle factors that are associated with brain health. Such factors include physical activities, social engagement, and cognitively stimulating exercises an individual engages in. These constructs are often measured by qualitative interviews, and psychometric assessments such as Lifestyle Activity Questionnaire (LAQ), Memory functioning questionnaire, omnibus measures like Victoria Longitudinal Study-Activity Lifestyle Questionnaire (VLS-ALQ). (Randolph, 2023). Neuropsychological tests evaluate cognitive strengths and weaknesses, guiding interventions and treatment plans. These assessments help tailor interventions to individual cognitive profiles, promoting cognitive resilience and wellbeing (Randolph, 2023).

Clinical Case Studies

There have been important foundational cases like those of Phineas Gage, H.M., Tan, etc., which have contributed to our understanding of the neurobiology of behavior. Case studies are often useful in conferring upon a better understanding of unique/specific illness and their functional implications on brain regions (Getz, 2014). For instance, in the case of Phineas Gage, researchers understood that an injury to the prefrontal cortex impairs an individual's social functioning, decision-making, and personality (Macmillan, 2000). Case studies can also focus on individuals who have overcome significant challenges or adversity and maintained high levels of wellbeing and cognitive health. These studies can shed light on the personal, social, and neural factors that support resilience and positive psychological outcomes. By studying these individuals in-depth, researchers can gain insights into the factors that contribute to optimal cognitive functioning (Patricia Pimental, 2017).

While case studies offer a rich and detailed understanding of individual experiences, it is important to note that their findings may not be generalizable to larger populations. However, when combined with other research methods, such as neuroimaging and longitudinal studies, case studies can contribute to a more comprehensive understanding of the factors that promote cognitive health and wellbeing (Randolph, 2013). An example in point is the case study of Solomon Shereshevskii. Luria in 1968 depicted that Shereshevskii had exceptional memory abilities, i.e., he could retain long lists of meaningless syllables, and displayed multiple forms of synesthesia, a perceptual phenomenon in which stimulation of one sensory pathway results in an involuntary stimulation in another sensory pathway (Fornazzari et al., 2018). This suggests that case studies of individuals with exceptional abilities could be considered as a method of understanding positive neuropsychological constructs.

Microscopic Evaluations

The process of microscopic evaluation dates back to the examination of pathological lesions in brain tissue by Emil Kraeplin in the 1800s. Microscopic evaluation involves harvesting cerebrospinal fluid, submerging the brain tissue in a protective solution to maintain its integrity, and allowing the brain tissue to freeze for further evaluation. The further evaluation process is carried out by administering staining techniques (Golgi stain, Nissl stain, etc.), which allow certain features of the brain tissue to be clearly observed (Getz, 2014). Research suggests that our understanding of neurodegenerative diseases like Alzheimer's and schizophrenia has advanced with the use of small-molecule staining techniques (Rosario et al., 2022). Regardless of its focus on pathological brain substrates, neuronal staining techniques have recently shifted toward mass spectrometry and kinetic histochemistry, which help in enhancing our understanding of ophthalmology (Rosario et al., 2022). This indicates a shift from the study of abnormality to the normal abilities of humans, hinting at the emergence of staining techniques and microscopic evaluations in positive neuropsychology. Microscopic methods such as histology or electron microscopy, although beneficial in neuroscience research, were not commonly applied in positive neuropsychology investigations. These techniques were typically utilized to explore the cellular and molecular mechanisms that influence brain structure and function, but now, gradually shift their focus onto studying the neural connections of positive psychological attributes and behaviors.

Electroencephalogram

EEG is a non-invasive, electrophysiological procedure in which electrodes are placed in a specified order to record the electrical activity of the neurons (Getz, 2014). In clinical neuropsychological settings, EEG is often used to examine the presence of abnormal neuronal discharges, a characteristic of epilepsy (Noachtar & Rémi, 2009). EEG can also determine whether there is a slowing of neuronal discharges, a characteristic of the organic state of delirium tremens (Wiegand et al., 2022). In addition, EEG is also used in sleep laboratories to understand disturbances in the stages of sleep, or the presence of sleep disorders like sleep apnea, narcolepsy, parasomnias, etc. (Lustenberger & Huber, 2012). In addition to these traditional uses of EEG, one of the promising developments in the field (Figure 2.1) has been the

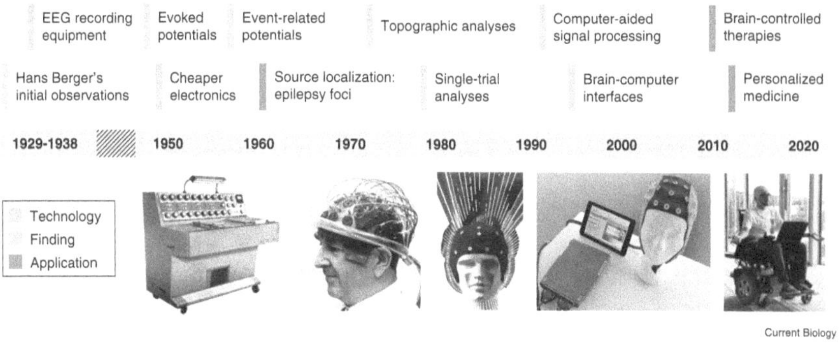

Figure 2.1 Evolution of Electroencephalography (Biasiucci et al., 2019)

incorporation of computational modelling to understand the functional brain correlates of stimulations of real-life situational interactions (Biasiucci et al., 2019).

An application of this technology in the field of positive neuropsychology would be the study of positive social interactions and corresponding brain activity as measured by EEG recordings. EEG is a valuable method used in positive neuropsychology research to investigate cognitive processes, emotional responses, and their interaction. A growing body of research also indicates the use of EEG recordings in the investigation of positive affect. For instance, in an opinion article by Gable et al. (2021), the authors reported that research studies have made use of alpha bands (recorded over the lateral prefrontal area) and beta bands (recorded over motor and premotor cortex) are considered as measures of approach motivation aspect of positive affect. In positive neuropsychology, EEG is utilized to study neural responses to positive affect, emotional processing, and cognitive tasks related to wellbeing and resilience (Gable et al., 2021). Its non-invasive nature, high-temporal resolution, and versatility make EEG an essential method for investigating the neural basis of positive psychological traits and behaviors.

Functional Magnetic Resonance Imaging

In the research of positive neuropsychology, fMRI is an effective neuroimaging technique that has been widely used to study the neural correlates of resilience, wellbeing, and optimal cognitive functioning (Roalf & Gur, 2017). The fMRI neuroimaging technique (Figure 3) works under the premise of the BOLD principle (Arthurs & Boniface, 2002). BOLD refers to blood-oxygen level-dependent changes where neuronal activity is measured in terms of the level of oxygen saturation in blood in response to cognitive or sensorimotor activity. When neurons become more active, there is an increased demand for oxygen, leading to a local increase in blood flow and changes in the magnetic properties of blood. Thus, this non-invasive procedure is a primary method used in cognitive experimental research involving cognitive and motor tasks, most often in the study of positive affect variables (Poldrack, 2008).

In positive neuropsychology, fMRI has been used to study various neural mechanisms of cognitive health and wellbeing such as brain regions involved in processing positive emotions, such as happiness, gratitude (Roalf & Gur, 2017), resilience (Bennett et al., 2016), and optimal cognitive functioning, such as creativity, memory, and problem solving.

The ability of fMRI to measure both cortical and subcortical activation is a key advantage in positive neuropsychology. This allows researchers to examine the role of deeper brain structures in positive psychological processes. In order to obtain a more thorough understanding of the neural mechanisms of wellbeing and cognitive health, researchers in positive neuropsychology often combine fMRI with other techniques, such as neuropsychological assessments and behavioral genetic testing (Roalf & Gur, 2017).

Positron Emission Tomography

The PET technology utilizes radiotracers that visualize and measure changes in glucose metabolism (Getz, 2014). This works on the premise that labeled isotopes often accumulate in relatively higher metabolic areas as compared to lower metabolic areas, which is then detected by PET scans (Purves & Williams, 2001). Clinical neuropsychology research has used PET scans to understand and compare brain activity while an individual is performing cognitive tests and at rest (Getz, 2014), and to understand abnormal brain activity by comparing the brains of healthy and experimental subjects (Al-Sharify et al., 2020; Figure 4).

Changes in brain metabolism and function associated with positive psychological traits, emotional regulation, and cognitive health can be identified with PET scans. PET scans can provide important insights into how the brain functions in relation to resilience and wellbeing by monitoring metabolism, enzyme activity, and receptor binding (Slough et al., 2016). A recent study has applied multimodal imaging (combination of fMRI and PET scans) to study neural correlates of happiness via autobiographical recall methods; the research observed activation in the anterior cingulate, prefrontal cortical, and insular brain regions (Suardi et al., 2016).

Brain Stimulation Techniques

Transcranial magnetic stimulation (TMS) is a non-invasive brain stimulation technique used to study brain activity and its role in mental health disorders, emotional reactions, and cognitive processes. Through the use of a metal coil positioned close to the scalp, TMS creates a rapidly fluctuating magnetic field that causes a small electric current to be induced in the brain tissue underneath. This type of stimulation can be delivered to different areas of the brain to measure variations in brain activity or to temporarily alter brain function.

This may throw light on the neural mechanisms underpinning a range of emotional and cognitive states.

In order to better understand attention, memory, visual processing, action planning, decision-making, and language processing, cognitive neuroscience researchers have turned to TMS. Research suggests that TMS as a neuromodulation technique is often used in the treatment of mood disorders, especially major depression; pragmatic clinical research trials still continue to investigate the exact process of action of TMS in major depression (Janicak & Dokucu, 2015).

Community-Based Research

Other than these traditional clinical neuropsychological research methodologies adapted to the study of positive psychological constructs, community-based research could be used to understand the cross-cultural diversity in the experience of positive psychological variables such as happiness and satisfaction. For instance, a research study by Oishi and Gilbert (2016) reported the presence of several differences in the experience of happiness: (1) the meaning and importance given to experiencing happiness differs across cultures and time periods; (2) the social predictors of happiness differ across cultures; and (3) finally, as in the above two levels, even the interventions necessary for facilitating happiness differ cross-culturally.

Thus, reviewing the above multitude of research techniques used in traditional clinical settings, and likewise adapted to the field of positive neuropsychology, one can surmise that interdisciplinary methodologies in the field still have a long way to go. Future research studies focus on implementing multimodal imaging techniques, and multilevel analyses incorporating several behavioral (surveys, rating scales, reaction times, etc.), structural and functional (CT, fMRI, PET, etc.), and community-based measures (cross-cultural research) to facilitate an efficient understanding of positive psychological constructs.

References

Al-Sharify, Z. T., Al-Sharify, T. A., Al-Sharify, N. T., & Yahya naser, H. (2020). A critical review on medical imaging techniques (CT and PET scans) in the medical field. *IOP Conference Series: Materials Science and Engineering*, *870*(1), 012043. https://doi.org/10.1088/1757-899x/870/1/012043

Arthurs, O. J., & Boniface, S. (2002). How well do we understand the neural origins of the fMRI bold signal? *Trends in Neurosciences*, *25*(1), 27–31. https://doi.org/10.1016/s0166-2236(00)01995-0

Bennett, M. R., Hatton, S., Hermens, D. F., & Lagopoulos, J. (2016). Behavior, neuropsychology and fMRI. *Progress in Neurobiology*, *145–146*, 1–25. https://doi.org/10.1016/j.pneurobio.2016.07.001

Biasiucci, A., Franceschiello, B., & Murray, M. M. (2019). Electroencephalography. *Current Biology*, *29*(3). https://doi.org/10.1016/j.cub.2018.11.052

Board of Directors. (2007). American Academy of Clinical Neuropsychology (AACN) practice guidelines for neuropsychological assessment and consultation. *The Clinical Neuropsychologist*, *21*(2), 209–231. https://doi.org/10.1080/13825580601025932

Csikszentmihalyi, M., Abuhamdeh, S., & Nakamura, J. (2014). Flow. *Flow and the Foundations of Positive Psychology*, 227–238. https://doi.org/10.1007/978-94-017-9088-8_15

Fornazzari, L., Leggieri, M., Schweizer, T. A., Arizaga, R. L., Allegri, R. F., & Fischer, C. E. (2018). Hyper memory, synaesthesia, savants Luria and Borges revisited. *Dementia & Neuropsychologia*, *12*(2), 101–104. https://doi.org/10.1590/1980-57642018dn12-020001

Gable, P. A., Paul, K., Pourtois, G., & Burgdorf, J. (2021). Utilizing electroencephalography (EEG) to investigate positive affect. *Current Opinion in Behavioral Sciences*, *39*, 190–195. https://doi.org/10.1016/j.cobeha.2021.03.018

Getz, G. (2014). *Applied biological psychology*. Springer Publishing Company, LLC.

Helwig, N., Yatsevich, D., Vetter, A. C., Wuttke, A. M., & Schmitz, B. (2020). A comparative review of current research methods in positive psychology. *European Journal of Applied Positive Psychology*, *4*(2), 1–31.

Janicak, P., & Dokucu, M. E. (2015). Transcranial magnetic stimulation for the treatment of major depression. *Neuropsychiatric Disease and Treatment*, *1549*. https://doi.org/10.2147/ndt.s67477

Lustenberger, C., & Huber, R. (2012). High density electroencephalography in sleep research: Potential, problems, future perspective. *Frontiers in Neurology*, *3*. https://doi.org/10.3389/fneur.2012.00077

Macmillan, M. (2000). Restoring Phineas Gage: A 150th retrospective. *Journal of the History of the Neurosciences*, *9*(1), 46–66. https://doi.org/10.1076/0964-704x(200004)9:1;1-2;ft046

Noachtar, S., & Rémi, J. (2009). The role of EEG in epilepsy: A critical review. *Epilepsy & Behavior*, *15*(1), 22–33. https://doi.org/10.1016/j.yebeh.2009.02.035

Oishi, S., & Gilbert, E. A. (2016). Current and future directions in culture and happiness research. *Current Opinion in Psychology*, *8*, 54–58. https://doi.org/10.1016/j.copsyc.2015.10.005

Patricia Pimental. (2017). The brave new world of positive neuropsychology. *Applied Neuropsychology: Adult*, *24*(2), 99. https://doi.org/10.1080/23279095.2016.1269489

Phan, H. P., Ngu, B. H., Chen, S. C., Wu, L., Shi, S., Lin, R., Shih, J., & Wang, H. (2020). Advancing the study of positive psychology: The use of a multifaceted structure of mindfulness for development. *Frontiers in Psychology*, *11*. https://doi.org/10.3389/fpsyg.2020.01602

Poldrack, R. A. (2008). The role of fMRI in cognitive neuroscience: Where do we stand? *Current Opinion in Neurobiology*, *18*(2), 223–227. https://doi.org/10.1016/j.conb.2008.07.006

Purves, D., & Williams, S. M. (2001). *Neuroscience*. Sinauer Associates.

Randolph, J. J. (Ed.). (2013). *Positive neuropsychology: Evidence-based perspectives on promoting cognitive health*. Springer Science + Business Media. https://doi.org/10.1007/978-1-4614-6605-5

Randolph, J. J. (2018). Positive neuropsychology: The science and practice of promoting cognitive health. *Applied Neuropsychology: Adult*, *25*(4), 287–294. https://doi.org/10.1080/23279095.2018.1457465

Randolph, J. J. (2023). *Positive neuropsychology evidence-based perspectives on promoting brain and Cognitive Health*. Springer International Publishing AG.
Roalf, D. R., & Gur, R. C. (November 2017). Functional brain imaging in neuropsychology over the past 25 years. *Neuropsychology*, *31*(8), 954–971. https://doi.org/10.1037/neu0000426. PMID: 29376672; PMCID: PMC5822440.
Rosario, A., Howell, A., & Bhattacharya, S. K. (2022). A revisit to staining reagents for neuronal tissues. *Annals of Eye Science*, *7*, 6. https://doi.org/10.21037/aes-21-31
Ryff, C. D. (2022). Positive psychology: Looking back and looking forward. *Frontiers in Psychology*, *13*. https://doi.org/10.3389/fpsyg.2022.840062
Seligman, M. E. (1972). Learned helplessness. *Annual Review of Medicine*, *23*(1), 407–412. https://doi.org/10.1146/annurev.me.23.020172.002203
Seligman, M. E., & Csikszentmihalyi, M. (2000). Positive psychology: An introduction. *American Psychologist*, *55*(1), 5–14. https://doi.org/10.1037//0003-066x.55.1.5
Slough, C., Masters, S. C., Hurley, R. A., & Taber, K. H. (2016). Clinical Positron Emission Tomography (PET) neuroimaging: Advantages and limitations as a diagnostic tool. *The Journal of Neuropsychiatry and Clinical Neurosciences*, *28*(2), A4–71. https://doi.org/10.1176/appi.neuropsych.16030044
Suardi, A., Sotgiu, I., Costa, T., Cauda, F., & Rusconi, M. (2016). The neural correlates of happiness: A review of pet and fMRI studies using autobiographical recall methods. *Cognitive, Affective, & Behavioral Neuroscience*, *16*(3), 383–392. https://doi.org/10.3758/s13415-016-0414-7
Wiegand, T. L., Rémi, J., & Dimitriadis, K. (2022). Electroencephalography in delirium assessment: A scoping review. *BMC Neurology*, *22*(1). https://doi.org/10.1186/s12883-022-02557-w

3 The Executive Brain

Nurturing Cognitive Skills for Success

Understanding Executive Functions

Cognitive executive functions refer to a set of higher-order cognitive processes that are responsible for the regulation and control of thought, emotions, behavior, and decision-making to achieve one's desired goals (Diamond, 2013). Executive functions encompass a range of cognitive functions that are crucial for adapting behavior and performing goal-directed actions. Abilities such as planning, initiating, monitoring, inhibiting, and adjusting behavior in response to changing stimuli are rooted in attentional control, working memory, cognitive inhibition, and cognitive flexibility forming the basis of executive functions (EFs) (Miyake et al., 2000). Cognitive executive functions are essential for goal-directed behavior and are critical for success in everyday life. They are also important for regulating emotions and managing stress. Working memory allows individuals to hold information in mind for short periods of time, while inhibitory control (IC) enables individuals to suppress irrelevant or inappropriate thoughts or behaviors. Cognitive flexibility allows individuals to switch between different tasks or mental sets, while attentional control allows individuals to focus on relevant information and ignore distractions. Together, these processes allow individuals to regulate their behavior and make decisions that are aligned with their goals and values.

The Diversity of Executive Functions

There are several different types of cognitive executive functions, each of which plays a unique role in human behavior and decision-making. The utility and diversity of these cognitive functions can be described by Miyake and Friedman's model of EFs (Miyake et al., 2012). The model suggests that cognitive functions can be divided into three core components: updating, inhibition, and shifting (Miyake et al., 2000). Updating refers to the ability to update and monitor representations within one's working memory. Inhibition refers to the control or suppression of responses as and when necessary and shifting involves one's ability to shift between tasks or mental sets

DOI: 10.4324/9781003477815-3

flexibly. Beyond the core components identified by Miyake and colleagues, EFs encompass a broader range of higher-order cognitive abilities such as planning, problem-solving, decision-making, and impulse control. Planning involves the ability to set goals, develop strategies to achieve those goals, and execute those strategies effectively. Problem-solving involves the ability to identify and define problems, generate potential solutions, and evaluate the effectiveness of those solutions. Decision-making involves the ability to weigh the costs and benefits of different options and choose the best course of action. Impulse control involves the ability to resist immediate temptations and delay gratification in pursuit of long-term goals.

Benefits of Executive Functions in Day-to-Day Life

Research has consistently highlighted the important implications of EFs in one's daily functioning. Executive functions are essential for everyday life, and deficits in these functions can lead to a range of problems, including poor academic and occupational performance, difficulties with social relationships, and mental health problems.

Understanding the importance of CFs in our personal and professional development can help us improve our cognitive abilities and lead a more fulfilling life. The ability to successfully plan, organize, inhibit inappropriate responses and flexibly shift between mental sets allows us to effectively solve problems and make decisions in a variety of contexts (Diamond, 2013) For example, when we are faced with a problem, CEFs, specifically planning and problem-solving skills, help us analyze the situation, break down complex tasks into manageable steps, anticipate potential obstacles, generate possible solutions, and choose the best course of action. Understanding CEF is essential for personal and professional development as it can help us improve our cognitive abilities and lead a more fulfilling life. Cognitive executive functions play a crucial role in our everyday life activities. From making decisions to solving problems, these functions are essential for our success and wellbeing. By understanding and improving these functions, we can enhance our productivity, efficiency, and overall quality of life.

Additionally, cognitive flexibility enables us to adapt to changing situations and think creatively when faced with challenges. By honing these skills through practice and training, we can improve our performance in various areas of life, including work, school, and relationships. Investing in developing our cognitive executive functions is an investment in ourselves that will pay off in the long run. So let's prioritize these skills and unlock our full potential in all aspects of life.

The Orchestra: Featuring Executive Functions

The human mind is a remarkable symphony, a complex orchestra of interconnected pathways and processes. Yet, behind the scenes resides a powerful conductor, guiding the flow of information and directing our cognitive efforts: the EFs. Nestled within the prefrontal cortex, these higher-order skills play a critical role in navigating the complexities of daily life, influencing our problem-solving, self-regulation, and decision-making abilities. To fully appreciate the executive symphony, it is essential to delve deeper and understand the unique instruments that comprise it: working memory, attention, cognitive flexibility, and IC.

Working Memory: Holding the Melody

Working memory is of crucial importance to musicians as it allows them to hold and manipulate the notes and melodies that make up the musical composition. It allows the maestro (EFs) to hold performance-relevant information as a guide to the performance. Working memory, the first chair of this cognitive orchestra, acts as the temporary storage and manipulation center for information. It allows us to hold onto vital details while actively processing them and weaving them into a coherent understanding. Imagine planning a surprise party for a loved one. Working memory allows you to juggle various pieces of information simultaneously—the guest list, the menu, the venue, and the decorations—and manipulate them to create a cohesive plan. Without this crucial function, the symphony of planning would quickly descend into discord, with essential details falling by the wayside. One prominent theoretical framework for understanding working memory is Baddeley and Hitch's Working Memory Model (1974). This model proposes three core components: the phonological loop, responsible for processing and maintaining auditory information; the visuospatial sketchpad, responsible for visual and spatial information; and the central executive, acting as the conductor of information flow, coordinating operations within the loop and sketchpad while also managing attention and decision-making. Additionally, the model posits the existence of a multimodal buffer, which acts as a temporary storage space for integrating information across different modalities.

Attention: Tuning the Instruments

Attention, the second chair, acts as the conductor's baton, directing the spotlight of awareness onto specific information. Just as a skilled conductor uses their baton to guide the musicians and maintain the flow of the performance, attention allows us to selectively focus on relevant details while filtering out distractions. It enables us to selectively focus on relevant details while filtering out the extraneous noise and distractions that constantly bombard us. Imagine studying for an important exam in a bustling coffee shop. Attention allows you to focus on the textbook content, silencing the chatter and background music, and directing your mental energy to the task at hand. Without this ability to focus, the symphony of learning quickly becomes a cacophony, hindering our ability to grasp complex concepts.

Inhibitory Control: Silencing the Dissonance

Inhibitory control, the percussion section within the executive orchestra, plays a critical role in maintaining the rhythm and structure of the performance. It allows us to manage impulsive urges and stay on track with our goals, ensuring that the music doesn't descend into chaotic improvisation. Imagine trying to focus on a challenging task while social media notifications entice you away. Inhibitory control helps you resist the urge to check your phone, allowing you to stay focused on the task at hand and achieve your goals. Without this ability to resist distractions, the symphony of productivity quickly becomes disrupted by the incessant noise of competing priorities.

Cognitive Flexibility: Adapting the Tempo

Cognitive flexibility refers to the ability to switch between different tasks, rules, and behaviors to correspond with the environment. Being one of the core components of EFs, cognitive flexibility allows individuals to switch between thinking, adjusting behavior, and engage in flexible problem solving and behavior. Similar to how a skilled musician smoothly transitions between different tempos and moods within a musical piece, cognitive flexibility involves changing mental gears and adapting to the changes in circumstances and demands. Cognitive flexibility, the resident oboist, provides the symphony with its adaptability. It empowers us to seamlessly adjust to changing situations and perspectives, ensuring that the performance continues harmoniously even when unexpected melodies arise. Imagine driving home on a familiar route when you encounter a sudden road closure. Cognitive flexibility allows you to quickly consider alternative routes, adjust your navigation plan, and maintain focus on reaching your destination. Without this agility, the symphony of life becomes rigid and inflexible, rendering us vulnerable to the disruptions that inevitably occur.

Planning and Organization: Orchestrating the Composition

Executive functions, like the conductor, must plan and organize the overall structure of the performance, and various musical elements and coordinate the musicians to successfully perform the composition. Just like a skilled conductor envisions and completes the composition and coordinates the various musical elements, the EF plans and formulates the sequence necessary to achieve a desired goal.

Emotional Control: Maintaining the Harmony

Similar to how a conductor is responsible for maintaining and balancing the harmony of the orchestra, the executive control is responsible for the role of emotional control and regulation. The EFs control emotions and impulses to maintain harmony in the "performance" of daily life, just as a conductor must make sure that all of the instruments and sections of the orchestra play in unison. Emotional control enables people to control their emotions, regulate and suppress impulsive thoughts and feelings, and react appropriately to circumstances. Keeping the "orchestra" of cognitive processes and behaviors in tune helps the EFs avoid dissonance or other disruptions that might make it difficult to accomplish tasks and achieve objectives.

Problem-Solving: The Conductor's Handbook

Problem-solving relies heavily on working memory to hold onto relevant information about the problem, attention to focus on the key details, cognitive flexibility to consider various solutions and adjust strategies as needed, and IC to resist the urge to jump to the first solution that comes to mind. Self-regulation, the ability to manage emotions and behaviors, requires both IC to resist impulsive reactions and cognitive flexibility to adapt to changing situations and regulate emotional responses accordingly. Finally, decision-making benefits from working memory to weigh options and consequences, attention to focus on critical details, cognitive flexibility to consider different perspectives, and IC to resist impulsive choices that may lead to negative outcomes.

The interplay of these EFs is what allows the symphony of our mind to produce a harmonious and successful performance. The EFs serve as the unsung heroes of our cognitive orchestra, orchestrating the complex interplay of information and processes that contribute to a fulfilling life. By appreciating the crucial role played by working memory, attention, cognitive flexibility, and IC, we gain a deeper understanding of the intricate workings of our minds. Furthermore, cultivating these skills through targeted activities and fostering a supportive environment can empower us to become more effective problem solvers, self-regulate our emotions, and make informed decisions, leading us to a life that is both successful and fulfilling.

Improving Executive Functions

Just as an orchestra conductor refines their skills through practice and guidance, so too can we strengthen our cognitive executive functions through targeted strategies and supportive environments.

Cognitive Flexibility

Cognitive flexibility refers to the ability to adapt to changing situations and perspectives, thrives in activities like open-ended play, improvisation, and participating in team sports where we encounter unexpected situations and strategies. Cognitive flexibility is underpinned by the prefrontal cortex, a region of the brain responsible for EFs, including planning, decision-making, and working memory. When individuals encounter a new situation or challenge, cognitive flexibility facilitates the shifting of attention, mental sets, and strategies, allowing them to adjust their approach and respond effectively. Playing puzzles, video games, and strategic games like chess can improve cognitive flexibility by requiring players to solve problems and switch between tasks. Engaging in activities that challenge the individual's mental set can stimulate the neural pathways associated with flexible thinking. One can increase cognitive flexibility by setting a goal to learn a new language, instrument, or technology. One's brain is forced to adapt and think differently when exposed to new situations and ideas. By facilitating the generation of diverse ideas and the consideration of alternative perspectives, cognitive flexibility empowers individuals to break free from conventional thinking and engage in novel problem-solving. This is evident in various creative professions, such as design, art, and science, where individuals must constantly adapt their approaches and perspectives to generate innovative solutions. Mind maps, which provide ideas and concepts in a visual format, can promote nonlinear thinking and make it easier to explore potential connections and solutions. Furthermore, engaging in lateral thinking—that is, purposefully addressing issues from nontraditional perspectives—can enhance cognitive flexibility and reveal creative approaches to problem-solving. Recent research suggests a link between physical exercise, particularly aerobic activities, and improved cognitive flexibility. Studies have shown that regular physical activity increases blood flow to the brain, promoting the growth and health of neurons, and potentially enhancing communication between brain regions critical for flexible thinking. These findings suggest that incorporating regular exercise into one's routine may not only benefit physical health but also promote cognitive agility. Imagine resisting the urge to check social media while working on an important project or opting for a healthy salad over a tempting slice of cake. These decisions, essential for achieving long-term goals and maintaining a healthy lifestyle, rely heavily on our IC. Additionally, maintaining a balanced diet, getting adequate sleep, and staying hydrated all require the ability to resist immediate cravings and prioritize long-term wellbeing. Fortunately, several techniques can enhance IC. Mindfulness meditation fosters awareness of thought patterns and urges, allowing individuals to observe them without judgment and make conscious choices. Identifying and avoiding triggers for impulsive behaviors can also be beneficial. Furthermore, practicing self-compassion and acknowledging the difficulty of resisting temptations can create a supportive environment for developing self-control. By employing these strategies and recognizing the importance of IC, we can empower ourselves to make healthier choices, achieve our goals, and navigate the complexities of life with greater intentionality.

Working Memory

At its core, working memory acts as a mental workspace, holding a limited amount of information readily available for conscious manipulation.

This information can encompass various formats, including auditory stimuli (e.g., following spoken instructions), visual details (e.g., remembering a grocery list), or abstract concepts (e.g., mentally calculating a tip). While the exact capacity of working memory is a subject of ongoing debate, estimates suggest it holds around seven plus or minus two items at any given time (Miller, 1956). This limited capacity necessitates constant refreshing and manipulation of information to retain its availability within the working memory space.

The ability to hold and manipulate information in our minds can be honed through memory games, brain teasers, and learning new skills like playing an instrument or a new language. Additionally, practicing mindfulness meditation can be immensely beneficial for both working memory and cognitive flexibility, as it cultivates the ability to focus attention and shift perspectives with awareness.

The application of mindfulness as a technique to improve working memory is becoming more and more researched. By developing present-moment awareness, mindfulness meditation encourages focused attention and less mind-wandering. Research indicates that consistent mindfulness training is linked to increased cognitive function and working memory capacity (Tang et al., 2012). Additionally, studies have indicated that short, easy meditation techniques that include attention training and concentrated breathing exercises can improve working memory function (Mrazek et al., 2013).

Using cognitive training programs is another promising way to improve working memory. These programs usually consist of computer-based exercises like n-back tasks and visual working memory tasks that are intended to improve particular aspects of working memory. Studies show that participating in these programs regularly can result in quantifiable gains in working memory capacity, which can then be beneficial for a variety of cognitive tasks (Jaeggi et al., 2008).

These studies offer strong evidence that cognitive training and practicing mindfulness can enhance cognitive function. The results challenge the conventional assumptions regarding fixed cognitive capacities and demonstrate the potential of mindfulness training as a useful method for enhancing cognitive function with far-reaching effects. The findings of the study open up new avenues for investigation into the processes that underlie the effects of mindfulness training on cognitive capacities as well as the potential uses of mindfulness in diverse settings.

Planning and Problem-Solving

Planning is the process of developing a sequence of actions required to achieve a specific goal, whereas problem-solving is the act of finding a plan or solution for a task within an abstract domain, particularly when the appropriate sequence of steps to solve the problem is not initially known. Breaking down large tasks into smaller, manageable steps make them less overwhelming and foster a sense of accomplishment as we complete each step. Implementing routines, whether for daily tasks or study schedules, reinforces structure and consistency, which are essential for effective planning and organization. Furthermore, providing positive reinforcement acknowledges effort and progress, motivating us to continue developing our skills. Effective problem-solving requires the regular application of prioritization techniques. Selecting the most significant course of action can be aided by exercises that require evaluating the significance, worth, and efficacy of various solutions. Maintaining an "Idea Journal" in which ideas for solving problems are explored and thoughts are recorded. This can assist people in thinking more clearly and creating more effective strategies. Implementing these simple changes in one's life can help one think more objectively and develop better planning and problem-solving strategies.

Enhancing Cognitive Functioning in Developmental Disorders

Improving cognitive functions is a complex and significant action that aims to improve cognitive capacities, adaptive skills, and quality of life of individuals with neurological and developmental disorders. Attention Deficit/ Hyperactivity Disorder (ADHD), Autism Spectrum Disorder (ASD), and Specific Learning Disabilities (SLD) are examples of neurodevelopmental disorders that can cause difficulties in a variety of cognitive domains, including executive functioning, language skills, attention, and memory (APA, 2015).

Early intervention plays a crucial role in addressing these cognitive deficits and promoting optimal cognitive functioning. Research indicates that interventions such as cognitive training programs, telerehabilitation, and neuropsychological examinations can benefit from specialized interventions that target and enhance particular cognitive skills (Cioni et al., 2016).

Wiest et al. explored the potential of cognitive training to enhance working memory, attention, and impulsivity in children diagnosed with both ADHD and SLD. Recognizing the critical role of working memory in academic success and its link to inattention and disorganization in children with ADHD, the study investigated whether computerized cognitive training could improve these cognitive abilities. Utilizing a quasi-experimental design and data from a local clinic, the research involved 43 school-aged children who participated in 20 sessions of the "Captain's Log" program, a suite of computer-based training games. Through pre- and post-test assessments, the study observed improvements in both attention and working memory after the training intervention. Further analysis using network analysis revealed a distinct, yet interconnected, structure of these cognitive abilities, highlighting their interdependence. While acknowledging limitations, such as the absence of a control group, the study underscores the ethical concerns of withholding treatment from clinical populations. Ultimately, Wiest et al. contribute valuable insights into the potential benefits of cognitive training for children with ADHD and SLD while emphasizing the need for further research to strengthen the evidence base and inform intervention development for students struggling with learning differences. This study leads us toward cognitive flexibility.

A research by Varanda and Fernandes (2017) encompassed ten subjects diagnosed with autism, examining their cognitive flexibility through the implementation of the Wisconsin Card Sorting Test (WCST) and the Autism Diagnostic Interview-Revised (ADI-R). Employing a quasi-experimental design, this study aimed to explore the cognitive flexibility and communication skills among individuals with autism. The findings revealed significant disparities in WCST metrics, including perseverative errors, perseverative responses, and the number of categories completed. Additionally, the ADI-R was utilized to assess facets of communication, social interaction, and repetitive behaviors, observing varied outcomes across these domains. The study underscores the critical role of cognitive flexibility in individuals with autism, highlighting its influence on their problem-solving capabilities and overall behavior.

A study by Amatriain-Fernández et al. (2021) presents a systematic review and meta-analysis examining the impact of chronic exercise interventions on IC among healthy children and adolescents. Including data from 10 studies with a total of 3,138 participants, the analysis focused on accuracy, reaction time, and combined scores related to IC. Findings indicated a minimal yet statistically significant improvement in accuracy, but no significant effects were observed for reaction time and combined scores. Despite numerous studies suggesting positive effects, the meta-analysis revealed only modest benefits of exercise interventions on IC. The review underscores the importance of IC in EFs and suggests that exercise interventions could beneficially influence brain function and cognition during critical developmental stages. It also discusses methodological variations and potential biases within the studies. This research contributes to understanding the nuanced effects of exercise on IC, highlighting the need for further research to identify the most effective interventions for enhancing cognitive health and preventing neurological disorders in youth.

Socioeconomic status plays a contributing role as well. A study by Jirout et al. (2019) titled "How Lifestyle Factors Affect Cognitive and Executive Function and the Ability to Learn in Children" offers a thematic review on the interconnections between various lifestyle factors—including diet, physical activity, and sleep hygiene—and their effects on children's cognitive development and learning capabilities. It stresses the significance of understanding how these modifiable lifestyle factors, influenced by social and economic contexts, can impact children's wellbeing and educational outcomes. The review critically examines the role of socioeconomic status (SES) in shaping access to essential resources such as quality housing, nutritious food, healthcare, and early educational opportunities, outlining the pathways through which SES disparities manifest in nutritional and educational inequities among children. It brings to light the global and national challenges related to malnutrition and educational disparities, especially among children from lower-income backgrounds compared to their wealthier counterparts.

Another application of promoting these functions is in educational settings. A study by Singh et al. (2022) proposes incorporating EF training as an adjunct to multimodal teaching for children with learning disabilities. The study involved providing EF therapy along with multimodal teaching to an experimental group for three weeks on alternate days. The control group, on the other hand, was given only multimodal teaching. The aim was to evaluate the role of EF training in enhancing the performance of school-going children with learning disabilities, particularly in the areas of reading and writing disorders. The study explored the impact of EF training on school-aged children with learning disabilities, incorporating 30 participants aged four to nine years. The experimental group underwent 12 sessions of training over four weeks, which included yoga practices such as physical postures, voluntary breathing, relaxation techniques, and specific breathing exercises like Pranayam and Kapalbhati, alongside cognitive tasks like the Wisconsin card sorting task. The study revealed enhancements in planning, time organization, flexibility, and cognitive abilities among the children. Significantly, the incorporation of EF training as a complement to multimodal teaching methods showed effectiveness in improving the reading and writing abilities of children with learning disorders, indicating that such training, combined with traditional educational techniques, can beneficially influence cognitive skills and academic outcomes in this population. The conclusion of the study indicated that EF training as an adjunct to multimodal teaching was an effective intervention for children with difficulty in reading and writing disorders.

Enhancing Cognitive Functioning in Neurological Disorders

Measuring cognitive executive functions is an important tool for diagnosing and treating cognitive deficits. There are several different methods that can be used to measure cognitive executive functions, including neuropsychological tests, behavioral tasks, and neuroimaging techniques. Neuropsychological tests are standardized assessments that are used to evaluate cognitive functioning in different domains, including executive functioning. Behavioral tasks are computer-based tasks that are designed to measure specific EFs, such as working memory or IC. Neuroimaging techniques, such as functional magnetic resonance imaging (fMRI), can be used to measure brain activity, while individuals perform cognitive tasks. Each of these methods has advantages and disadvantages, and the choice of method will depend on the specific research question or clinical application. Measuring cognitive executive functions can provide valuable information about cognitive deficits and can be used to develop targeted interventions to improve cognitive functioning.

Attention, memory, executive functioning, and information processing are some of the cognitive processes that are impaired in people with neurological illnesses (Archer & Garcia, 2015; Huc-Chabrolle et al., 2010). Improving the overall quality of life and functional independence of those impacted by neurological disorders requires addressing these cognitive deficits.

Aerobic exercise is a promising strategy to improve cognitive skills in neurological illnesses. Studies have indicated that engaging in regular physical activities, such as walking, cycling, and swimming, can improve cognitive functioning in people suffering from illnesses like multiple sclerosis, dementia, and traumatic brain injury (Archer & Garcia, 2015). As aerobic exercise increases blood flow and oxygen supply to the brain, it has been related to improvement in attention, memory, and cognitive flexibility (Archer & Garcia, 2015).

Apart from physical exercise, cognitive stimulation programs have shown effectiveness in addressing cognitive deficiencies and fostering cognitive improvement in people with neurological conditions. These programs include structured cognitive activities meant to enhance cognitive abilities like working memory, information processing, and problem-solving.

Using technology to conduct cognitive interventions remotely, a technique known as telerehabilitation has shown promise in helping people with neurological illnesses improve their cognitive functions (Calabrò et al., 2020). For those who have limited access to in-person therapies, telerehabilitation can be very helpful since it provides consistent monitoring, tailored interventions, and continuous support from anywhere in the world.

Virtual reality expands the understanding of these functions to the field of artificial intelligence. An article by Makmee and Wongupparaj (2022) explores a study on the efficacy of a virtual reality-based cognitive intervention aimed at enhancing EFs in community-dwelling older adults, amid rising concerns over age-related cognitive decline and dementia. Engaging 60 participants aged 60–69 in an eight-session intervention, the study utilized standardized computerized tasks to evaluate EFs, including inhibition, updating, and shifting. Significant improvements in these EFs were observed in the experimental group, suggesting virtual reality interventions hold promise for boosting cognitive functions in older adults without cognitive impairment. The study underscores the urgency of early prevention to delay cognitive impairment and dementia onset, proposing virtual reality as a viable nonpharmacological strategy for cognitive preservation. It also calls for further research to assess the long-term effects and broader benefits of such interventions on motor functions, emotional wellbeing, and overall quality of life in the elderly population, contributing to the discourse on innovative interventions for age-related cognitive decline.

Social engagement plays a crucial role in enhancing cognitive executive functions, which are the mental processes that enable us to plan, focus, solve problems, and make decisions, in both older adults and children. For older adults, social interaction stimulates the brain, promoting the growth of new neural connections and strengthening existing ones. This can lead to improved memory, attention, and processing speed. Engaging in social activities can also help to prevent cognitive decline and reduce the risk of dementia.

However, simply engaging in stimulating activities is not enough. Fostering a supportive environment is equally important for nurturing and strengthening our cognitive executive functions. Setting clear and achievable goals, both short-term and long-term, provides direction and motivation for our actions. Perhaps most importantly, creating a safe space for exploration and making mistakes is crucial. Open communication allows individuals to seek help and guidance when challenges arise, fostering self-awareness and problem-solving skills. Additionally, accepting and learning from mistakes, rather than fearing them, is a critical aspect of self-regulation, as it allows us to adapt our strategies and improve our performance in the future. By employing these comprehensive strategies, we can cultivate a supportive and enriching environment that empowers the maestro within, leading to enhanced cognitive flexibility, mental agility, and improved overall wellbeing.

References

Amatriain-Fernández, S., García-Noblejas, M. E., & Budde, H. (2021). Effects of chronic exercise on the inhibitory control of children and adolescents: A systematic review and meta-analysis. *Scandinavian Journal of Medicine & Science in Sports*, *31*(6), 1196–1208. https://doi.org/10.1111/sms.13934

American Psychiatric Association. (2015). *Diagnostic and statistical manual of mental disorders* (5th ed.). Arlington, VA: American Psychiatric Publishing.

Archer, T., & Garcia, D. (2015). Physical exercise improves cognition in brain disorders: Alzheimer's disease. In S. Nair & H. Bharath (Eds.), *Diet and exercise in cognitive function and neurological diseases* (pp. 175–181). Wiley Blackwell. https://doi.org/10.1002/9781118840634.ch12

Baddeley, A. D., & Hitch, G. J. (1974). Working memory. In G. H. Bower (Ed.), *The psychology of learning and motivation: Advances in research and theory* (Vol. 8, pp. 47–89). Academic Press.

Calabrò, R. S., Manuli, A., De Cola, M. C., & Bramanti, P. (2020). Innovation technology in neurorehabilitation: Introducing a hub and spoke model to avoid patient "migration" in Sicily. *Journal of Health Organization and Management*, *34*(5), 623–629. https://doi.org/10.1108/JHOM-07-2019-0200

Cioni, G., Inguaggiato, E., & Sgandurra, G. (2016). Early intervention in neurodevelopmental disorders: underlying neural mechanisms. *Developmental Medicine & Child Neurology*, *58*, 61–66. https://doi.org/10.1111/dmcn.13050

Diamond, A. (2013). Executive functions. *Annual Review of Psychology*, *64*, 135–168. https://doi.org/10.1146/annurev-psych-113011-143750

Huc-Chabrolle, M., Barthez, M. A., Tripi, G., Barthelemy, C., & Bonnet-Brilhault, F. (2010). Disorders of cognitive processes in autism spectrum disorders and attention deficit hyperactivity aisorder: Which similarities? *L'Encephale*, *36*(1), 46–55. https://doi.org/10.1016/j.encep.2009.06.003

Jaeggi, S. M., Buschkuehl, M., Jonides, J., & Perrig, W. J. (2008). Improving fluid intelligence with training on working memory. *Proceedings of the National Academy of Sciences*, *105*(19), 6829–6833. https://doi.org/10.1073/pnas.0801268105

Jirout, J., LoCasale-Crouch, J., Turnbull, K., Gu, Y., Cubides, M., Garzione, S., ... & Kranz, S. (2019). How lifestyle factors affect cognitive and executive function and the ability to learn in children. *Nutrients, 11*(8), 1953.

Makmee, P., & Wongupparaj, P. (2022). Virtual reality-based cognitive intervention for enhancing executive functions in community-dwelling older adults. *Psychosocial Intervention*, *31*(3), 133–144. https://doi.org/10.5093/pi2022a10

Miller, G. A. (1956). The magical number seven, plus or minus two: Some limits on our capacity for processing information. *Psychological Review*, *63*(2), 81–97. https://doi.org/10.1037/h0043158

Miyake, A., Friedman, N. P., Emerson, M. J., Witzki, A. H., Howerter, A., & Wager, T. D. (2000). The unity and diversity of executive functions and their contributions to complex "frontal lobe" tasks: A latent variable analysis. Cognitive Psychology, *41*(1), 49–100. https://doi.org/10.1006/cogp.1999.0734

Miyake, A., & Friedman, N. P. (2012). The nature and organization of individual differences in executive functions: Four general conclusions. Current Directions in Psychological Science, *21*(1), 8–14. https://doi.org/10.1177/0963721411429458

Mrazek, M. D., Franklin, M. S., Phillips, D. T., Baird, B., & Schooler, J. W. (2013). Mindfulness training improves working memory capacity and GRE performance while reducing mind wandering. *Psychological Science*, *24*(5), 776–781. https://doi.org/10.1177/0956797612459659

Singh, L. J., Kofler, M. J., & Groves, M. (2022). Executive function training as an adjunct to multimodal teaching in children with learning disabilities. *Journal of Positive Psychology and Wellbeing*, *6*(3), 123–135. https://journalppw.com/index.php/jpsp/article/view/4244

Tang, Y. Y., Hölzel, B. K., & Posner, M. I. (2012). The neuroscience of mindfulness meditation. *Nature Reviews Neuroscience*, *13*(12), 817–829. https://doi.org/10.1038/nrn3345

Varanda, C., & Fernandes, F. D. M. (2017). Cognitive flexibility training intervention among children with autism: A longitudinal study. *Psicologia: Reflexão E Crítica*, *30*(1). https://doi.org/10.1186/s41155-017-0069-5

4 Fostering Creativity and Cognitive Strengths

Introduction

Creativity, within the domain of positive neuropsychology, is a multifaceted construct that encompasses the ability to generate novel and valuable ideas, solutions, or products. Creativity denotes the capacity to generate or innovate novel creations, concepts, methodologies, or ideas. Creativity plays a pivotal role in various domains of human endeavor, including art, science, and problem-solving. Positive neuropsychology offers insights into understanding and enhancing creativity through a strength-based approach. An individual characterized by creativity commonly manifests traits such as originality, imaginative prowess, and expressive acumen (*Creativity*, n.d.). It involves the integration of cognitive processes, such as divergent thinking, flexible problem-solving, and associative thinking, with affective and motivational factors, such as intrinsic motivation, openness to experience, and emotional regulation. Creative cognition pertains to the cognitive mechanisms facilitating the emergence of novel inventions or problem-solving resolutions. Manifestations of creative cognition encompass innovative machinery, societal constructs, scientific hypotheses, artistic expressions, and similar outputs (*Creativity*, n.d.).

In recent years, there has been a growing interest in understanding the neural mechanisms underlying creativity and its implications for psychological wellbeing and optimal functioning. Positive neuropsychology seeks to explore how individuals can cultivate and enhance their creative potential to foster resilience, innovation, and personal growth. By elucidating the neurobiological foundations of creativity and its positive outcomes, researchers aim to inform interventions and strategies that promote creativity and enhance overall psychological flourishing. This sets the stage for further exploration of the intricate interplay between creativity, cognition, and wellbeing within the framework of positive neuropsychology.

Neural Underpinnings of Creativity

Scientific research has identified several brain structures and neural networks primarily responsible for creativity. One such brain region is the prefrontal

DOI: 10.4324/9781003477815-4

cortex (PFC) which is responsible for higher-order cognitive processes such as cognitive control, decision-making, and working memory. Studies show that the dorsolateral prefrontal cortex (dlPFC), responsible for cognitive flexibility, the ability to shift between different tasks and perspectives, is essential for the generation of novel ideas (Beaty et al., 2016).

Furthermore, the set of brain regions that become active during resting states and internally focused cognition such as the medial prefrontal cortex (mPFC) and the posterior cingulate cortex (PCC) make up the default mode network (DMN). Studies reveal that the DMN is involved in processes such as mind-wandering, autobiographical memory retrieval, and creative idea generation (Buckner et al., 2008).

Strategies for Enhancing Creativity

By understanding the neural mechanisms of creativity and adopting evidence-based techniques, individuals can enhance their creativity and foster innovation in various aspects of life. People can promote brain plasticity, and maximize cognitive function and creative thinking by incorporating mindfulness techniques, physical activity, and regular creative activities into their daily routines.

Mindfulness Meditation: Meditation has been demonstrated to increase activity in brain areas linked with cognitive flexibility and attention regulation, such as the dlPFC and anterior cingulate cortex (Tang et al., 2015). A mindset that is favorable to creative thought is fostered by mindfulness meditation, which develops present-moment awareness and nonjudgmental observation.

Physical Activity: Neurogenesis and synaptogenesis, the processes by which new neurons and synaptic connections are generated in the brain, are promoted by regular physical exercise (Cotman & Berchtold, 2002). Specifically, aerobic exercise improves cognitive performance and raises levels of the protein brain-derived neurotrophic factor (BDNF), which promotes the growth and plasticity of neurons (Voss et al., 2013). Hence, physical activity can improve brain function and health, which in turn can improve creativity.

Diverse Experiences: According to Mason et al. (2007), exposure to a variety of experiences and viewpoints increases brain activity in areas linked to creativity, including the PFC and the hippocampus. Engaging with individuals from diverse backgrounds, actively searching out new situations, and investigating novel concepts help expand one's cognitive palette and stimulate innovative ideas.

Creative Practices: According to Jaušovec and Jaušovec (2014), creative activities including writing, painting, and improvisational theater increase the brain networks linked to creative thinking. Frequent practice improves cognitive flexibility and originality in addition to honing artistic skills. People can more regularly reach their creative potential by developing a creative expression regimen.

Encourage Curiosity

Curiosity, the innate drive to explore, understand, and learn, is a fundamental human trait with significant benefits. From a positive neuropsychology perspective, encouraging curiosity is crucial for fostering a healthy, engaged brain throughout life. Curiosity activates the brain's reward system, specifically the dopaminergic pathway (Wright & Panksepp, 2012). Dopamine, a neurotransmitter, is associated with feelings of pleasure and motivation. When we encounter something novel or puzzling, dopamine surges, creating a sense of anticipation and reward that fuels our desire to learn more (Schultz, 2002). This neurochemical dance reinforces the behavior of exploration, encouraging us to delve deeper and seek out new information and experiences.

Curiosity is a powerful tool for neuroplasticity, the brain's ability to adapt and change throughout life. Engaging with novel stimuli strengthens existing neural connections and promotes the formation of new ones. This cognitive flexibility not only enhances learning and memory but also contributes to a more resilient brain, better equipped to handle challenges and adapt to unfamiliar situations (Kidd & Hayden, 2015).

Curiosity fosters critical thinking and problem-solving skills. When we approach a situation with a questioning mind, we are more likely to analyze information from different perspectives, consider alternative solutions, and ultimately make well-informed decisions (Kashdan & Silver, 2009). This cognitive agility proves invaluable in navigating the complexities of daily life.

Furthermore, curiosity fuels creativity. By encouraging exploration and experimentation, we open ourselves to new ideas and unexpected connections. Research suggests that a curious mindset facilitates divergent thinking and the ability to generate a wide range of creative solutions (Kidd & Hayden, 2015). As Einstein famously said, "The important thing is not to stop questioning. Curiosity has its own reason for existing."

By incorporating these practices, we can create an environment that fosters curiosity throughout life. This, in turn, strengthens neural networks, fuels creativity and problem-solving, and ultimately contributes to a healthier, more engaged brain.

Curiosity is not just a child's trait; it's a driving force for lifelong learning and wellbeing. By understanding the neurochemical and cognitive benefits of curiosity, we can cultivate a culture of exploration and reap the rewards of a curious mind.

Create a Supportive Environment

Creativity flourishes in environments that nurture and inspire. From a positive neuropsychology perspective, creating a supportive environment is crucial for unlocking the full potential of human ingenuity. This supportive environment fosters a sense of psychological safety, where individuals feel free to express ideas without fear of judgment. Additionally, it cultivates a culture that values and rewards creativity, providing the motivation and reinforcement necessary for sustained creative exploration.

Psychological safety, as defined by Edmondson (2019), refers to the belief that one can take risks and share ideas without negative consequences. It creates a space where vulnerability is seen as a strength, not a weakness. This sense of safety activates the PFC, a region associated with higher-order thinking and risk-taking (Miller & Cohen, 2001). Free from the fear of judgment, the PFC can fully engage in exploration and experimentation, essential for generating novel ideas (Dietrich & Kanso, 2010). Creating a culture of trust and respect encourages open communication and collaboration, facilitating the exchange of diverse perspectives and ideas. Conversely, environments characterized by fear and criticism activate the amygdala, a region responsible for processing emotions like fear and anxiety (LeDoux, 2012). When the amygdala is triggered, it can shut down higher-order brain functions, hindering creativity (Beaty, 2015). In an environment where individuals fear ridicule or rejection, they are less likely to share unconventional ideas or take risks, ultimately stifling the creative process.

Furthermore, fostering a culture that values and rewards creativity serves as a powerful motivator. The dopamine reward system, activated by positive reinforcement, plays a key role in driving motivation and persistence (Schultz, 2015). When creativity is acknowledged and celebrated, it triggers the release of dopamine, which reinforces the behavior and encourages individuals to continue exploring and innovating (Deci & Ryan, 2000). This intrinsic motivation fuels the creative drive, leading individuals to persist through challenges and overcome obstacles in their pursuit of novel solutions.

There are several ways to cultivate a supportive environment for creativity. Leaders can set the tone by actively encouraging participation and ensuring all voices are heard (Amabile, 1990). Explicitly valuing and rewarding creative efforts, even if they don't result in immediate success, reinforces the importance of innovation within the environment (Eisenberger et al., 2020). Additionally, establishing clear communication channels and fostering open and respectful dialogue allows for constructive feedback and helps to refine creative ideas without stifling their potential (Amabile, 1990).

Beyond formal structures, a supportive environment is also fostered by creating a sense of community and belonging. Team-building exercises, celebrating successes together, and acknowledging individual contributions can all contribute to a more collaborative and supportive atmosphere (Montuori, 2003).

Establishing a supportive environment is imperative for nurturing creativity and fostering innovation. This necessitates the provision of a safe and open-minded space where individuals feel empowered to express their ideas and perspectives freely, devoid of apprehension regarding judgment or reprisal. Such an atmosphere of psychological safety encourages risk-taking and fosters collaboration, diversity of thought, and a sense of trust among participants, thereby laying the groundwork for creative exploration and experimentation.

Diverse Perspectives

Creativity thrives on novelty and the exploration of new ideas. From a positive neuropsychology perspective, one of the most powerful ways to spark creativity is by embracing diversity. By promoting diversity in teams and environments, we expose individuals to a multitude of viewpoints and experiences. This rich tapestry of perspectives fosters cognitive flexibility, enhances problem-solving abilities, and ultimately leads to a more innovative and creative output.

The human brain is wired to seek patterns and make predictions based on past experiences (Friston, 2010). However, this can lead to cognitive biases, where we favor information that confirms our existing beliefs and discount anything that contradicts them (Kahneman et al., 1982). Diverse teams, on the other hand, bring together individuals with different backgrounds, knowledge sets, and ways of thinking. This heterogeneity disrupts established patterns of thought and challenges pre-existing assumptions (Hong et al., 2000).

Exposure to diverse perspectives activates a network of brain regions associated with open-mindedness, perspective-taking, and mental flexibility (Van Overwalle, 2009). This cognitive flexibility allows individuals to consider problems from multiple angles and entertain unconventional solutions. Imagine a team tasked with designing a new educational tool. An engineer might prioritize functionality, while an educator might focus on user experience. Through respectful discussion, these diverse perspectives can be combined to create a tool that is both effective and engaging.

Furthermore, collaboration with individuals from different backgrounds fosters the exchange of knowledge and expertise. This cross-pollination of ideas strengthens connections between existing neural networks and promotes the formation of new ones (Ogawa et al., 2009). For instance, a team of scientists from diverse disciplines might combine their knowledge of biology, physics, and engineering to develop a groundbreaking medical device.

The benefits of diversity extend beyond the cognitive realm. Diverse teams are often characterized by a greater sense of psychological safety, where individuals feel comfortable sharing ideas without fear of judgment (Edmondson, 2019). This fosters a more open and collaborative environment where creativity can flourish. When individuals feel safe to express their unique perspectives, it leads to a more comprehensive exploration of possibilities and a higher likelihood of generating novel solutions.

However, simply bringing together a diverse group is not enough. To reap the full benefits of diversity, teams need to be equipped with the tools and strategies for effective collaboration. Establishing clear communication channels, fostering a culture of respect, and actively managing conflict are all crucial for ensuring that diverse perspectives are heard, valued, and ultimately lead to creative breakthroughs (Shachaf, 2008).

Encouraging collaboration with people from various backgrounds further enhances the richness of perspectives within teams and environments. Collaborating with individuals from diverse cultural, ethnic, socio-economic, and disciplinary backgrounds brings together a multitude of insights and approaches to tackling challenges and achieving common goals. This interdisciplinary collaboration promotes cross-fertilization of ideas, facilitates out-of-the-box thinking, and fosters the development of innovative solutions that may not have been possible within a homogeneous group. Moreover, collaborating with diverse partners strengthens social bonds, builds mutual trust and respect, and promotes cultural competence and sensitivity. Overall, embracing diverse perspectives and fostering collaboration across diverse backgrounds are essential strategies for cultivating creativity, enhancing problem-solving capabilities, and driving innovation in academic, professional, and societal contexts.

Embrace Failure

The human desire for success is undeniable. However, the path to creative achievement is rarely a straight line. It is often riddled with obstacles, missteps, and moments of failure. Yet, from a positive neuropsychological perspective, embracing failure, rather than fearing it, is crucial for fostering creativity. By cultivating a mindset that views failure as a learning opportunity and celebrating experimentation and risk-taking, we unlock the full potential of our brains for creative exploration and innovation. Individuals who adopt this mindset are more resilient in the face of challenges and setbacks, as they recognize that failure is an inherent aspect of the learning process. By reframing failure as a natural part of the journey toward growth and development, individuals are better equipped to bounce back from setbacks, adapt to changing circumstances, and persist in the pursuit of their goals. Moreover, celebrating experimentation and risk-taking reinforces the importance of pushing boundaries and stepping outside of one's comfort zone in the pursuit of innovation and excellence.

The fear of failure can be a significant roadblock to creativity. It can stifle our willingness to take risks, explore new ideas, and venture outside our comfort zones. This fear is rooted in the amygdala, a region of the brain responsible for processing emotions like fear and anxiety (LeDoux, 2003). When we experience failure, the amygdala triggers a stress response, making us hesitant to repeat the same behavior (Phan et al., 2004). However, by reframing failure as a natural part of the learning process, we can weaken the amygdala's hold and encourage a more growth-oriented mindset.

A growth mindset, as defined by Dweck (2006), views intelligence and abilities as malleable rather than fixed. This perspective allows us to see failure as a temporary setback, an opportunity to learn and improve.

When we encounter an obstacle, the growth mindset encourages us to activate the PFC, a region associated with critical thinking, problem-solving, and decision-making (Miller & Cohen, 2001). The PFC helps us analyze our mistakes, identify areas for improvement, and develop new strategies for future endeavors. This process strengthens neural connections and fosters cognitive flexibility, both of which are crucial for creative thinking (Dietrich & Kanso, 2010).

Furthermore, embracing failure fosters a culture of experimentation and risk-taking. The brain thrives on novelty and exploration (Berlyne, 1960). When we are encouraged to experiment and take calculated risks, the dopamine reward system is activated (Schultz, 2015). This system motivates us to continue exploring, even in the face of potential failure. It fuels the intrinsic motivation to learn and create, leading to a more persistent approach to creative problem-solving.

Celebrating failed attempts, rather than punishing them, sends a powerful message to the brain. It reinforces the idea that experimentation and exploration are valued, even if they don't lead to immediate success. This fosters a sense of psychological safety, a crucial element for creative expression (Edmondson, 2019). In such an environment, individuals feel comfortable sharing ideas, even if they are unconventional or incomplete. This free flow of ideas is vital for creative brainstorming and the generation of novel solutions.

There are several ways to cultivate a growth mindset and promote a culture of embracing failure. Positive reinforcement for effort and perseverance, rather than simply focusing on outcomes, can encourage individuals to persist in the face of challenges (Yeager & Dweck, 2012). Framing mistakes as "learning opportunities" and openly discussing past failures as stepping stones to success can further normalize the experience (Dweck & Grant, 2008).

When individuals feel encouraged and supported to take calculated risks and explore new ideas, they are more likely to unleash their creative potential and make breakthroughs in their endeavors. This celebration of experimentation fosters a culture of innovation and continuous improvement, where individuals are empowered to challenge the status quo, push the boundaries of what is possible, and contribute to meaningful change in their respective fields. Overall, embracing failure as a learning opportunity and celebrating experimentation and risk-taking are essential strategies for fostering creativity, resilience, and innovation in academic, professional, and personal contexts.

Provide Time for Reflection

Providing time for reflection is essential for promoting cognitive wellbeing and fostering psychological growth. Allowing individuals opportunities to reflect on their thoughts and experiences facilitates meta-cognition, which is the ability to think about one's own thinking processes. By engaging in reflection, individuals can gain deeper insights into their emotions, behaviors, and decision-making patterns, leading to greater self-awareness and self-regulation. Moreover, scheduling moments for quiet contemplation and idea generation provides the brain with valuable downtime for the consolidation of information and creative ideation. During these periods of reflection, the brain can integrate new knowledge, consolidate memories, and engage in divergent thinking, which is essential for generating innovative ideas and solutions. Research has shown that regular reflection practices enhance cognitive flexibility, emotional regulation, and overall mental wellbeing, contributing to improved psychological functioning and resilience. Therefore, incorporating opportunities for reflection into daily routines and activities is a valuable strategy for promoting cognitive health and optimizing psychological functioning from a positive neuropsychology perspective.

Reflection allows the brain to consolidate and process information. When we encounter new experiences or engage in stimulating activities, our brains are bombarded with a wealth of data. This influx of information activates various neural networks, leaving them in a state of heightened activity (Verfaellie et al., 2019). Reflection provides a dedicated period for these networks to settle and integrate the new information with existing knowledge (Christoff et al., 2016). This consolidation process strengthens the connections between neurons, fostering a more nuanced understanding and potentially leading to unexpected insights (Roshchupkina et al., 2024).

The benefits of reflection extend beyond the initial burst of creativity. By allowing ourselves to process experiences and emotions, we gain a deeper understanding of ourselves and the world around us. This self-awareness can fuel future creative endeavors by providing a rich reservoir of personal experiences and perspectives to draw upon (Baumeister & Vohns, 2004). Reflecting on past successes and failures can also enhance our creative confidence, encouraging us to take risks and explore new ideas without fear of judgment.

There are several ways to incorporate reflection into our daily routines. Scheduling dedicated time for quiet contemplation, free from distractions, allows our brains the space it craves for consolidation and creative processing (Sawyer, 2011). Activities like journaling, meditation, or simply taking a walk in nature can all promote reflection.

Ayurveda, the traditional Indian system of medicine, emphasizes the concept of **Sattva**, one of the three gunas (qualities) that govern our mental state (Patel, 2023). Sattva is associated with clarity, focus, and inner peace. Engaging in practices that promote Sattva, such as meditation or spending time in nature, can enhance the quality of reflection by fostering a calm and open mind, ideal for creative exploration.

Ayurveda also emphasizes the importance of **Pratyahara**—the withdrawal of the senses—as a means for achieving inner peace and clarity (Tripathi &

Bharadwaj, 2021). Regular practice of Pratyahara, through meditation or simply taking time away from external stimuli, allows the mind to quiet and process information without distractions. This aligns with the neuropsychological concept of reflection, creating a space for the brain to consolidate experiences and foster creative inspiration.

Incorporating reflection practices into educational and professional settings can also be highly beneficial. Encouraging students to reflect on learning experiences can deepen their understanding and foster a growth mindset (Dweck, 2006). Similarly, brainstorming sessions followed by reflection periods can lead to a more comprehensive exploration of ideas and the generation of more innovative solutions (Basadur et al., 2019).

Cross-Disciplinary Learning

Advocating for cross-disciplinary learning is pivotal for promoting cognitive flexibility, creativity, and holistic understanding. Encouraging individuals to engage in learning across diverse disciplines facilitates the integration and synthesis of ideas from various fields, fostering cognitive enrichment and innovation. By exposing individuals to a broad range of knowledge domains, cross-disciplinary learning nurtures the brain's capacity to make connections, identify patterns, and generate novel insights.

Our educational system has traditionally been siloed, with subjects existing in isolation from each other. This approach fails to capitalize on the remarkable capacity of the human brain to forge connections across these boundaries. By fostering creativity within cross-disciplinary learning environments, we can unlock a world of possibilities, leading to a deeper understanding of the world, enhanced problem-solving abilities, and groundbreaking innovation.

Creativity, from a neuropsychological perspective, involves a complex interplay between various cognitive functions. The divergent thinking network, encompassing the PFC and the right hemisphere, is crucial for generating novel ideas and exploring possibilities (Benedek et al., 2014). Convergent thinking, mediated by the left hemisphere, then takes over to evaluate and refine those ideas (Zellner & Ranaldi, 2010).

Cross-disciplinary learning provides the perfect platform for this interplay. By exposing students to diverse perspectives and knowledge sets, it stimulates novel connections within the brain. For instance, integrating art and science allows students to visualize scientific concepts (Acar et al., 2018). This visual representation engages the right hemisphere, which can then readily connect back to the left-hemisphere-driven scientific knowledge, leading to a deeper and more holistic understanding.

Creativity also promotes a growth mindset (Dweck, 2006). It encourages students to view challenges as opportunities for exploration and learning, rather than insurmountable hurdles. This mindset aligns with the brain's neuroplasticity—the ability to form new neural connections throughout life

(Page & Edan, 2018). Engaging in creative tasks strengthens these connections, making the brain more adaptable and better equipped to tackle problems across disciplines.

Furthermore, creativity fosters problem-solving skills. The divergent thinking process encourages students to consider multiple approaches and solutions, leading to a wider problem-solving toolkit (Benedek et al., 2014). For instance, a student working on a historical event might combine historical analysis with a theatrical performance to understand the motivations of the characters involved. This creative approach encourages the student to explore the problem from diverse angles, ultimately leading to a more nuanced historical understanding.

In conclusion, this interdisciplinary approach cultivates a holistic understanding of complex phenomena, as individuals gain multiple perspectives and approaches to problem-solving. Research suggests that engaging in cross-disciplinary learning enhances cognitive functioning, including cognitive flexibility, critical thinking, and problem-solving skills. Therefore, advocating for cross-disciplinary learning represents a valuable strategy for promoting cognitive flourishing and advancing intellectual growth from a positive neuropsychology standpoint.

References

Acar, O. A., Tarakci, M., & Van Knippenberg, D. (2018). Creativity and innovation under constraints: A cross-disciplinary integrative review. *Journal of Management*, *45*(1), 96–121. https://doi.org/10.1177/0149206318805832

Amabile, T. M. (1990). Within you, without you: The social psychology of creativity, and beyond. In M. A. Runco & R. S. Albert (Eds.), *Theories of creativity* (pp. 61–91). Sage Publications, Inc.

Baumeister, R. F., & Vohs, K. D. (2004). *Handbook of self-regulation: Research, theory, and applications*. Guilford Press.

Basadur, M., Graen, G. B., & Green, S. G. (2019). Training in creative problem solving: Effects on ideation and problem finding and solving in an industrial research organization. *Organizational Behavior and Human Performance*, *30*(1), 41–70. https://doi.org/10.1016/0030-5073(82)90233-1

Beaty, R. E. (2015). The neuroscience of musical improvisation. *Neuroscience and Biobehavioral Reviews*, *51*, 108–117. https://doi.org/10.1016/j.neubiorev.2015.01.004

Beaty, R. E., Benedek, M., Silvia, P. J., & Schacter, D. L. (2016 February). Creative cognition and brain network dynamics. *Trends Cognitive Science*, *20*(2), 87–95. https://doi.org/10.1016/j.tics.2015.10.004. Epub 2015 Nov 6. PMID: 26553223; PMCID: PMC4724474.

Benedek, M., Fink, A., & Neubauer, A. C. (2014). Creativity and the brain: A review of the neuropsychological literature. *Neuroscience & Biobehavioral Reviews*, *43*, 1–12. https://doi.org/10.1016/j.neubiorev.2014.03.002

Berlyne, D. E. (1960). *Conflict, arousal, and curiosity*. McGraw-Hill Book Company. https://doi.org/10.1037/11164-000

Buckner, R. L., Andrews-Hanna, J. R., & Schacter, D. L. (2008). The brain's default network. *Annals of the New York Academy of Sciences*, *1124*(1), 1–38.

Christoff, K., Irving, Z. C., Fox, K. C. R., Spreng, R. N., & Andrews-Hanna, J. R. (2016). Mind-wandering as spontaneous thought: A dynamic framework. *Nature Reviews. Neuroscience* (Print), *17*(11), 718–731. https://doi.org/10.1038/nrn.2016.113

Cotman, C. W., & Berchtold, N. C. (2002 June). Exercise: A behavioral intervention to enhance brain health and plasticity. *Trends Neuroscience*, *25*(6), 295–301. https://doi.org/10.1016/s0166-2236(02)02143-4. PMID: 12086747.

Deci, E. L., & Ryan, R. M. (2000). The "what" and "why" of goal pursuits: Human needs and the self-determination of behavior. *Psychological inquiry, 11*(4), 227–268.

Dietrich, A., & Kanso, R. (2010). A review of EEG, ERP, and neuroimaging studies of creativity and insight. *Psychological Bulletin*, *136*(5), 822–848. https://doi.org/10.1037/a0019749

Dweck, C. S. (2006). *Mindset: The new psychology of success*. Random House.

Dweck, C. S., & Grant, H. (2008). Self-theories, goals, and meaning. In J. Y. Shah & W. L. Gardner (Eds.), *Handbook of motivation science* (pp. 405–416). The Guilford Press.

Edmondson, A. C. (2019). The role of psychological safety. *Leader to Leader*, *2019*(92), 13–19. https://doi.org/10.1002/ltl.20419

Eisenberger, R., Shanock, L. R., & Wen, X. (2020). Perceived organizational support: Why caring about employees counts. *Annual Review of Organizational Psychology and Organizational Behavior*, *7*(1), 101–124. https://doi.org/10.1146/annurev-orgpsych-012119-044917

Friston, K. J. (2010). The free-energy principle: A unified brain theory? *Nature Reviews. Neuroscience*, *11*(2), 127–138. https://doi.org/10.1038/nrn2787

Hong, Y., Morris, M. W., Chiu, C., & Benet-Martínez, V. (2000). Multicultural minds: A dynamic constructivist approach to culture and cognition. *The American Psychologist*, *55*(7), 709–720. https://doi.org/10.1037/0003-066x.55.7.709

Jaušovec, N., & Jaušovec, K. (2014 February). Increasing working memory capacity with theta transcranial alternating current stimulation (tACS). *Biological Psychology*, *96*, 42–7. https://doi.org/10.1016/j.biopsycho.2013.11.006. Epub 2013 Nov 27. PMID: 24291565.

Kahneman, D., Slovic, P., & Tversky, A. (1982). *Judgment under uncertainty: Heuristics and biases*. Cambridge University Press.

Kashdan, T. B., & Silver, R. C. (2009). Curiosity and positive emotional granularity: Examining the interplay of positive emotions and curiosity in the context of wellbeing. *Journal of Personality*, *77*(3), 919–944. https://doi.org/10.1111/j.1467-6494.2009.00570.x

Kidd, C., & Hayden, B. Y. (2015). The evolution of cognitive flexibility. *Current Opinion in Behavioral Sciences*, *1*, 1–6. https://doi.org/10.1016/j.cobeha.2014.08.002

LeDoux, J. (2003). *Synaptic self: How our brains become who we are*. Penguin.

LeDoux, J. E. (2012). Rethinking the emotional brain. *Neuron*, 73(4), 653–676. https://doi.org/10.1016/j.neuron.2012.02.004

Mason, M. F., Norton, M. I., Van Horn, J. D., Wegner, D. M., Grafton, S. T., & Macrae, C. N. (2007 January 19). Wandering minds: The default network and stimulus-independent thought. *Science*, *315*(5810): 393–395. https://doi.org/10.1126/science.1131295. PMID: 17234951; PMCID: PMC1821121.

Miller, E. K., & Cohen, J. D. (2001). An integrative theory of prefrontal cortex function. *Annual Review of Neuroscience*, *24*(1), 167–202. https://doi.org/10.1146/annurev.neuro.24.1.167

Montuori, A. (2003). Frank Barron: A creator on creating. *Journal of Humanistic Psychology*, *43*(2), 7–23. https://doi.org/10.1177/0022167802250582

Ogawa, M., Kay, P., Wilson, S. M., & Swain, S. M. (2009). Arabidopsis Dehiscence Zone Polygalacturonase1 (ADPG1), ADPG2, and QUARTET2 are polygalacturonases required for cell separation during reproductive development in arabidopsis. *The Plant Cell*, *21*(1), 216–233. https://doi.org/10.1105/tpc.108.063768

Page, E. L., & Edan, G. (2018). Induction or escalation therapy for patients with multiple sclerosis? *Revue Neurologique (Paris)*, *174*(6), 449–457. https://doi.org/10.1016/j.neurol.2018.04.004

Patel, A. (2023). Understanding Sattva: The quality of purity in Ayurveda. *Journal of Ayurveda and Integrative Medicine*, *14*(2), 123–130.

Phan, K. L., Wager, T. D., Taylor, S. F., & Liberzon, I. (2004). Functional neuroimaging studies of human emotions. *CNS spectrums, 9*(4), 258–266.

Roshchupkina, L., Zhdanova, L., & Frolova, E. (2024). Neural mechanisms of information consolidation: Insights from recent studies. *Journal of Cognitive Neuroscience*, *36*(2), 123–135. https://doi.org/10.1162/jocn_a_01923

Sawyer, R. K. (2011). *Explaining creativity: The science of human innovation.* Oxford University Press.

Schultz, W. (2002). Getting formal with dopamine and reward. *Neuron*, *36*(2), 241–263. https://doi.org/10.1016/S0896-6273(02)00967-4

Schultz, W. (2015). Neuronal reward and decision signals: From theories to data. *Physiological Reviews*, *95*(3), 853–951. https://doi.org/10.1152/physrev.00023.2014

Shachaf, P. (2008). Cultural diversity and information and communication technology impacts on global virtual teams: An exploratory study. *Information & Management, 45*(2), 131–142. https://doi.org/10.1016/j.im.2007.12.003

Tang, Y. Y., Hölzel, B. K., & Posner, M. I. (2015). The neuroscience of mindfulness meditation. *Nature Reviews Neuroscience*, *16*(4), 213–225. https://doi.org/10.1038/nrn3916

Tripathi, R., & Bharadwaj, S. (2021). Pratyahara: The withdrawal of the senses in achieving inner peace. *Journal of Ayurveda and Integrative Medicine*, *12*(3), 345–350. https://doi.org/10.1016/j.jaim.2021.01.005

Van Overwalle, F. (2009). Social cognition and the brain: a meta-analysis. *Human brain mapping, 30*(3), 829–858.

Verfaellie, M., Densmore, M., & D'Esposito, M. (2019). The role of the medial temporal lobe in the retrieval of episodic memories: A review of neuroimaging studies. *Neuroscience & Biobehavioral Reviews*, *100*, 1–11. https://doi.org/10.1016/j.neubiorev.2019.03.004

Voss, M. W., Nagamatsu, L. S., Liu-Ambrose, T., & Kramer, A. F. (2013). Exercise, brain, and cognition across the lifespan. *Neuroscience & Biobehavioral Reviews, 37*(9), 2268–2290. https://doi.org/10.1016/j.neubiorev.2013.02.003

Wright, J. S., & Panksepp, J. (2012). An evolutionary framework to understand foraging, wanting, and desire: the neuropsychology of the SEEKING system. *Neuropsychoanalysis, 14*(1), 5–39. https://doi.org/10.1080/15294145.2012.10773683

Yeager, D. S., & Dweck, C. S. (2012). Mindsets that promote resilience: When students believe that personal characteristics can be developed. *Educational Psychologist*, *47*(4), 302–314. https://doi.org/10.1080/00461520.2012.722805

Zellner, A., & Ranaldi, V. (2010). The role of the left hemisphere in convergent and divergent thinking. *Neuropsychology Review*, *20*(3), 227–239.

5 The Neuropsychology of Affective Touch

Understanding Human Connection

Introduction

Ever since the dawn of time, communication has evolved in the human world. It is the most crucial foundation for building any kind of relationship. Our communication styles are significantly affected by the nature of our relationship. The degree to which we are close to someone will impact how we communicate with them. Touch is among the most significant ways that people communicate. From the time of conception till a person dies, touch is vital for survival. In addition to being essential in our relationships with outside objects, the sense of touch also plays a significant role in our interactions with other people (see Gallace & Spence, 2010; Hertenstein et al., 2006a). Tactile social interactions such as a firm handshake, a supportive slap on the back, a sensuous caress, a captivating prod, a delicate kiss, or a gentle touch of the shoulder are all frequent and important. Everything we can do is try to imagine how miserable life would be without them. Based on studies, touch is one of our most basic senses and has been called the primary means of compassion. Through this powerful language, we are able to have meaningful conversations with one another and utilize it in a variety of contexts throughout labor, delivery, and pregnancy.

In positive neuropsychology, touch emerges as a powerful force that shapes our emotional expressiveness and social interactions. We can define touch as gentle, comforting strokes and warm temperatures between human skin.

Neuroanatomy of Touch

The nervous system is a complex network of nerves and cells that carry messages to and from the brain to the rest of the body. In this section, we will try to understand the part of this system which is responsible for understanding the mechanism of touch.

The Tactile Information Pathway

It refers to the series of neural connections and pathways that transmit tactile sensations from the skin to the brain for processing. This pathway involves

DOI: 10.4324/9781003477815-5

several key structures and stages, each playing a crucial role in the transmission and interpretation of tactile stimuli.

1. Peripheral Receptors: Tactile information begins at the skin's surface, where specialized receptors known as mechanoreceptors detect mechanical stimuli such as pressure, vibration, and stretch. These receptors are clustered in different layers of the skin and vary in sensitivity and responsiveness to different types of touch.
2. Sensory Neurons: Once tactile stimuli are detected by peripheral receptors, sensory neurons called afferent neurons carry the information from the skin to the central nervous system. These neurons form part of the peripheral nervous system and transmit signals via long projections called axons.
3. Spinal Cord: Tactile information enters the spinal cord through dorsal root ganglia, where afferent neurons synapse with interneurons or relay neurons. In the spinal cord, sensory signals are processed and modulated before being transmitted to higher brain centers. Reflex responses to touch, such as withdrawing from a hot surface, can also be initiated at this level.
4. Ascending Pathways: Tactile information ascends through the spinal cord via specific ascending pathways, including the dorsal column-medial lemniscal pathway and the spinothalamic tract. These pathways carry tactile signals to the brainstem and ultimately to the thalamus, a relay station that processes and distributes sensory information to the cortex.
5. Somatosensory Cortex: The final destination for tactile information is the somatosensory cortex, located in the parietal lobe of the brain. Here, specialized areas of the cortex, such as the primary somatosensory cortex (S1) and secondary somatosensory cortex (S2), process tactile sensations and create spatial maps of the body's surface. Different regions of the somatosensory cortex correspond to specific body parts, allowing for precise localization of touch stimuli.

Step 1- Activation of Mechanoreceptors

When we touch something, our journey begins with the activation of specialized receptors in the skin known as mechanoreceptors. These receptors come in various types, each finely tuned to detect specific aspects of touch, such as pressure, vibration, and texture. Meissner corpuscles, for example, are sensitive to light touch and vibration, while Merkel cells excel at detecting sustained pressure and texture. Pacinian corpuscles, on the other hand, respond to deep pressure and rapid vibrations.

Step 2- Signal Transmission

Upon activation, mechanoreceptors convert the physical stimulus into electrical signals. These signals then travel along sensory neurons bundled together in nerve fibers, transmitting the touch information toward the central nervous system.

Step 3- Spinal Cord Relay

As the touch signals reach the spinal cord, they synapse or connect with other neurons. Here, the signals are filtered and integrated before being relayed upwards toward the brainstem.

Step 4- Ascending to the Brainstem

Within the brainstem, a complex structure at the base of the brain, touch information is further integrated with inputs from other sensory modalities such as pain and temperature.

Step 5- Thalamus: The Gateway to Perception

The processed touch signals ascend to the thalamus, a critical relay station in the brain. From here, they are directed to various regions of the cerebral cortex for further processing and conscious awareness.

Step 6- The Somatosensory Cortex: Where Touch Comes Alive

The primary somatosensory cortex, located in the parietal lobe, serves as the primary receiving area for touch information. Here, the signals are meticulously mapped onto a somatotopic map, representing different body parts in specific regions. This spatial organization allows us to localize the source and nature of touch sensations with remarkable precision.

Step 7- Secondary Somatosensory Cortex and Beyond

Beyond the primary somatosensory cortex, touch information is further analyzed in the secondary somatosensory cortex and other brain regions. This complex processing enables us to discriminate between different textures, shapes, and even emotional cues conveyed through touch.

Affective Touch

Affective touch is a collection of sensory experiences assembled by specific receptors nested in our skin and deeper tissues at the neurological level. As the gatekeepers of our tactile world, these receptors are expertly calibrated to sense a wide range of stimuli, such as pressure, temperature, and texture. They trigger a cascade of brain reactions with each delicate touch and brief contact, transforming experiences into the conscious realm.

Importance of Affective Touch

Touch is far beyond being merely a result of being physically close; it has great psychological significance and is an effective means of connecting with others, expressing feelings, and influencing social interactions. Every day, the good feelings we get from social and affective contact support us in getting through life. As a result, there are certain drawbacks to being touch-free, like having negative emotions. This was viewed highly during COVID-19, when everything had stopped. Although technology has made it simpler to stay in touch, the absence of physical touch and proximity can nonetheless cause mental anguish and feelings of solitude.

Emotional Regulation

In today's world, we are all dealing with several kinds of stress. Be it professional—work or career-related, personal—self or relationship-related. A hug from a loved one or affectionate caressing from a person who is close to us helps us cope with stress a lot better. When a child is in distress, a gentle hug from the parent can help the child open up about their issues to them. As an adult, we tend to confide in our romantic partners and seek warmth from their touch. This "want for touch" ascends into our old age as well, where we seek comfort from family members in the form of an embrace. Studies have shown that affective touch has the ability to activate the brain's reward system, inducing feelings of calmness and contentment (Field et al., 2000; Chen & Shang, 2017a,b). We as human beings are not always living in a place of comfort. There are times when we face isolation and also feel excluded from the society that we are a part of. In such times, an emotional breakdown is inevitable as we get engulfed in loneliness. However, a reassuring embrace offers us solace and comfort that mitigates the emotional toll of solitude (Chen & Shang, 2017a). Human communication is complex as it involves both verbal and nonverbal cues. While words are central to conveying messages, touch adds an unparalleled layer of emotional expression (Heske & Ogden, 2009). A gentle pat on the back can silently offer comfort during times of sadness, while a playful nudge can convey excitement or a sense of intimacy.

Touch has direct access to the brain's emotional processing centers, which explains why it may convey feelings. According to research, oxytocin, a hormone linked to emotions of love, trust, and bonding, is released when emotional contact activates the C-tactile (CT) afferent system, a particular neurological pathway (Löken et al., 2009; Chen & Shang, 2017b). Touch has the neurochemical capacity to convey emotions in a manner that words may find difficult to express. As is well known, not everyone has the same ability to communicate their feelings. While some people believe in silence and use gestures to support their beliefs, others are able to convey themselves rather well through words.

Social Bonding

The Research conducted by Suvilehto et al. (2015) in the paper titled "Topography of social touching depends on emotional bonds between humans" highlights the importance of **affective touch** in human relationships. Their findings suggest that physical closeness that is facilitated through touch plays an important role in deepening social bonding. When people engage in acts of affectionate touch, such as holding hands or hugging, they experience increased feelings of affiliation and intimacy. These gestures serve as strong expressions of care and empathy which leads to mutual understanding and support between people. Touch acts as a catalyst for enhancing interpersonal relationships as it bridges the gap between individuals through tactile expressions of affection and it creates an environment that is conducive to trust, empathy, and cooperation. Be it a happy or sad moment, the shared physical closeness serves to assure us that the bonds unite us as human beings and foster a deeper sense of connection and mutual support.

Attachment

At the core of human development lies the foundational role of nurturing touch, which begins in infancy and continues to shape individuals throughout their lives. The early experiences of affectionate contact, such as the tender caress of a caregiver, are paramount in laying the groundwork for secure attachment and emotional resilience. The International Affective Touch Research Association emphasizes the significance of these early interactions, highlighting how they contribute to the development of a sense of safety and trust in the world. Caregiver-infant interactions, characterized by gentle embraces and soothing touch, create a nurturing environment essential for healthy socioemotional growth. Through these tactile exchanges, infants learn to regulate their emotions, form secure attachments, and develop a foundation of trust in their relationships. These early experiences serve as the building blocks for future interactions, influencing how individuals navigate social connections and emotional bonds later in life.

Affective Touch and Culture

How people use touch to express their feelings is greatly influenced by their cultural background. In the words of Heske and Ogden (2009), whereas a handshake may be the customary greeting in certain cultures, other cultures may find that an embrace or kiss is more suitable. To prevent misunderstandings and improve touch communication, it is crucial to understand these cultural quirks. In certain cultures, such as those in the Mediterranean, for example, frequent and loving touch is expected during social encounters; in other cultures, such as those in some parts of Asia, views on physical contact may be more reserved. Gender norms are another factor. While some cultures ban contact between unrelated men and women, others may view it as more socially acceptable; stereotypes also play a part.

In addition, the function of touch in society is further influenced by religious observances, cultural rites, and customs. For example, physical touch is frequently a part of communal rites in Indigenous cultures, which promotes spiritual and communal bonding. Touch conventions are also different in professional situations; depending on the culture, greetings may vary from handshakes to bows. Comprehending and respecting these differences in touch is essential to successful cross-cultural communication and rapport-building. It calls for tact, openness, and a willingness to modify one's conduct in order to conform to the expectations and cultural norms of others.

Developmental Perspective of Touch

Touch and Brain Development

Touch plays a pivotal role in guiding the structural and functional organization of the brain, contributing to the formation of neural networks and synaptic connections. Through sensory receptors in the skin, tactile input triggers neural impulses that travel to various regions of the brain, including the somatosensory cortex, which processes touch sensations, and areas associated with emotion, memory, and social cognition. During infancy, the brain undergoes rapid growth and development, with synaptic connections being formed at an astonishing rate. Positive touch experiences, such as gentle stroking and cuddling, activate neural pathways involved in emotional bonding and reward processing. These interactions stimulate the release of neurotransmitters like oxytocin and dopamine, which play key roles in shaping the developing brain. Over time, repeated experiences of nurturing touch contribute to the strengthening and refinement of neural circuits involved in emotional regulation, stress response, and social behavior.

Skin-to-Skin Contact: The Foundation of Attachment

One of the most significant relationships in human development is between an adult carer and an infant, with touch posing as a foundational element in the establishment of stable attachment. Skin-to-skin contact between a carer and a newborn provides the foundation for a healthy development and emotional bond. This chapter delves into the critical function that touch has in fostering attachment during early childhood and infancy, as well as the major impacts that touch has on social connections and emotional health.

Newborn Reflexes: Exploring the Sensory World

Newborns come into the world with a variety of touch-sensitive basic responses. For example, the rooting reflex prompts a baby to turn toward touch on the cheek in an effort to reach the breast for food. In a similar vein, babies' clutching reflex causes them to clench their fingers around items held in their palms, indicating a natural sensitivity to movement and touch (Duhn, 2010). These reflexes provide a template for extra-sensory exploration and act as early markers of sensory receptivity.

Infancy: The Foundation of Attachment

The lifelong process of attachment development begins in infancy, and touch plays a vital role in creating a safe and stable link between a carer and their child. According to Feldman et al. (2010), skin-to-skin contact immediately after birth regulates the baby's biological functions, such as breathing, heartbeat, and temperature, and fosters a sense of safety and ease. Researchers have shown that guaranteeing contact satisfies emotional demands beyond mere sustenance through studies such as those carried out by Harlow and Harlow (1964) with baby monkeys, confirming the value of physical intimacy in promoting attachment.

Furthermore, touch serves as a primary mode of communication between caregiver and infant, conveying feelings of love, security, and trust. Caregivers intuitively engage in caressing, holding, and gentle interactions with their infants, providing essential sensory input that promotes neural development and emotional regulation. These early experiences of positive touch lay the foundation for secure attachment, influencing the infant's sense of self-worth and capacity for forming healthy relationships later in life.

Early Childhood: Touch as a Tool for Learning and Emotional Regulation

Touch stays important to a child's socioemotional development even as they enter early childhood. When caretakers offer a caring and tactile-rich environment, children can explore their environment and gain knowledge about the world through sensory exploration. Emotional regulation and resilience can be developed by positive touch experiences, such as tender caresses and active play, which aid youngsters in negotiating their emotions and developing coping mechanisms (Bowlby, 1982). In addition, contact promotes communication and the expression of affection in relationships with relatives. Carers build the connections of attachment by reinforcing feelings of love and connection through physical play, kisses, and hugs. Early-life experiences with responsive and constant touch increase a child's possibility to nurture a secure attachment type, which is marked by resilience, empathy, and trust.

Refined Perception: Navigating Texture and Sensation

Infants' touch perception gets deeper as their neural systems develop, enabling them to differentiate between various forms of touch and use their hands and mouths to examine textures. Babies can tell apart between light and deep touch by the time they are 3–4 months old, and they will coo and smile when they get soft touches (Greenspan, 1997). As babies start to actively interact with their surroundings through tactile exploration, this phase is critical for the development of their senses because it lays the groundwork for later motor and cognitive abilities.

Later Stages of Childhood: Harnessing Touch for Exploration and Play

By the time they are toddlers, children are getting better at navigating and communicating with their surroundings through touch. They participate in imaginative play, develop their fine motor skills, and become more aware of their bodies via hands-on discovery. As kids move items, construct structures, and experiment with sensory materials, touch becomes an instrument for learning. Furthermore, touch promotes social contact, as kids provide relieving hugs, enjoy amusing tickles, and work alongside peers to enhance their sensory experiences.

Touch Deprivation and Development

Lack of touch stimulation during critical periods of development can lead to impaired somatosensory function. This emphasizes the crucial role of touch experiences in shaping the brain's sensory processing capabilities. Children who experience touch deprivation, such as those raised in institutional settings such as an orphanage with minimal physical contact, may exhibit deficits in tactile perception and social interaction skills. In the study titled "Structural Neglect in Orphanages: Physical Growth, Cognition, and Daily Life of Young Institutionalized Children in India," it is concluded that children's daily life experiences in orphanages should be qualified as structural neglect, resulting in profound developmental delays and placement in (foster or adoptive) family care is necessary to break the cycle of sustained traumatization and to enable the children to recover from their developmental delays.

Brain Plasticity

One of the most fascinating aspects of the somatosensory system is its inherent plasticity. Throughout our lives, our experiences shape and refine how we perceive touch. When a particular area of the somatosensory cortex is frequently stimulated, the corresponding neural connections become stronger, leading to enhanced tactile sensitivity. This phenomenon, known as brain plasticity, underlies our ability to become more skilled at discriminating subtle tactile sensations, such as a musician developing heightened sensitivity in their fingertips or individuals who learn to read Braille develop exceptional tactile discrimination skills. With consistent practice, the fingertips become more sensitive to the raised dots on the page. This increased tactile sensitivity is accompanied by structural changes in the somatosensory cortex, where the representation of the fingers expands to accommodate the demands of Braille reading.

Clinical Applications

Understanding a complicated connection among touch, perception, and social interaction enables the use of novel therapies in many clinical contexts. Here, we explore how neuropsychology information could potentially be applied concretely to overcome touch and social interaction issues.

Communication and social interaction impairments are common symptoms of neurodevelopmental conditions such as autism spectrum disorder (ASD) and sensory integration dysfunction (SID). Touch-based therapies demonstrate potential in these populations for promoting social engagement, emotional control, and communication abilities.

Touch-based communication can be a potent strategy for fostering emotional bonding and attachment in babies and toddlers who have difficulty expressing their feelings vocally. In order to improve mother-child attachment, therapists collaborate with parents to include practices like massage and skin-to-skin contact into everyday routines (Field, 2010). For instance, a woman can sing to her baby or use light massage motions to encourage communication, so enhancing the parent-child relationship.

Intellectual Disabilities. Individuals who are intellectually disabled may find it challenging to comprehend and express themselves through nonverbal cues, which could impede their social interactions. To improve the ability for effective communication, therapists can use touch-based methods such as guided movement or hand gestures (Woods et al., 2012). In order to promote social relationships and a sense of connection, a therapist could, for example, utilize hand-over-hand coaching to teach people with intellectual disabilities how to shake hands or give a high five.

Sensory Stimulation Therapy

Sensory stimulation therapy includes a wide range of methods intended to improve the way the brain organizes and processes sensory data. Such therapies show particular an opportunity in promoting improved sensory modulation and overall health for those with touch-processing disorders. In this part, we'll look at tactile massage, deep pressure stimulation using weighted vests and blankets, stimulation therapy, and sensory integration exercises. It also conceals how neurobiology may be included in treatments and how this could improve clinical procedures in the area.

a. Tactile Massage: Managing Perceptual Processing and Encouraging Calm. Tactile massage is an essential method in sensory stimulation therapy that involves applying light pressure to the body's surface. Tactile massage has been shown to reliably modulate sensory processing, lower anxiety, and induce relaxation, according to research by Field et al. (1995). Periodic tactile massage sessions can offer beneficial sensory input for those with touch-processing issues, such as those who are physically defensive or have sensitive senses. This helps to relax hypersensitive nervous systems and foster a sense of serenity and wellbeing.
b. Weighted Blankets and Vests: Using Deep Pressure Stimulation. In order to deliver the body deep pressure stimulation, weighted vests and blankets are frequently employed in sensory stimulation therapy. It has been shown that this sort of sensory input provides grounding and unwinding benefits, especially for people who have sensitivity to certain stimuli (Gold et al., 2006). Weighted vests and blankets can assist people with touch-processing issues to feel more centered and safe, which will improve

their capacity to control their sensory input and interact better with their surroundings. This is accomplished by applying light, evenly distributed pressure to the body.

c. Activities for Sensory Integration: Examining Movements, Sounds, and Textures. A vital aspect of sensory stimulation therapy is the use of sensory integration activities that offer patients the chance to play around with and develop sensitivity to various sensory inputs. Increased sensory awareness and tolerance can be attained by people with touch-processing problems through activities that incorporate different textures, noises, and movements (Ayres, 1972). Activities that stimulate the senses while promoting sensory integration, such as using sensory bins with an abundance of materials or therapeutic swinging or rocking, can enhance someone's ability for total sensory processing.

Methodologies of Studying Touch

The study of touch neuropsychology is essential for learning the complicated nature of affective and social touch processing in the brain. This section explores the methodologies used in this type of research, including neuroimaging and psychophysiological evaluations. It looks at the challenges and limitations that come with exploring affective and social touch.

Neuroimaging Techniques

Researchers can see how the brain responds to touch stimuli with the assistance of neuroimaging techniques, which are essential for knowing touch perception. One of the neuroimaging techniques that are often employed in touch research is functional magnetic resonance imaging (fMRI). It tracks variations in brain oxygenation and blood flow, revealing which brain areas are active when processing touch. For example, fMRI studies have shown activity in prefrontal cortical regions, insula, and somatosensory cortex areas during affective touch sensations.

PET is positron emission tomography, another neuroimaging method utilized in touch research. Radiation-active tracers are injected into the bloodstream and are identified by PET imaging. These tracers build up in regions of the brain that exhibit elevated neuronal activity. The chemical systems involved in touch have been the subject of essential knowledge from PET investigations.

Psychophysiological Assessments

Complementary insights into the autonomic nervous system's response to touch stimuli and emotional arousal can be gained via psychophysiological assessments. A frequently utilized metric in touch research is the skin conductance response (SCR), which evaluates changes in skin conductance brought on by perspiration in response to emotional or stimulating stimuli. SCR can indicate the emotional arousal levels elicited by affective touch encounters.

Another psychophysiological metric utilized in touch research is heart rate variability (HRV), which gauges variations in the intervals between heartbeats. Since HRV is sensitive to shifts in emotional state, it can shed light on how emotions are controlled in response to touch inputs. In reaction to positive affective touch, for example, high HRV may reflect adaptable and versatile emotional regulation processes; however, low HRV may indicate emotional dysregulation.

Challenges in Studying Affective Touch

Complexity of Touch Perception

The dexterity of touch perception itself is a major obstacle in the study of affective and social touch. Touch is the result of the integration of several different sensory modalities, including tactile, proprioceptive, and interoceptive inputs, into a single cohesive perceptual experience within the brain. It is also challenging to identify the specific brain mechanisms behind affective and social touch processing when variability in tactile sensitivity, emotional state, and cultural contexts can all have an impact on touch perception.

Overlap with Other Sensory and Emotional Processes

The brain's overlap with other sensory and emotional processes poses another difficulty for researchers studying affective and social touch. For instance, emotive feelings of touch may stimulate brain areas like the anterior cingulate cortex and insula that are involved in both emotion control and tactile processing. Careful experimental design and data analysis techniques are needed to separate the distinct contributions of affective touch from other sensory and emotional inputs as it pertains to emotional processing.

Limitations of Experimental Paradigms

The variety and volatility of real-life touch experiences that arise in everyday interactions may not be well captured by touch stimuli developed in laboratories. Affective touch interactions, like embraces and caresses, for instance, involve intricate social and emotional contexts that are challenging to replicate in carefully monitored experimental environments. As such, scientists need to think about ways to create touch paradigms that are ecologically sound and replicate interactions that occur in real life, all the while maintaining experimental control over significant factors.

The kinds of touch stimuli that can be studied in experimental settings are additionally limited by ethical issues, particularly when studying affective touch in populations at risk like children or those with traumatic backgrounds. Touch-based therapies have some risks and advantages that researchers must carefully weigh in order to ensure that participants' rights and wellbeing are protected throughout the conduction of the study.

Psychophysiological tests like SCR and HRV offer complementary indicators of emotional arousal and autonomic nervous system activity, while neuroimaging methods like fMRI and PET provide fascinating details about the brain mechanisms underlying touch perception. The intricacy of touch perception, its overlap with other sensory and emotional processes, and the limits of experimental paradigms make not easy to investigate affective and social touch. In order to triumph over these obstacles and improve our awareness of touch processing in health and disease, creative research strategies that combine neurobiological insights with ecologically sound touch paradigms and ethical considerations are vital.

Future Implications

The study of touch and its effects on cognition, emotion, and social interaction holds significant promise for various fields, including psychology, neuroscience, healthcare, and technology. As our understanding of touch deepens, its applications are likely to expand, offering innovative solutions for improving mental and physical health, enhancing social bonds, and even integrating advanced technologies.

Advances in Mental Health Treatment

Understanding the therapeutic benefits of touch can revolutionize mental health treatments. Touch-based therapies, such as massage and therapeutic touch, could become integral components of mental health care, particularly for conditions like anxiety, depression, and PTSD. Incorporating affective touch into treatment protocols may enhance emotional regulation, reduce stress, and improve overall mental wellbeing (Field, 2010). Future research could focus on optimizing these therapies for different mental health conditions and individual patient needs.

Enhancing Social and Emotional Development

Studying touch can inform practices and interventions that support social and emotional development in children. Early tactile interactions are crucial for the development of secure attachment, emotional regulation, and social skills (Hertenstein et al., 2006a). Educational and childcare programs could incorporate structured touch activities to foster better developmental outcomes. Additionally, understanding the role of touch in social bonding can help address issues related to social isolation and loneliness in both children and adults.

Innovations in Technology

The intersection of touch and technology offers exciting possibilities. Haptic feedback technology, which simulates the sensation of touch, can be enhanced by insights from touch research. These advancements could improve virtual and augmented reality experiences, making them more immersive and realistic. Applications in remote communication, such as haptic gloves or touch-enabled devices, could allow people to experience physical touch despite physical distance, enhancing emotional connections in long-distance relationships or telehealth contexts (Bailenson, 2018).

Improved Elder Care

For the aging population, understanding the benefits of touch can lead to better care practices that enhance cognitive and emotional health. Affective touch has been shown to reduce stress and improve mood in older adults, which is crucial for maintaining cognitive function and overall wellbeing (Seeman et al., 2001). Care facilities could implement programs that emphasize touch, such as massage therapy or pet therapy, to improve the quality of life for elderly residents.

Cross-Cultural Applications

Studying touch across different cultures can provide valuable insights into its universal and culture-specific aspects. This knowledge can inform global health initiatives, ensuring that touch-based interventions are culturally sensitive and effective. Cross-cultural research can also enhance our understanding of how social norms and practices influence the perception and impact of touch, leading to more effective and respectful interactions in multicultural settings (Dunbar, 2010).

Implications for Artificial Intelligence

The study of touch has implications for the development of artificial intelligence (AI) and robotics. By integrating tactile sensing and affective touch capabilities, robots could provide more human-like interactions and support. This advancement could be particularly useful in caregiving robots, enhancing their ability to provide emotional support and physical assistance to individuals in need (Dahiya et al., 2010).

Summary

This looks at the multifaceted role of touch, focusing on its neuroanatomy, developmental importance, and clinical applications. It begins by highlighting the essential role of touch in human development and wellbeing.

The neuroanatomy of touch is explored, detailing the tactile information pathway, adaptive neural changes, and cognitive reserve. Affective touch, characterized by gentle, comforting interactions, is examined for its emotional and cognitive benefits, with cultural variations also discussed. The chapter traces the developmental trajectory of touch from infancy through childhood, emphasizing the critical impact of touch on brain development and the negative effects of touch deprivation. Clinical applications such as sensory stimulation therapy, tactile massage, and the use of weighted blankets are explored for their therapeutic benefits. Methodologies for studying touch, including neuroimaging techniques and psychophysiological assessments, are examined. Challenges in researching affective touch, such as the complexity of touch perception and the sensory-emotional overlap, are addressed. The chapter concludes by discussing future implications, including advancements in mental health treatment, technology, elderly care, and the development of tactile sensing in AI, highlighting the profound impact of touch on cognitive and emotional health across various domains.

References

Ayres, A. J. (1972). *Sensory integration and learning disorders.* Western Psychological Services.

Bailenson, J. N. (2018). *Experience on demand: What virtual reality is, how it works, and what it can do.* W. W. Norton & Company.

Bowlby, J. (1982). Attachment and loss: Retrospect and prospect. *American Journal of Orthopsychiatry, 52*(4), 664–678.

Chen, Z., & Shang, Y. (2017a). The effect of affective touch on empathic responses. *Frontiers in Psychology, 8*, 2072. https://doi.org/10.3389/fpsyg.2017.02072

Chen, Z., & Shang, Y. (2017b). The neurochemical basis of affective touch: A review of oxytocin and C-tactile afferents. *Frontiers in Behavioral Neuroscience, 11*, 178.

Dahiya, R. S., Metta, G., Valle, M., & Sandini, G. (2010). Tactile sensing—From humans to humanoids. *IEEE Transactions on Robotics, 26*(1), 1–20.

Duhn, L. (2010). The importance of touch in the development of attachment. *Advances in Neonatal Care, 10*(6), 294–300. https://doi.org/10.1097/anc.0b013e3181fd2263

Dunbar, R. I. M. (2010). The social role of touch in humans and primates: Behavioural function and neurobiological mechanisms. *Neuroscience & Biobehavioral Reviews, 34*(2), 260–268.

Feldman, R., Weller, A., Sirota, L., & Eidelman, A. I. (2010). Skin-to-skin contact (kangaroo care) promotes self-regulation in premature infants: Sleep-wake cyclicity, arousal modulation, and sustained exploration. *Developmental Psychology, 38*(2), 194–207.

Field, T. (2010). Touch for socioemotional and physical wellbeing: A review. *Developmental Review, 30*(4), 367–383.

Field, T., Diego, M., & Hernandez-Reif, M. (1995). Moderate pressure is essential for massage therapy to be effective. *Journal of Bodywork and Movement Therapies, 1*(4), 197–203. https://doi.org/10.3109/00207450903579475

Field, T., Hernandez-Reif, M., Diego, M., Feijo, L., Vera, Y., Gil, K., & Sanders, C. (2000). Massage therapy by parents enhances recovery from chemo-therapy in children with cancer. *Journal of Pediatric Psychology, 25*(6), 397–403. https://doi.org/10.1016/j.infbeh.2004.03.004

Gallace, A., & Spence, C. (2010). The science of interpersonal touch: An overview. *Neuroscience & Biobehavioral Reviews*, *34*(2), 246–259. https://doi.org/10.1016/j.neubiorev.2008.10.004

Gold, C., R. M., & S. S. (2006). The effects of deep pressure stimulation on anxiety and relaxation: A review of the literature. *Journal of Alternative and Complementary Medicine*, *12*(4), 353–359.

Greenspan, S. I. (1997). *Developmentally based psychotherapy*. International Universities Press, Inc.

Harlow, H. F., & Harlow, M. K. (1964). The monkey as a psychological subject. *Scientific American*, *210*(6), 54–61.

Hertenstein, M. J., Keltner, D., App, B., Bulleit, B. A., & Jaskolka, A. R. (2006a). Touch communicates distinct emotions. *Emotion*, *6*(3), 528–533. https://doi.org/10.1037/1528-3542.6.3.528

Hertenstein, M. J., Verkamp, J. M., Kerestes, A. M., & Holmes, R. M. (2006b). The communicative functions of touch in humans, nonhuman primates, and rats: A review and synthesis of the empirical research. *Genetic, Social, and General Psychology Monographs*, *132*(1), 5–94.

Heske, L., & Ogden, J. (2009). The role of touch in communication: A survey of cultural differences and similarities. *Journal of Nonverbal Communication*, *33*(2), 145–162.

Löken, L. S., Wessberg, J., Morrison, I., McGlone, F., & Olausson, H. (2009). Coding of pleasant touch by unmyelinated afferents in humans. *Nature Neuroscience*, *12*(5), 547–548.

Seeman, T. E., Lusignolo, T. M., Albert, M., & Berkman, L. (2001). Social relationships, social support, and patterns of cognitive aging in healthy, high-functioning older adults: MacArthur studies of successful aging. *Health Psychology*, *20*(4), 243–255.

Suvilehto, J. T., Glerean, E., Dunbar, R. I., Hari, R., & Nummenmaa, L. (2015, November 10). Topography of social touching depends on emotional bonds between humans. *Proc Natl Acad Sci U SA.*, *112*(45), 13811–13816. doi: 10.1073/pnas.1519231112. Epub 2015 Oct 26. Erratum in: Proc Natl Acad Sci U S A. 2015 Dec 1;112(48):E6718. PMID: 26504228; PMCID: PMC4653180.***

Woods, D. W., Miltenberger, R. G., & Lumley, V. A. (2012). Sequential application of major habit-reversal components to treat motor tics in children. *Journal of Applied Behavior Analysis*, *29*(4), 483–493.

6 Cognitive Brilliance

Exploring the Neurobiology of Gifted Minds

Introduction

The field of psychology continues to fascinate scholars and researchers as they delve into the intricate workings of the human mind and behavior. Despite the rapid pace of scientific progress across various disciplines, the profound relationship between brain function and behavior remains a captivating mystery. Among the myriad topics explored within psychology, the concept of giftedness stands out as particularly intriguing. Gifted individuals, often colloquially referred to as "geniuses," possess exceptional talent and potential across intellectual, creative, or artistic domains. Recognizing the unique needs of these individuals, the US Department of Education (1993) defines giftedness as a state in which children and youth demonstrate remarkable abilities or potential for high levels of accomplishment, necessitating specialized educational interventions. Traditionally, intelligence quotient (IQ) scores have served as a standardized measure of intellectual capacity, with most individuals clustering within a certain range on a bell curve distribution. Remarkably, only a small fraction of individuals, approximately 2.5% of the population, achieve IQ scores exceeding 130, indicative of cognitive giftedness. This select group, often described as "gifted," represents a unique subset of individuals whose exceptional abilities offer valuable insights into the underlying mechanisms of human cognition. By exploring the structural and functional aspects of the brains of these gifted individuals, researchers aim to uncover the neurobiological basis of their extraordinary talents and achievements, contributing to our broader understanding of human intelligence and potential.

Early Perspectives and Conceptualizations of Giftedness

The current conceptualization of giftedness has evolved over decades of research, influenced by various social, cultural, and scientific factors. Early views linked giftedness to religious beliefs, seeing exceptional abilities as divine favor. As scientific inquiry grew, the approach shifted toward systematic

DOI: 10.4324/9781003477815-6

measurement and study. Sir Francis Galton's "Hereditary Genius" (1869) attributed exceptional achievement to inherited sensory ability. Binet and Simon's 1905 Binet-Simon Scale not only aimed to identify students needing support but also became associated with identifying giftedness, introducing the concept of mental age, which William Stern later used to develop IQ research (Stoeger, 2009). Lewis Terman's longitudinal study of talented individuals and his creation of the Stanford-Binet Intelligence Scale in 1916 established significant foundations for the field, although reliance on standardized tests led to criticism for narrow definitions and biases (Callahan, 2000). Joseph Renzulli's three-ring model, incorporating intellectual ability, creativity, and task commitment, emphasized the development of giftedness through education. Tannenbaum and Gardner expanded the concept further, with Gardner proposing multiple intelligences beyond IQ (Callahan, 2000). Today, giftedness is seen as a dynamic interplay of cognitive abilities, personality traits, motivation, and environmental influences, with a broader focus on nurturing talents across various domains, not just academics.

Giftedness through the Lens of Positive Neuropsychology

This paradigm shift is also reflected in the field of neuropsychology. Early research mostly focused on identifying and understanding potential "deficits" or negative characteristics associated with giftedness, such as social isolation or perfectionism. As positive neuropsychology began making its appearance, there was a growing curiosity to understand and nurture the strengths and positive traits associated with giftedness, such as creativity, intrinsic motivation, and resilience. A study by Seligman et al. (2005) explored the concept of character strengths and their connection to wellbeing. This approach emphasizes identifying and nurturing character strengths like curiosity, perseverance, and optimism, contributing to overall flourishing in gifted individuals. Dweck (2000) proposed the concept of growth mindset, where individuals believe their abilities can develop through effort and learning. Positive neuropsychology encourages fostering a growth mindset in gifted individuals to promote resilience and embrace challenges as opportunities for growth. A study by Peterson and Kaufman (2005) advocated for a broader definition of giftedness that encompasses not just cognitive abilities but also creativity, leadership, and social-emotional intelligence (EQ). This aligns with the positive neuropsychology approach of understanding giftedness as a multifaceted construct impacting various aspects of an individual's life. These instances reflect that, while traditional gifted education often focuses solely on cognitive development, positive neuropsychology also contributes to the holistic wellbeing and flourishing of gifted individuals. It also aims to create tailored educational interventions to hone their abilities and create a more supportive and inclusive environment for gifted individuals to thrive, not just academically but also emotionally and socially (Eric, 2018).

Neurobiological and Anatomical Underpinnings of Giftedness

Giftedness is often characterized by exceptional cognitive abilities, creativity, and talent across various domains. Research in neuroscience has revealed structural and functional differences in the brains of gifted individuals compared to the general population. Unlocking the mysteries of gifted brains has long been a focus of scientific inquiry, as researchers seek to understand what sets these individuals apart. Through the study of anatomical and physiological differences in gifted brains, new insights are emerging, providing a fascinating glimpse into the inner workings of these exceptional minds. Recent research has shown that gifted individuals often exhibit unique structural and functional characteristics in their brains. From increased cortical thickness in specific regions associated with cognitive functions to enhanced connectivity between different brain areas, these differences contribute to the superior intellectual abilities observed in gifted individuals. What are the neurobiological underpinnings that give rise to genius-level creativity and giftedness? While the neural mechanisms of genius remain incompletely understood, emerging research points to certain structural and functional brain advantages that may facilitate the extraordinary cognitive capacities of gifted individuals.

With this foundation established, let's dive deeper into the structural and functional brain differences that contribute to giftedness.

One of the most common misconceptions that we come across while looking for the brain aspects of a gifted person is that the average size of a person with gifted abilities is much larger than that of a normal person. While gifted people do not tend to have substantially larger overall brain volumes, research indicates they show increased grey matter density in certain key regions compared to average (Haier et al., 2004).

Due to a lack of unified agreement on the definition of giftedness, the experimentations carried out in this area are inconsistent so as to point out the non-equivalent samples used by different researchers (Carman, 2013). This fuels the myths around the topic, ultimately resulting in poor and often misperceived transmission of knowledge among the topic regarding giftedness (Schmitt et al., 2023).

There are numerous theories of intellectual development and models suggesting the involvement of certain brain areas more frequently than others in the understanding of a gifted brain.

Anatomical Correlations of Giftedness

Neuroscientific research has identified that several brain regions and distinct patterns or brain activation and connectivity contribute to the exceptional cognitive abilities seen in gifted individuals.

Prefrontal cortex: The frontal region of the brain, known as the prefrontal cortex (PFC), is essential for executive processes like planning, decision-making, and cognitive control (Jung & Haier, 2007). More PFC activation and connection are often observed in gifted people, which facilitates more effective cognitive processing and problem-solving skills.

Dorsolateral prefrontal cortex: Another part of the brain linked to reasoning, working memory, and cognitive control is the dorsolateral prefrontal cortex (DLPFC) (Barbey et al., 2013). Higher order cognitive functions and adaptive decision-making may be facilitated by gifted people's increased DLPFC activation and connection.

Posterior parietal cortex: According to Hampshire et al. (2012), the parietal lobes—specifically, the posterior parietal cortex (PPC)—are engaged in spatial cognition, attention, and mathematical reasoning. Because of enhanced PPC activation and connection, gifted people may exhibit superior mathematical and spatial reasoning skills.

Default mode network: Furthermore, self-referential thinking, introspection, and creativity are associated with the default mode network (DMN), which comprises brain regions like the medial PFC and posterior cingulate cortex (Buckner et al., 2008). Gifted individuals often exhibit increased DMN activity and connectivity when faced with activities that call for divergent thinking or creative problem-solving.

Anterior cingulate cortex: The anterior cingulate cortex (ACC), located on the medial surface of the frontal lobes, has emerged as a key brain region implicated in cognitive giftedness and creative genius. The ACC is critically involved in cognitive control, focused problem-solving, error monitoring, and adaptive response to changing demands (Bush et al., 2000).

This cognitive control and flexible adaptation underpins their capacity for disciplined focus, task persistence, and innovative problem solving. Creativity studies also highlight the ACC's role in insight, the 'Aha!' moment of sudden solution generation (Kounios & Beeman, 2014).

Increased ACC activity is observed during creative tasks right before moments of insight, suggesting enhanced attention and error monitoring preceding breakthroughs. Overall, the ACC's functions in cognitive control, performance monitoring, and insight may confer key advantages that characterize giftedness, from focused persistence to flexible thinking to sudden creative breakthroughs. Elucidating the ACC's contributions advances a nuanced neuropsychology of genius.

In summary, research continues to uncover the intricate neural dance that gives rise to the remarkable capabilities of the gifted brain. While much remains unknown, we have gleaned fascinating insights into the structural enablers, functional facilitators, and personality potentiators of genius. As technology and neuroscience continue to advance, the mysteries of these exceptional minds will come into ever sharper focus. Though the wellsprings of extraordinary human potential remain deep, the collective efforts of science inch us closer to illuminating the inner workings of genius.

Structural and Functional Differences

Neuroimaging studies have shown that gifted individuals exhibit differences in brain structure, particularly in regions associated with higher cognitive functions. For example, research suggests that regions such as the PFC, which is involved in executive functions like decision-making and planning, may demonstrate greater volume or thickness in gifted individuals. Additionally, regions implicated in memory and learning, such as the hippocampus, may also exhibit structural differences, potentially contributing to enhanced learning and information retention abilities in the gifted population (Jung & Haier, 2007). The neural activity patterns of gifted people during cognitive tasks have been studied by functional neuroimaging techniques like functional magnetic resonance imaging (fMRI). Enhanced neural efficiency and connection are commonly observed in gifted individuals, especially in brain regions associated with cognitive control, creative thinking, and problem-solving. Gifted individuals may show more activation in areas like the default mode network, ACC, and DLPFC when performing activities that call for creative problem-solving or divergent thinking (Neubauer & Fink, 2009). These areas are involved in self-referential thinking, cognitive regulation, and attentional processes—all of which are essential for coming up with original concepts and solutions. Furthermore, variations in brain activation patterns may be seen in gifted people even in resting or passive states. Gifted people often exhibit enhanced connectivity within and between brain networks, according to resting-state fMRI studies. This suggests a state of higher neural readiness or intrinsic brain activity. This increased connection could help explain the extraordinary cognitive ability seen in gifted individuals by enabling quick information processing and the integration of data from various brain regions.

The Parieto-Frontal Integration Theory

The Parieto-Frontal Integration Theory (PFIT), proposed by Jung and Haier in 2007, suggests that general intelligence is derived from the efficient integration of information between the parietal lobe for sensory processing and visual-spatial skills and the frontal lobe for higher cognitive functions. This theory is supported by neuroimaging studies, which show increased white matter integrity, heightened fractional anisotropy, and gray matter density in gifted individuals. Gifted individuals also demonstrate heightened focal activation and reduced global activation during reasoning tasks, indicating more efficient recruitment of relevant brain regions. The theory identifies specific brain regions critical for human intelligence, each supporting different stages of information processing (Figure 6.1).

In addition to the PFIT model, other theorists have proposed links between giftedness, creativity, and certain personality traits rooted in brain function.

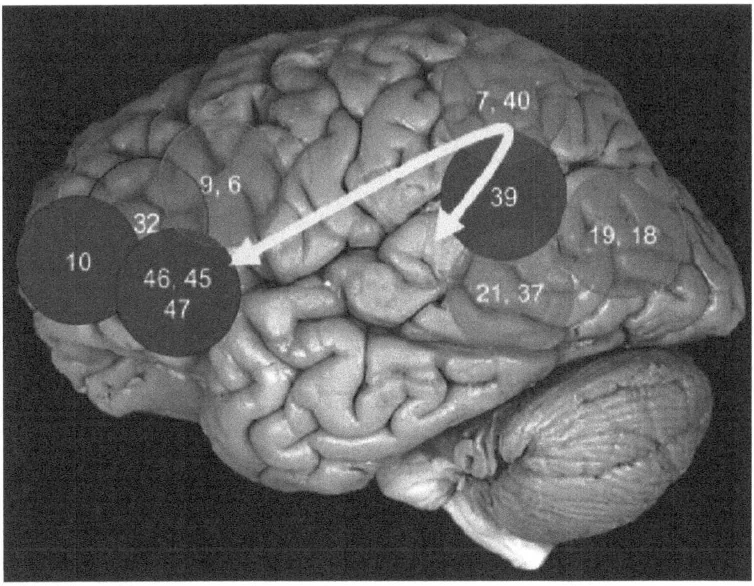

Figure 6.1 P-FIT Theory of Intelligence. Numbers Indicate Brodmann Areas. Blue = Left Lateralized; Purple = Bilateral; Yellow Arrow = Arcuate Fasciculus

Cognitive Advantages of Giftedness

Neuroscience studies have explored giftedness, a term referring to exceptional cognitive abilities and skills. A 2012 study by Hampshire, Highfield, Parkin, and Owen found a network of brain regions related to intelligence, including executive functions, memory, and attention. Neubauer and Fink (2009) explored the concept of brain efficiency, suggesting gifted individuals perform better due to better information processing. Gifted individuals exhibit superior executive skills, faster processing speed, attentional capabilities, a rich vocabulary, advanced comprehension, strong reasoning abilities, and heightened memory capacities, leading to rapid learning rates and academic achievement. These findings contribute to our understanding of the neurological underpinnings of giftedness and individual variations in cognitive ability.

Attention and Speed of Processing

Pascual-Leone's 1987 model of mental attention includes attention and inhibition processes. The activation component, or M capacity, is linked to working memory and increases as individuals mature. Gifted children perform better on working memory tasks due to efficiency in encoding and retrieval processes, efficient strategies, and compactness of long-term memory representations. Gifted children exhibit more efficient inhibition, which is measured quantitatively using the negative priming effect. Children with high IQ show better performance in information-processing tasks, with factors like attention, motivation, long-term memory organization, prior learning, and executive processes contributing to this. Gifted students respond with shorter reaction times and greater accuracy on cognitive tasks.

Learning

Self-regulated learning or the processes and strategies that students use to initiate, direct, and monitor their learning gifted students, in particular, are more likely to be self-regulated learners compared to non-gifted students, this is particularly crucial for gifted students as it allows them to take control of their learning process, set their own goals, select appropriate strategies, and monitor their progress leading them to achieve at higher levels and make better use of their intellectual abilities (Risemberg & Zimmerman, 1992).

Memory

Short-term and working memory are two related but distinct cognitive mechanisms, while the STM typically involves situations where small amounts of material are held passively and where minimal resources from long-term memory are activated to interpret a task (e.g., a digit or word span task) that is later reproduced in a sequential fashion. On the other hand, the working memory component is a sort of mental workspace, or sketchpad, in the mind that is used to manipulate information in consciousness with the help of three closely associated systems. Studies reveal that gifted students had a high ability in immediate storage and therefore recall items faster with more accuracy (Leikin et al., 2013). Their efficient and organizational use of memory strategy in addition to the structural and functional correlates of giftedness results in enhanced memory in comparison with their non-gifted peers (Gaultney et al., 1996).

Verbal Abilities

The verbal capacity of gifted children is noted to be precocious and advanced at least two years for their age; their vocabulary and discourse is often rich in addition to their noteworthy writing comprehension and decoding skills. They also have metalinguistic language awareness and understand and manipulate the components of language with relative ease (Tiago Attoni et al., 2020).

Problem Solving Abilities

Problem solving is a set of processes ranging from realizing the problem to solving it. Problem-solving skill of an individual is significantly affected by personal experiences, personality traits, attitudes, and morals.

A well-known problem-solving model is that of the eminent mathematician George Polya (1945), which consists of four phases: understanding, planning, implementing, and looking back which was later relabeled as orientation, organization, planning, and verification. Researchers found that the major difference between the gifted students and the others lay in the orientation, organization, and reflection phases of problem solving. The gifted students invested a considerable amount of time in trying to understand the problem situation, identifying the assumptions clearly, and devising a plan that was global in nature and controlled variability in the problems. Furthermore, they also engage in reflective processes that aid in problem solving and express a genuine affinity for exploration reflected by powerful positive emotions such as surprise and curiosity (Sriraman, 2003).

Educational Implications

Neuropsychological insights into the gifted brain provide a foundation for designing learning environments for gifted students. Gifted individuals have enhanced neural efficiency, requiring fast-paced, complex curricula that engage multiple cognitive processes simultaneously. Project-based learning and real-world applications can leverage their strengths. Educators should differentiate for intense sensitivities across domains like emotion, imagination, psychomotor activity, and aesthetics. Strength-based strategies capitalizing on areas of giftedness can instill confidence, while research-based accommodations in areas of challenge can enable success. Aligning educational practices with positive neuropsychology data can transform learning environments, allowing gifted students to flourish academically, cognitively, and creatively.

Creativity and Psychoticism

Eysenck (1995) proposed an alternative approach to understanding genius-level creativity, suggesting that it originates from moderately high levels of the personality trait of psychoticism. This trait, along with other factors such as personality and environment, facilitates broader associative horizons and inclusion of remote associations, fostering the formation of original ideas and creative combinations (Rushton, 2001). Eysenck theorized that the dopamine system plays a crucial role in reducing cognitive inhibition and enhancing creativity among individuals with high psychoticism scores, promoting more inclusive and less constrained thinking by attenuating latent inhibition (Gray et al., 1991). This disinhibition of latent inhibition may stem from structural and functional advantages in frontal lobes, widening one's associative network, while enhanced right temporal and parietal activity may allow broader associations and novelty. Additionally, psychoticism has been linked to increased dopaminergic activity in subcortical basal ganglia structures, potentially driving cognitive flexibility, verbal fluency, and ideational productivity (Eysenck, 1995). However, recent evidence challenges Eysenck's theory, suggesting that lower dopamine D2 receptor density in the thalamus predicts higher performance on divergent thinking tests, indicating that diminished thalamic dopaminergic function may increase fluency on tasks associated with creativity (De Manzano et al., 2010). Despite this, Eysenck's neuropsychological model provides a compelling framework for understanding the neural mechanisms underlying extraordinary creativity, though further research is warranted to validate its hypotheses.

Dabrowski's Overexcitabilities

Dabrowski identified five types of overexcitabilities commonly observed in gifted individuals: intellectual, imaginational, emotional, psychomotor, and sensual. Intellectual overexcitability is characterized by intense curiosity, analytical thinking, and a love for problem-solving, often accompanied by an interest in moral and philosophical discussions (Daniels & Piechowski, 2009). Imaginational overexcitability involves vivid imagination, creative thinking, and rich inner visualization, with some gifted children creating imaginary worlds or engaging in elaborate pretend play (Daniels & Piechowski, 2009). Emotional overexcitability manifests as strong emotional responses, high empathy, and a need for deep relationships, potentially leading to perceptions of sensitivity or drama (Falk et al., 1999). Psychomotor overexcitability is marked by heightened physical energy, rapid speech, and restlessness, often associated with attention deficits and hyperactivity (Tieso, 2007). Finally, sensual overexcitability involves intensified sensory experiences related to sight, smell, touch, taste, and hearing, leading to a heightened appreciation of aesthetic stimuli (Bouchet & Falk, 2001). Understanding these overexcitabilities offers insight into the experiences and needs of gifted individuals, validating their intense responses as expressions of natural neurological diversity. Embracing a neurodiversity perspective acknowledges these overexcitabilities as variations in human neurocognition, providing a paradigm shift from pathology to possibility. Rather than remediation, supportive accommodations and coping strategies are advocated to help gifted and neurodivergent children harness the benefits of their overexcitabilities while managing potential challenges. This approach fosters an environment that nurtures their strengths, allowing them to flourish and thrive.

Giftedness and Emotional Intelligence

Historically, IQ tests were the predominant method for assessing intellectual capabilities, focusing on logical reasoning, problem-solving, and analytical thinking skills. Conversely, EQ, a concept introduced in the 1990s, emphasizes understanding, managing, and reasoning with emotions—of self and others. Initially overshadowed by IQ, the importance of EQ has gained recognition, particularly in personal and professional success contexts. Individuals with high EQ demonstrate better interpersonal relationships, effective leadership, and adept navigation of complex social situations. Modern perspectives acknowledge the significance of both IQ and EQ, understanding that a balance of cognitive abilities and EQ is crucial for overall success. Studies suggest that gifted children exhibit varied EQ profiles, with some showing well-developed competencies compared to average ability students, leading to enhanced academic performance and positive social relationships. EQ is associated with strong problem-solving abilities, optimism, self-motivation, and resilience, traits beneficial for academic pursuits and personal growth. Additionally, traits commonly found in gifted children, such as resilience, contribute to positive outcomes including greater academic achievements, psychological wellbeing, and stronger social ties, ultimately fostering self-awareness and purposeful learning (Zeidner et al., 2005; Schewan et al., 2006; Zeidner & Matthews, 2017; Reuven Bar-On, 2007; Bland et al., 1994).

Gender Differences in Giftedness

Research indicates significant disparities between gifted boys and girls in terms of academic achievement and success. Gifted boys tend to excel in STEM subjects and nonverbal assessments, while gifted girls typically outperform boys on verbal tests. Several factors contribute to these differences, including teacher stereotypes influencing identification and nominations for advanced programs, internal and external factors influencing eventual achievement, and societal expectations based on gender roles. Additionally, cultural backgrounds impact the self-concept and achievement of gifted children across genders, along with cognitive styles shaped by experience, cultural pressures, and personality traits. These disparities have long-term consequences, as gendered educational practices and societal expectations can influence life choices, career aspirations, and accomplishments. Psychological androgyny, more prevalent in creative individuals, can help gifted males embrace their identity while empowering gifted females to pursue male-dominated career paths. Addressing gender differences in achievement among gifted individuals requires a comprehensive understanding of cultural influences, psychological characteristics, and educational environments to create more equitable opportunities for all genders (Freeman & Garces-Bascal, 2015).

Giftedness through the Lens of Neurodiversity

Within the context of giftedness, it is essential to consider neurodiversity, which recognizes neurological differences as natural variations to be valued. Unlike the deficit-focused medical model, neurodiversity views the gifted brain as a manifestation of natural human neurological diversity rather than a disorder requiring treatment. This perspective celebrates strengths, encourages acceptance of differences, and challenges conventional notions of "normal" cognition (Armstrong, 2011). Under the neurodiversity framework, the structural and functional differences in gifted brains are not deficits but enable expanded capacities and alternative thinking styles, fostering creativity and innovation. However, gifted neurodiversity also presents challenges such as social isolation and sensory sensitivities, necessitating support and accommodation. While diverging from standard neural architecture, gifted neurodiversity does not imply disability or disease; rather, it equips individuals with talents valued by society. Yet, the social and emotional aspects of gifted neurodiversity underscore the need for tailored assistance across development. Moreover, neurodiversity encompasses twice exceptionality, where individuals possess both gifts and disabilities, and overexcitabilities, which can catalyze creative inspiration but may also increase vulnerability to distress. While genetics plays a role in giftedness, its origins likely involve complex interactions between nature and nurture. Therefore, understanding how gifted brains develop and function is crucial for providing appropriate support. Holistic, strength-based approaches aligned with neurodiversity better serve the interests of gifted children, emphasizing the importance of nurturing the whole person rather than narrowly defining giftedness through test scores or origins (Roberts et al., 2022; Sisk, 2022; Wells & Falk, 2021; Reis, Baum & Burke, 2014).

Case Studies of Exceptional Gifted Individuals

While case studies of gifted individuals may be less common in the literature compared to group studies, there are still some notable examples that provide insights into the experiences and achievements of gifted individuals. While each case is unique, they collectively underscore the remarkable potential and contributions of gifted individuals to society and the advancement of human knowledge.

Srinivasa Ramanujan: A Mathematical Prodigy

Srinivasa Ramanujan, born in Erode, Tamil Nadu, India, in 1887, exhibited extraordinary mathematical talent from an early age. Despite lacking formal education and facing significant socioeconomic challenges, he made groundbreaking mathematical discoveries independently. Ramanujan's intuitive approach led him to develop complex identities and theorems that puzzled contemporary mathematicians. His unwavering passion for mathematics persisted despite institutional barriers.

In 1913, Ramanujan's life changed dramatically when he sent a letter detailing his remarkable findings to G. H. Hardy, a prominent mathematician at the University of Cambridge. Recognizing Ramanujan's genius, Hardy brought him to England, where they collaborated on pioneering mathematical projects. At Cambridge, Ramanujan made substantial contributions to number theory, infinite series, and mathematical analysis. His work on modular forms, mock theta functions, and partitions of numbers profoundly influenced mathematical thought and laid the groundwork for future research.

Though Ramanujan's life was brief, his legacy endures, inspiring mathematicians and scholars worldwide. His natural talent, relentless determination, and passion for mathematics exemplify the transformative power of human intelligence.

The Life of Marie Curie

Marie Curie, born in 1867 in Warsaw, Poland, exhibited extraordinary intelligence and curiosity from a young age, challenging societal norms that restricted women's access to higher education. She defied these limitations by enrolling at the Sorbonne University in Paris, where she excelled in physics and mathematics. Curie's exceptional talent led her to pioneer the study of radioactivity, a term she coined. Alongside her husband Pierre, she discovered the elements radium and polonium, earning her the first Nobel Prize awarded to a woman in 1903. This achievement shattered barriers and opened doors for future women in science.

Curie's brilliance extended beyond her scientific discoveries. During World War I, she developed mobile X-ray units to treat wounded soldiers, demonstrating her adaptability and innovation. In 1911, she won a second Nobel Prize in Chemistry for her work on radium and polonium. Her research on radioactivity revolutionized fields such as medicine, energy, and military technology, fundamentally altering our understanding of the universe.

Despite modern recognition of her exceptional intellect, the limited scientific knowledge and tools of her time, coupled with the infancy of brain studies, leave us with little information on the neurobiological correlates of her genius. Nonetheless, Curie's contributions laid the foundation for oncology and radioactive research, marking her as a pivotal figure in scientific history.

Behind Leonardo da Vinci's Genius

Leonardo da Vinci's life and work seamlessly integrated diverse disciplines, producing iconic art like the Mona Lisa and The Last Supper while making groundbreaking contributions to anatomy, architecture, engineering, and aeronautics. His exceptional cognitive abilities, such as heightened perceptual skills and prodigious memory, were key to his achievements. However, Catani and Mazzarello (2019) suggest that da Vinci might have struggled with attention deficit and hyperactivity disorder (ADHD), citing his chronic procrastination and mind wandering, traits noted by contemporaries and biographers. These ADHD traits, while fueling his creativity, often hindered his ability to complete projects. Despite challenges like left-handedness, dyslexia, and atypical brain lateralization, which may have influenced his artistic abilities, da Vinci's resilience and profound impact on history remain undisputed. His life offers insights into the neuropsychological mechanisms of giftedness and creative genius, highlighting the boundless potential of the human mind.

Summary

This chapter begins by presenting early perspectives on giftedness, which laid the foundation for contemporary understandings. It then examines giftedness through the lens of positive neuropsychology, emphasizing the strengths and unique cognitive profiles of gifted individuals. The neurobiological underpinnings are explored, focusing on anatomical correlations, structural and functional brain differences, and the PFIT. These sections reveal how specific brain regions and networks contribute to the cognitive advantages observed in gifted individuals, such as superior attention, rapid processing speed, enhanced learning and memory, advanced verbal abilities, and exceptional problem-solving skills.

This chapter also delves into the educational implications of these findings, advocating for tailored educational approaches that accommodate the distinctive needs of gifted students. The relationship between creativity and psychoticism is analyzed, suggesting that certain traits associated with psychoticism may enhance creative capacities. Dabrowski's theory of overexcitabilities is discussed, highlighting how heightened sensitivities in various domains can both enrich and challenge the lives of gifted individuals.

EQ is examined, with a focus on how gifted individuals often exhibit advanced emotional competencies that complement their cognitive abilities. Gender differences in giftedness are addressed, considering how societal and cultural factors influence the recognition and development of talents in boys and girls. The neurodiversity paradigm is introduced, advocating for the acceptance and celebration of neurological differences rather than viewing them as deficits.

Finally, this chapter presents case studies of three extraordinary individuals: Srinivasa Ramanujan, Marie Curie, and Leonardo da Vinci. These case studies illustrate the diverse manifestations of giftedness and the profound impact that gifted individuals can have across various fields. Through these comprehensive explorations, this chapter provides a nuanced understanding of giftedness, emphasizing both the remarkable capabilities and the unique challenges faced by gifted individuals.

References

Armstrong, T. (2011). *The power of neurodiversity: Unleashing the advantages of your differently wired brain* (published in hardcover as Neurodiversity). Hachette

Attoni, T. M., Coelho, R., Martins, R. C., Lemos, L., Fernandes, L. S., Francis, T., Fernandes, S., & Fideles, K. (2020). The language aspects of children with high abilities/giftedness: An integrative literature review. *Revista CEFAC*, *22*(6). https://doi.org/10.1590/1982-0216/20202269320

Barbey, A. K., Colom, R., & Grafman, J. (2013). Distributed neural system for emotional intelligence revealed by lesion mapping. *Social Cognitive and Affective Neuroscience*, *8*(4), 369–378.

Bar-On, R. (2007). The impact of emotional intelligence on giftedness. *Gifted Education International*, *23*(2), 122–137. https://doi.org/10.1177/026142940702300203

Bland, L. C., Sowa, C. J., & Callahan, C. M. (1994). An overview of resilience in gifted children. *Roeper Review*, *17*(2), 77–80. https://doi.org/10.1080/02783199409553629

Bouchet, N., & Falk, R. (2001). The relationship among giftedness, gender, and overexcitability. *Gifted Child Quarterly*, *45*(4), 260–267. https://doi.org/10.1177/001698620104500404

Buckner, R. L., Andrews-Hanna, J. R., & Schacter, D. L. (2008). The brain's default network: Anatomy, function, and relevance to disease. *Annals of the New York Academy of Sciences*, *1124*(1), 1–38.

Bush, G., Luu, P., & Posner, M. I. (2000). Cognitive and emotional influences in anterior cingulate cortex. *Trends in Cognitive Sciences*, *4*(6), 215–222. https://doi.org/10.1016/s1364-6613(00)01483-2

Callahan, C. M. (2000). *Intelligence and giftedness*. Cambridge University Press eBooks (pp. 159–175). https://doi.org/10.1017/cbo9780511807947.009

Carman, C. A. (2013). Comparing apples and oranges. *Journal of Advanced Academics*, *24*(1), 52–70. https://doi.org/10.1177/1932202x12472602

Catani, M., & Mazzarello, P. (2019). Grey Matter Leonardo da Vinci: A genius driven to distraction. *Brain*, *142*(6), 1842–1846. https://doi.org/10.1093/brain/awz131

Daniels, S., & Piechowski, M. M. (2009). *Living with intensity: Understanding the sensitivity, excitability, and emotional development of gifted children, adolescents, and adults*. Great Potential Press, Inc.

De Manzano, Ö., Červenka, S., Karabanov, A. N., Farde, L., & Ullén, F. (2010). Thinking outside a less intact box: Thalamic dopamine D2 receptor densities are negatively related to psychometric creativity in healthy individuals. *PLoS ONE*, *5*(5), e10670. https://doi.org/10.1371/journal.pone.0010670

Duncan, S. (n.d.). Neuroscience of giftedness: Physiology of the brain. *Gro-Gifted*. Retrieved from https://gro-gifted.org/the-neuroscience-of-giftedness/

Dweck, C. S. (2000). *Self-theories: Their role in motivation, personality, and development*. Psychology Press.

Eric. (2018). *ERIC ED603050: Examining gifted students' mental health through the lens of positive psychology PDF*. Retrieved from https://zlibrary.to/dl/eric-ed603050-examining-gifted-students-mental-health-through-the-lens-of-positive-psychology

Eysenck, H. J. (1995). *Genius: A natural history of creativity*. Cambridge University Press.

Falk, R. F., Lind, S., Miller, N. B., Piechowski, M. M., & Silverman, L. K. (1999). *The Overexcitability Questionnaire-Two (OEQII): Manual, scoring system, and questionnaire*. Denver, CO: Institute for the Study of Advanced Development.

Freeman, J., & Garces-Bascal, R. M. (2015). Gender differences in gifted children. In M. Neihart, S. I. Pfeiffer, & T. L. Cross (Eds.), *The social and emotional development of gifted children: What do we know?* Prufrock Press Inc. Retrieved from https://www.joanfreeman.com/pdf/Freeman-Garces-Bascal-on-gender-2015.pdf

Gaultney, J. F., Bjorklund, D. F., & Goldstein, D. (1996). To be young, gifted, and strategic: Advantages for memory performance. *Journal of Experimental Child Psychology*, *61*(1), 43–66. https://doi.org/10.1006/jecp.1996.0002

Gray, J. A., Feldon, J., Rawlins, J. N. P., Hemsley, D. R., & Smith, A. (1991). The neuropsychology of schizophrenia. *Behavioral and Brain Sciences*, *14*(1), 1–20. https://doi.org/10.1017/s0140525x00065055

Haier, R. J., Jung, R. E., Yeo, R. A., Head, K., & Alkire, M. T. (2004). Structural brain variation and general intelligence. *NeuroImage*, *23*(1), 425–433. https://doi.org/10.1016/j.neuroimage.2004.04.025

Hampshire, A., Highfield, R. R., Parkin, B. L., & Owen, A. M. (2012). Neural correlates of intelligence. *NeuroImage*, *60*(1), 587–595.

Retrieved from http://www.jstor.org/stable/3696292

Jung, R. E., & Haier, R. J. (2007). The Parieto-Frontal Integration Theory (P-FIT) of intelligence: Converging neuroimaging evidence. *Behavioral and Brain Sciences*, *30*(2), 135–154. https://doi.org/10.1017/s0140525x07001185.

Kounios, J., & Beeman, M. (2014). The cognitive neuroscience of insight. *Annual Review of Psychology*, *65*(1), 71–93. https://doi.org/10.1146/annurev-psych-010213-115154

Leikin, M., Paz-Baruch, N., & Лейкин, P. (2013). Memory abilities in generally gifted and excelling-in-mathematics adolescents. *Intelligence*, *41*(5), 566–578. https://doi.org/10.1016/j.intell.2013.07.018

Neubauer, A. C., & Fink, A. (2009). Intelligence and neural efficiency. *Neuroscience & Biobehavioral Reviews*, *33*(7), 1004–1023. https://doi.org/10.1016/j.neubiorev.2009.04.001

Ramanujan, S. (1913). *Collected papers of Srinivasa Ramanujan*. Cambridge University Press.

Reis, S. M., Baum, S. M., & Burke, E. M. (2014). An operational definition of twice-exceptional learners. *Gifted Child Quarterly*, *58*(3), 217–230. https://doi.org/10.1177/0016986214534976

Risemberg, R., & Zimmerman, B. J. (1992). Self-regulated learning in gifted students. *Roeper Review*, *15*(2), 98–101. https://doi.org/10.1080/02783199209553476

Roberts, J. L., Inman, T. F., & Robins, J. H. (2022). *Introduction to gifted education*. Taylor & Francis.

Rushton, J. P. (2001). A scientometric appreciation of H. J. Eysenck's contributions to psychology. *Personality and Individual Differences*, *31*(1), 17–39. https://doi.org/10.1016/s0191-8869(00)00235-x

Schewan, J. M., & Barlow, J. H. (2006). Emotional intelligence and its role in the development of resilience in children. *Journal of Child Health Care*, *10*(2), 139–150.

Schmitt, A., Wollschläger, R., Sarrasin, J. B., Masson, S., Fischbach, A., & Schiltz, C. (2023). Neuromyths and knowledge about intellectual giftedness in a highly educated multilingual country. *Frontiers in Psychology*, *14*. https://doi.org/10.3389/fpsyg.2023.1252239

Peterson, J. S., & Kaufman, J. C. (2005). Gifted and Talented. In *Encyclopedia of Applied Developmental Science* (pp. 449–452). SAGE Publications, Inc. https://dx.doi.org/10.4135/9781412950565.n177

Seligman, M. E., Steen, T. A., Park, N., & Peterson, C. (2005). Positive psychology progress: empirical validation of interventions. *American Psychologist*, *60*(5), 410.

Sisk, D. (2022). *Gifted education, creativity and leadership development*. Mdpi AG.

Sriraman, B. (2003). Mathematical giftedness, problem solving, and the ability to formulate generalizations: The problem-solving experiences of four gifted students. *The Journal of Secondary Gifted Education*, *14*(3), 151–165. https://doi.org/10.4219/jsge-2003-425

Stoeger, H. (2009). Identifying giftedness: The role of the Binet-Simon Scale. *Gifted Child Quarterly*, *53*(3), 190–197. DOI:10.1007/978-3-319-78592-9_3

Tieso, C. L. (2007). Patterns of overexcitabilities in identified gifted students and their parents. *Gifted Child Quarterly*, *51*(1), 11–22. https://doi.org/10.1177/0016986206296657

Wells, C., & Falk, R. (2021). The origins and conceptual evolution of overexcitability. *Psychologia Wychowawcza*, *62*(20), 23–44. https://doi.org/10.5604/01.3001.0015.3816

Zeidner, M., & Matthews, G. (2017). Emotional intelligence in gifted students. *Gifted Education International*, *33*(2), 163–182. https://doi.org/10.1177/0261429417708879

Zeidner, M., Shani-Zinovich, I., Matthews, G., & Roberts, R. D. (2005). Assessing emotional intelligence in gifted and non-gifted high school students: Outcomes depend on the measure. *Intelligence*, *33*(4), 369–391. https://doi.org/10.1016/j.intell.2005.03.001

7 The Science of Love

Decoding the Neuropsychological Basis of Human Connection

Introduction

Love, as described by Dr. Barbara L. Fredrickson, is multifaceted in nature, encompassing a diverse array of emotions such as affection, attachment, commitment, intimacy, passion, and romance (Fredrickson, 2001). This conceptualization challenges the notion of love as a singular entity, highlighting its complexity and depth. While historically rooted in biological imperatives for reproduction and survival, love has undergone a remarkable transformation throughout human history, shaped by societal, cultural, and individual influences. However, despite its rich tapestry of experiences, popular culture often oversimplifies love, reducing it to fleeting emotions and superficial connections. Yet, love's essence extends beyond romantic relationships, encompassing various forms such as parental love, self-love, spiritual love, and compassionate love (Sternberg, 1988). These diverse manifestations of love enrich our lives and contribute to our overall wellbeing. In the realm of positive psychology, love is recognized as integral to positive relationships, fostering connection, communication, and support (Park et al., 2016). Moreover, positive neuropsychology explores the cognitive benefits of love, studying its impact on brain function and mental health (Pimental, 2017). Love is intricately linked to positive emotions, contributing to psychological resilience, happiness, and overall life satisfaction (Izard, 1977). Through the lens of positive neuropsychology, love offers valuable insights into how positive experiences shape the brain and promote cognitive health and flourishing. As such, understanding the multifaceted nature of love enriches our comprehension of human emotions and experiences, fostering greater empathy, connection, and wellbeing in society.

Neural Mechanisms of Love

Love is a profound and complex phenomenon that elicits a cascade of emotions and sensations when we gaze upon the face of someone we deeply care about. Recent studies have delved into the neural mechanisms underlying love, revealing a fascinating interplay of brain activity. While previous

DOI: 10.4324/9781003477815-7

research focused on rodents, current investigations center on unraveling the intricacies of love within the human brain. Prairie voles serve as models for understanding the neurobiology of pair-bond formation, shedding light on the roles of neurotransmitters like dopamine and serotonin, as well as hormones such as oxytocin (OT), vasopressin, cortisol, testosterone, and estrogen. By examining the neuroanatomical aspects and chemical pathways involved, we gain deeper insights into the neurological foundations of love.

Neuroanatomical Underpinnings of Love

The brain structures involved in love have been extensively studied by researchers, shedding light on the neurobiological underpinnings of this complex emotion. According to recent research findings, love primarily activates specific brain regions associated with reward, motivation, and emotion regulation.

The ventral tegmental area (VTA) and the caudate nucleus are key brain regions consistently associated with romantic love. These areas are part of the brain's reward pathway and are involved in regulating the release of dopamine, a neurotransmitter linked to pleasure and reward (Aron et al., 2005). Other brain regions implicated in romantic love include the anterior cingulate cortex (ACC), insula, hippocampus, nucleus accumbens (NAC), amygdala, and hypothalamus. These regions are involved in processing emotions, motivation, and social cognition, contributing to the complex experience of love (Bartels & Zeki, 2000). Studies have shown that when individuals are in love, there is increased activation in the VTA, striatum, NAC, and other regions associated with reward and pleasure. These neural patterns of romantic love are universal across genders, cultures, and sexual orientations (Zeki, 2007). The release of neurotransmitters such as dopamine, OT, and vasopressin plays a significant role in romantic attachment and bonding. These neuromodulators are involved in the rewarding and pleasurable aspects of love as well as in promoting feelings of attachment and closeness (Insel & Young, 2001).

Neurotransmitters

Dopamine, a neurotransmitter central to various physiological and psychological functions, is intricately linked to reward, desire, addiction, and euphoric states (Zeki, 2007). Released by the hypothalamus and produced in brain regions like the substantia nigra and VTA, dopamine induces a "feel good" state and is crucial in forming relationships and sexual experiences (Acevedo & Aron, 2014a,b). In maternal love and long-term relationships, dopamine activation extends to reward-associated brain areas, along with regions rich in serotonin receptors, influencing mood regulation and emotional processing (Zeki, 2007). This suggests that romantic partners trigger reinforcement learning responses, motivating individuals to engage in relationship-maintaining behaviors (Acevedo & Aron, 2014a,b).

Similarly, serotonin, another neurotransmitter, regulates mood, appetite, and sleep, impacting feelings of wellbeing associated with love. Changes in serotonin levels, along with corticosteroids, drive stress-related emotions in the initial phases of love. Genetic factors also influence serotonin receptors, contributing to obsessive aspects of love (Tafet et al., 2001; Emanuele et al., 2007). Additionally, OT and vasopressin, often termed "love hormones," play crucial roles in social bonding and pair bonding, influencing attachment, trust, and commitment in romantic relationships (Gonzaga et al., 2006).

Together, these neurotransmitters provide insights into the complex mechanisms underlying the emotional and behavioral aspects of love.

In addition to dopamine, serotonin, OT, and vasopressin, several other neurotransmitters contribute to the experience of love. Endorphins, for example, are often referred to as "feel-good" chemicals because they produce feelings of pleasure and reduce pain perception (Young & Wang, 2004). These neurotransmitters are released during activities such as hugging, kissing, or engaging in intimate moments with a romantic partner, further enhancing the emotional connection and bonding experienced in love relationships. Additionally, adrenaline, also known as epinephrine, is released during moments of excitement or arousal, such as during the initial stages of falling in love or when experiencing romantic gestures from a partner. Adrenaline heightens physiological responses, including increased heart rate and perspiration, which can intensify feelings of attraction and desire (Zeki, 2007). Furthermore, endocannabinoids, which are neurotransmitters that resemble chemicals found in cannabis, play a role in regulating mood, pleasure, and memory (Pimental, 2017). These neurotransmitters are released during positive experiences and may contribute to the rewarding aspects of love, enhancing the overall enjoyment and satisfaction derived from romantic relationships. Overall, the intricate interplay of these neurotransmitters underscores the complexity of love as a multidimensional emotional experience shaped by various neurochemical processes in the brain.

The hypothalamic–pituitary–adrenal (HPA) axis, a critical neuroendocrine system governing stress response, comprises the hypothalamus, pituitary gland, and adrenal glands. Heightened HPA axis activity is observed, especially during the early stages of romantic love (Marazziti & Canale, 2004). OT and vasopressin, crucial to bonding, exert opposing effects on the HPA axis—OT decreases while vasopressin increases its activity (Legros, 2001). In long-term relationships, OT likely contributes to reduced stress levels and diminished HPA axis activity compared to the initial love stages (De Boer et al., 2012). Cortisol, known as the "stress hormone," is implicated in the body's stress response. Individuals in new romantic relationships exhibit higher cortisol levels, suggesting that falling in love induces stress and arousal (Marazziti & Canale, 2004). Conversely, long-term relationships are associated with decreased stress levels and increased security, leading to reduced cortisol levels (Esch & Stefano, 2005). Testosterone, primarily produced in the testicles for males and ovaries for females, plays a role in romantic love and pair bonding (Marazziti & Canale, 2004). Men in new relationships have lower testosterone levels, while women show elevated levels, indicating a temporary alteration of gender-based hormonal differences during early love experiences (Marazziti & Canale, 2004). Additionally, physical proximity in relationships affects testosterone levels in women, highlighting the complex interaction between hormones and relationship dynamics (van Anders & Watson, 2007). These findings underscore the dynamic regulation of hormones in romantic relationships and its impact on stress responses and bonding.

Evolutionary Phases of Romantic Love

Love, particularly in romantic relationships, progresses through different phases, as described by theorists like Robert Sternberg and psychologists like García (García, 1998; Sternberg, 2007). The initial phase, known as "Being in Love" or the honeymoon phase, is marked by heightened passion, intimacy, and commitment (García, 1998). During this phase, cortisol levels increase, while testosterone levels decrease, and serotonin levels remain low (García, 1998). Additionally, nerve growth factor levels are elevated in individuals experiencing romantic love, influencing activity in the HPA axis and stress responses (Zeki, 2007). In the subsequent "Passional Love" phase, stress levels decrease while passion, intimacy, and commitment remain high (García, 1998). Finally, "Companionate Love" is characterized by a decline in passion but sustained intimacy and commitment (García, 1998).

OT and vasopressin play significant roles in reinforcing and maintaining pair bonds throughout these phases (Starka, 2007). Love and compassion share neurobiological pathways involving neurotransmitters like dopamine, OT, and endogenous opioids, contributing to pleasurable sensations and rewarding outcomes (Esch & Stefano, 2011). An fMRI study on unconditional love identified brain regions like the middle insula and posterodorsal ACC as active during experiences of unconditional love, alongside other cortical and subcortical regions (Beauregard et al., 2009).

The joy experienced in love impacts a network of cortical and subcortical structures within the limbic and paralimbic regions, influencing cognition, emotion, and autonomic functions (Esch et al., 2004). This intricate connection reflects a positive reinforcement mechanism in the brain throughout various stages of love, highlighting its profound effects on cognitive, emotional, and physiological aspects.

Maternal and Romantic Love

Maternal attachment represents a vital and enduring social bond essential for offspring survival (Dębiec, 2007a,b). This form of love, characterized by tender intimacy and selflessness, shares behavioral similarities with both parent-infant and adult romantic attachments (Bartels & Zeki, 2004). Both maternal and romantic love serve a common evolutionary purpose of promoting species maintenance and individual bonding, activating overlapping brain regions associated with the reward system (Figure 7.1). However, maternal love uniquely involves face-specific activation and distinct hypothalamic engagement, while both forms suspend judgment and involve cortical de-activation (Bartels & Zeki, 2004; Zeki, 2007).

The OT system plays a central role in various human attachments, including maternal and romantic bonds (Love, 2014). OT and vasopressin, with distinct brain distributions, contribute to maternal behavior and pair bonding, reflecting commonality between mother–child attachment and long-term adult bonding (Winslow et al., 1993; Kendrick, 2000; Insel & Young, 2001; Curtis & Wang, 2003). Specific neural activation in the ACC reflects maternal feelings of empathy and the urge to care for offspring (Bartels & Zeki, 2004).

Hormonal priming during pregnancy, involving the synthesis of OT and other neurochemicals, contributes to the establishment of maternal attachment (Panksepp, 1998; Lim et al., 2006). The neural mechanisms underlying maternal love exhibit cortical deactivation similar to romantic love, affecting regions associated with judgment formation and negative emotions (Bartels & Zeki, 2004). This suggests shared neurohormonal control between maternal and romantic love (Bartels & Zeki, 2004).

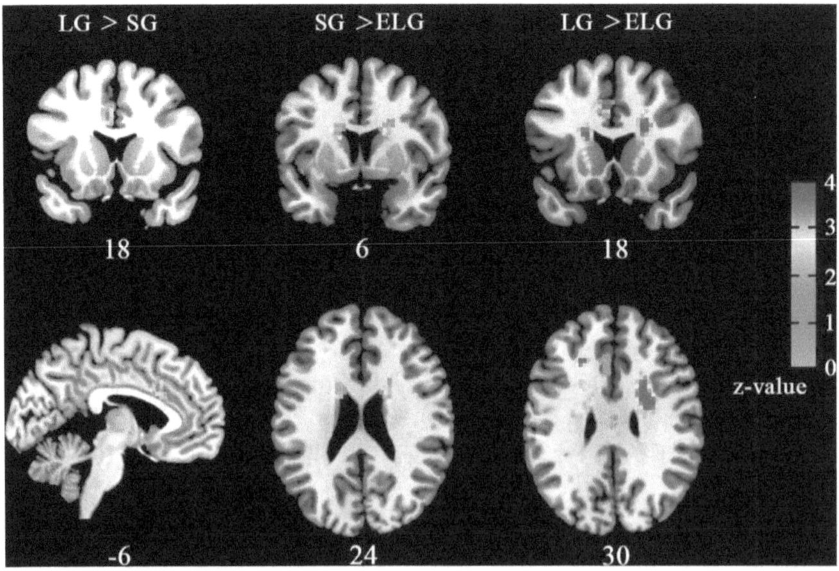

Figure 7.1 Altered Regional Homogeneity in Brain Areas of In-Love and Ended-Love Groups (Song et al., 2015)

Research on human attachments underscores the neurobiological systems shaped by the mother–offspring relationship during early sensitive periods, contributing to mammalian bonding (Carter, 2014). Continuity in these systems underlies human bonds, repurposing the basic machinery established by the parent-offspring bond for other attachments throughout life (Feldman, 2016).

Love and Cognition

Throughout life, human bonds wield transformative power, capable of ameliorating early negative relationships through subsequent benevolent ones. The remarkable plasticity of the human social brain allows subsequent attachments to reorganize neural networks, partially mitigating the impacts of adverse early experiences (Feldman, 2016). Research delving into the neural mechanisms associated with compassion training demonstrates its positive effects on affective experiences, eliciting neural activity in regions linked to positive affect and affiliation (Klimecki et al., 2013). This suggests that compassion training engenders functional neural plasticity, augmenting positive affect in response to others' distress.

There exists evidence supporting a causal relationship between being in love and human cognition, with subliminal exposure to romantic love bolstering cognitive processes (Bianchi-Demicheli et al., 2006). Love, akin to passion, is construed as a goal-directed state with motivational and reward components (Aron & Aron, 1986; Fisher, 1998, 2004; Aron et al., 2005). Exposure to love primes enhances subsequent performance on mentalizing tasks and memory tasks pertaining to beloved-related information (Langeslag et al., 2008, 2015). Furthermore, companionate love may yield both constructive and inhibiting impacts on creativity, fostering solidarity and cooperation while potentially impeding innovative problem-solving (Yang & Hung, 2015).

The experience of love transiently deactivates brain areas associated with higher cognitive functions, while ongoing research endeavors to elucidate its potential in enhancing cognitive abilities and overall cognitive health.

Love as a Social Glue in Communities

Love serves as a potent social adhesive within communities, nurturing connection, empathy, and cooperation, thereby enhancing collective wellbeing (Zeki, 2007). Positive social interactions fortified by love contribute to a more positive community atmosphere, fostering resilience in confronting challenges (Zeki, 2007). OT and vasopressin play pivotal roles in fostering social connections and influencing social behavior contributing to bonding and shaping learning and memory within social contexts (Carter, 1998; Insel & Young, 2001). Studies on prairie voles, known for their monogamous nature, elucidate the significance of vasopressin in forming lifelong social bonds (Pfaff et al., 2008). Additionally, societal norms surrounding love impact social interactions and behaviors, with contemporary shifts emphasizing individual choice and emotional compatibility (Zeki, 2007).

Love and Stress: A Paradox?

Love, despite its rewarding capacities, can evoke both positive and negative stress responses, influencing physiological and emotional states. Physical symptoms associated with love, such as increased heart rate, sweating, and changes in appetite and sleep, contribute to stress experiences, observed both in the early stages of falling in love and during breakups (Marazziti & Canale, 2003). The reality of relationships often deviates from idealized expectations, leading to emotional turbulence during breakups, characterized by sadness, anger, and physical discomfort (Marazziti & Canale, 2003). This emotional upheaval triggers the body's stress response, resulting in elevated levels of stress hormones like cortisol.

Love and pleasure possess stress-reducing properties, facilitating positive behaviors and motivations (Esch & Stefano, 2005). OT, a key player in love physiology, exerts anxiolytic effects and inhibits stress response activity, contributing to stress reduction (Carter, 1998). Long-term relationships have been shown to decrease stress levels and enhance feelings of security, promoting overall wellbeing (Esch & Stefano, 2005).

Chronic stress, however, can lead to depression and inhibit the formation of new bonds and attachments (Esch et al., 2002). Despite the initial stress response observed in the early stages of love, the formation of social attachment fosters physiological states that reduce anxiety and negative sensations over time (Marazziti & Canale, 2003).

The intricate relationship between stress and love underscores its paradoxical nature—a potential source of stress yet also a means of stress reduction (Marazziti & Canale, 2003). The activation of the HPA axis post-stressful experiences is correlated with the formation of social attachment, contributing to diminished anxiety and associated negative sensations (Marazziti & Canale, 2003).

Love and Addiction: A Trap?

Love and addiction exhibit similarities in terms of neural pathways, particularly involving dopaminergic systems, leading to the question:

Is love addictive? While distinctions exist, such as in the context of artificial drug ingestion, the term "addicted to love" encapsulates the complex interplay between love-related behaviors and substance-related dependencies (Edwards & Self, 2006).

Studies indicate that the dopaminergic pathways associated with love and pair bond formation share similarities with those involved in addictive behaviors (Insel, 2003; Young & Wang, 2004). Key components of the brain's reward-learning system, like the NAC and ventral pallidum, play essential roles in both love and addiction (Insel, 2003).

Neural activity resembling addiction responses is observed in individuals facing rejection, with heightened activity in regions associated with craving and addiction, such as the NAC and orbitofrontal/prefrontal cortex (Fisher et al., 2010). Additionally, the angular gyrus, implicated in romantic love, has been linked to cigarette craving, further suggesting overlapping neural systems between romantic rejection and addictive behaviors (Brody et al., 2007).

The Link Between Love and Reduced Anxiety and Depression

The positive emotion of love has proven effective in enhancing mood and alleviating feelings of anxiety. The reinforcing nature of positive experiences associated with love may explain its connection to reduced levels of anxiety and depression, promoting overall positive affective states.

Activation and deactivation patterns in the lateral prefrontal cortices, influenced by the pleasure associated with love, contribute to a decrease in depression and an improvement in mood, essentially fostering a sense of happiness (Davidson et al., 2003).

OT and prolactin play a role in reducing anxiety, acting on various brain sites, and have demonstrated the ability to decrease stress responsiveness at multiple levels—neuronal, neuroendocrine, and behavioral (Pfaff et al., 2008). Numerous studies have highlighted the neuromodulatory role of OT in response to anxiety-inducing stimuli, suggesting its potential in addressing the pathogenesis of depression. This has led to the proposal of intranasal OT as a potential treatment for anxiety and depressive disorders (De Cagna et al., 2019).

The Heart of Wellbeing: How Love Nurtures Our Mental Health

Love is crucial in fostering mental wellbeing. It is a powerful buffer against stress, strengthening our emotional resilience and promoting feelings of security and belonging. Studies have shown that individuals experiencing love often report elevated levels of wellbeing, including happiness, satisfaction, and purpose. This positive emotional state can be linked to an increased lifespan and improved physical health. Additionally, the sense of connection and support fostered by love can motivate individuals to adopt healthier habits, further contributing to overall wellbeing. It is important to remember that love is a multifaceted concept, and the specific ways it benefits our mental and physical health can vary depending on the nature of the relationship and individual circumstances.

The cultivation of mental wellbeing involves several strategies aimed at nurturing self-compassion, fostering strong social connections, and engaging with supportive communities.

Self-compassion and self-care: Prioritizing self-love and engaging in mindfulness activities can alleviate stress, reduce anxiety, and enhance self-awareness (Neff, 2003). Embracing regular exercise, maintaining a wholesome diet, ensuring sufficient sleep, and pursuing personal hobbies contribute to overall physical and mental wellbeing (Sarris et al., 2014). Journaling and intentional breaks facilitate introspection and personal growth (Adams et al., 2008).

Strong social connections: Spending quality time with loved ones fosters a sense of belonging and support (Holt-Lunstad et al., 2010). Open communication, active listening, and setting healthy boundaries are essential for maintaining healthy relationships (Gottman & Silver, 1999). Prioritizing meaningful connections over superficial ones helps cultivate authentic relationships (Berscheid & Reis, 1998).

Social support and community engagement: Joining social groups and engaging in community activities reduce feelings of isolation and promote peer support (Thoits, 2011). Community engagement provides a sense of purpose and belonging while combating social isolation (Thoits, 2011).

Summary

Love, a complex emotion with profound implications for human wellbeing, is explored through its neurobiological underpinnings and evolutionary significance. Neuroimaging studies reveal intricate neural circuits associated with love, while neurotransmitters like dopamine and OT modulate its emotional and reward aspects. From initial attraction to long-term attachment, romantic love traverses distinct evolutionary phases, shaped by genetic predispositions and social influences. Parallels between maternal and romantic love underscore their shared neurobiological substrates, influencing cognition and promoting social cohesion within communities. While love may mitigate stress and reduce anxiety and depression through its positive influence on emotional regulation and social support, its addictive nature raises questions about potential pitfalls. Ultimately, love emerges as a fundamental aspect of human experience, nurturing resilience and wellbeing through its profound impact on mental health and social connection.

References

Acevedo, B. P., & Aron, A. (2014a). Love as a reward: A function of liking, learning, and motivation. *Social and Personality Psychology Compass*, *8*(7), 383–393.

Acevedo, B. P., & Aron, A. P. (2014b). Romantic love, pair-bonding, and the dopaminergic reward system. In M. Mikulincer & P. R. Shaver (Eds.), *Mechanisms of social connection: From brain to group* (pp. 55–69). American Psychological Association. https://doi.org/10.1037/14250-004

Adams, K. B., Leibbrandt, S., & Moon, H. (2008). A critical review of the literature on social and leisure activity and wellbeing in later life. *Ageing & Society*, *28*(6), 1–23.

Algoe SB, Kurtz LE, Grewen K. Oxytocin and Social Bonds: The Role of Oxytocin in Perceptions of Romantic Partners' Bonding Behavior. Psychol Sci. 2017 Dec;28(12):1763–1772. doi: 10.1177/0956797617716922. Epub 2017 Oct 2. PMID: 28968183; PMCID: PMC5734372.

Aron, A., & Aron, E. N. (1986). *Love and the expansion of self: Understanding attraction and satisfaction*. Hemisphere Publishing Corp.

Aron, A., Fisher, H. E., Mashek, D. J., Strong, G., Li, H., & Brown, L. L. (2005). Reward, motivation, and emotion systems associated with early-stage intense romantic love. *Journal of Neurophysiology*, *94*(1), 327–337.

Bartels, A., & Zeki, S. (2000). The neural basis of romantic love. *Neuroreport*, *11*(17), 3829–3834.

Bartels, A., & Zeki, S. (2004). The neural correlates of maternal and romantic love. *NeuroImage*, *21*(3), 1155–1166. https://doi.org/10.1016/j.neuroimage.2003.11.003

Beauregard, M., Courtemanche, J., Paquette, V., & St-Pierre, É. L. (2009). The neural basis of unconditional love. *Psychiatry Research: Neuroimaging*, *172*(2), 93–98. https://doi.org/10.1016/j.pscychresns.2008.11.003

Berscheid, E., & Reis, H. T. (1998). Attraction and close relationships. In D. T. Gilbert, S. T. Fiske, & G. Lindzey (Eds.), *The handbook of social psychology* (4th ed., Vol. 2, pp. 193–281). McGraw-Hill.

Bianchi-Demicheli, F., Grafton, S. T., & Ortigue, S. (2006). The power of love on the human brain. *Social Neuroscience*, *1*(2), 90–103.

Booth, A., Granger, D. A., Mazur, A., & Kivlighan, K. T. (2006). Testosterone and Social Behavior. Social Forces, 85(1), 167–191. http://www.jstor.org/stable/3844412

Brody, A. L., Mandelkern, M. A., Olmstead, R. E., Jou, J., Tiongson, E., Allen, V., Scheibal, D., London, E. D., Monterosso, J. R., Tiffany, S. T., Korb, A., Gan, J. J., & Cohen, M. S. (2007). Neural substrates of resisting craving during cigarette cue exposure. *Biological Psychiatry*, *62*(6), 642–651. https://doi.org/10.1016/j.biopsych.2006.10.026

Carter, C. S. (1998). Neuroendocrine perspectives on social attachment and love. *Psychoneuroendocrinology*, *23*(8), 779–818.

Carter, C. S. (2014). Oxytocin pathways and the evolution of human behavior. *Annual Review of Psychology*, *65*, 17–39. https://doi.org/10.1146/annurev-psych-010213-115110

Curtis, J. T., & Wang, Z. (2003). The neurochemistry of pair bonding. *Current Directions in Psychological Science*, *12*(2), 49–53. https://doi.org/10.1111/1467-8721.01224

Davidson, R. J., Kabat-Zinn, J., Schumacher, J., Rosenkranz, M., Muller, D., Santorelli, S. F., Urbanowski, F., Harrington, A., Bonus, K., & Sheridan, J. F. (2003). Alterations in brain and immune function produced by mindfulness meditation. *Psychosomatic Medicine*, *65*(4), 564–570. https://doi.org/10.1097/01.PSY.0000077505.67574.E3

De Boer, A., Van Buel, E. M., & Ter Horst, G. J. (2012). Love is more than just a kiss: A neurobiological perspective on love and affection. *Neuroscience*, *201*, 114–124. https://doi.org/10.1016/j.neuroscience.2011.11.017

De Cagna, F., Fusar-Poli, L., Damiani, S., Rocchetti, M., Giovanna, G., Mori, A., Politi, P., & Brondino, N. (2019). The role of intranasal oxytocin in anxiety and depressive disorders: A systematic review of randomized controlled trials. *Clinical Psychopharmacology and Neuroscience*, *17*(1), 1–11. https://doi.org/10.9758/cpn.2019.17.1.1

Dębiec, J. (2007a). A synaptic model of memory: Long-term potentiation in the amygdala. *Neuron*, *55*(5), 724–736. https://doi.org/10.1016/j.neuron.2007.08.016
Dębiec, J. (2007b). From affiliative behaviors to romantic feelings: A role of nanopeptides. *FEBS Letters*, *581*(14), 2580–2586. https://doi.org/10.1016/j.febslet.2007.03.095
Edwards, S., & Self, D. W. (2006). Monogamy: Dopamine ties the knot. *Nature Neuroscience*, *9*(1), 7–8.
Emanuele, E., Brondino, N., Pesenti, S., Re, S., & Geroldi, D. (2007). Genetic loading on human loving styles. *Neuro Endocrinology Letters*, *28*(6), 815–821.
Esch, T., & Stefano, G. B. (2005). The neurobiology of love. *Neuroendocrinology Letters*, *26*(3), 175–192.
Esch, T., & Stefano, G. B. (2011). The neurobiological link between compassion and love. *Medical Science Monitor: International Medical Journal of Experimental and Clinical Research*, *17*(3), RA65–75. https://doi.org/10.12659/msm.881441
Esch, T., Guarna, M., Bianchi, E., Zhu, W., & Stefano, G. B. (2004). Commonalities in the central nervous system's involvement with complementary medical therapies: Limbic morphinergic processes. *Medical Science Monitor: International Medical Journal of Experimental and Clinical Research*, *10*(6), MS6–17.
Esch, T., Stefano, G. B., Fricchione, G. L., & Benson, H. (2002). The role of stress in neurodegenerative diseases and mental disorders. *Neuroendocrinology Letters*, *23*(3), 199–208.
Feldman, R. (2016). The neurobiology of mammalian parenting and the biosocial context of human caregiving. *Hormones and Behavior*, *77*, 3–17. https://doi.org/10.1016/j.yhbeh.2015.10.001
Fisher, H. (2004). *Why we love: The nature and chemistry of romantic love*. Henry Holt and Company.
Fisher, H. E. (1998). Lust, attraction, and attachment in mammalian reproduction. *Human Nature*, *9*(1), 23–52. https://doi.org/10.1007/s12110-998-1010-5
Fisher, H. E., Brown, L. L., Aron, A., Strong, G., & Mashek, D. (2010). Reward, addiction, and emotion regulation systems associated with rejection in love. *Journal of Neurophysiology*, *104*(1), 51–60. https://doi.org/10.1152/jn.00784.2009
Fredrickson, B. L. (2001). The role of positive emotions in positive psychology: The broaden-and-build theory of positive emotions. *American Psychologist*, *56*(3), 218–226. https://doi.org/10.1037/0003-066X.56.3.218
García, C. Y. (1998). Temporal course of the basic components of love throughout relationships. *Psychology in Spain*, *2*, 76–86.
Gonzaga, G. C., Turner, R. A., Keltner, D., Campos, B., & Altemus, M. (2006). Romantic love and sexual desire in close relationships. *Emotion*, *6*(2), 163–179. https://doi.org/10.1037/1528-3542.6.2.163
Gottman, J. M., & Silver, N. (1999). *The seven principles for making marriage work*. Harmony.
Holt-Lunstad, J., Smith, T. B., & Layton, J. B. (2010). Social relationships and mortality risk: A meta-analytic review. *PLoS Medicine*, *7*(7), e1000316.
Insel TR. Is social attachment an addictive disorder? Physiol Behav. 2003 Aug;79(3):351-7. doi: 10.1016/s0031-9384(03)00148-3. PMID: 12954430.
Insel, T. R., & Young, L. J. (2001). The neurobiology of attachment. *Nature Reviews Neuroscience*, *2*(2), 129–136. https://doi.org/10.1038/35053579

Izard, C. E. (1977). Differential emotions theory. In C. E. Izard (Ed.), *Human emotions* (pp. 43–66). Springer. https://doi.org/10.1007/978-1-4899-2209-0_3

Kendrick, K. M. (2000). Oxytocin, motherhood and bonding. *Experimental Physiology, 85*(s1). https://doi.org/10.1111/j.1469-445X.2000.tb00014.x

Klimecki, O. M., Leiberg, S., Lamm, C., & Singer, T. (2013). Functional neural plasticity and associated changes in positive affect after compassion training. *Cerebral Cortex, 23*(7), 1552–1561. https://doi.org/10.1093/cercor/bhs142

Langeslag, S. J. E., Franken, I. H. A., & Van Strien, J. W. (2008). Dissociating love-related attention from task-related attention: An event-related potential oddball study. *Neuroscience Letters, 431*(3), 236–240. https://doi.org/10.1016/j.neulet.2007.11.044

Langeslag, S. J. E., Olivier, J. R., Köhlen, M. E., Nijs, I. M., & Van Strien, J. W. (2015). Increased attention and memory for beloved-related information during infatuation: Behavioral and electrophysiological data. *Social Cognitive and Affective Neuroscience, 10*(1), 136–144. https://doi.org/10.1093/scan/nsu034

Legros, J.-J. (2001). *Inhibitory effect of oxytocin on corticotrope function in humans: Are vasopressin and oxytocin ying–yang neurohormones?*

Lim, M. M., Wang, Z., & Olazabal, D. E. (2006). Oxytocin and vasopressin: Their role in social behavior and attachment. *Psychoneuroendocrinology, 31*(9), 1029–1041. https://doi.org/10.1016/j.psyneuen.2006.05.004

Marazziti, D., & Canale, D. (2003). The role of serotonin in love. *Clinical Neuropsychiatry, 1*(1), 1–6.

Marazziti, D., & Canale, D. (2004). The neurobiology of love. *Clinical Neuropsychiatry, 1*(1), 33–38.

Neff, K. D. (2003). The development and validation of a scale to measure self-compassion. *Self and Identity, 2*(3), 223–250. https://doi.org/10.1080/15298860309027

Panksepp, J. (1998). *Affective neuroscience: The foundations of human and animal emotions.* Oxford University Press.

Peterson, Christopher. (2009). Character Strengths: Research and Practice. Journal of College and Character. 10. 10.2202/1940-1639.1042.

Pfaff, D. W., et al. (2008). The role of vasopressin in social bonding: Evidence from studies on prairie voles. *Journal of Neurobiology, 68*(1), 1–10. https://doi.org/10.1002/neu.20547

Pimental, P. A. (2017). Positive neuropsychology: A review of the literature and future directions. In I. M. Pagotto (Ed.), *Neurobiology of abnormal emotion and motivated behaviors: Integrating animal and human research* (pp. 137–154). Academic Press.

Sarris, J., O'Neil, A., Coulson, C. E., Schweitzer, I., & Berk, M. (2014). Lifestyle medicine for depression. *BMC Psychiatry, 14*(1), 1–13. https://doi.org/10.1186/1471-244X-14-107

Song, H., Zou, Z., Kou, J., Liu, Y., Yang, L., Zilverstand, A., Federico d'Oleire Uquillas, & Zhang, X. (2015). Love-related changes in the brain: a resting-state functional magnetic resonance imaging study. *Frontiers in Human Neuroscience, 9.* https://doi.org/10.3389/fnhum.2015.00071

Starka, L. (2007). The role of oxytocin and vasopressin in the regulation of social behavior. *Physiological Reviews, 87*(2), 431–462. https://doi.org/10.1152/physrev.00008.2006

Sternberg, R. J. (1986). A triangular theory of love. Psychological Review, 93(2), 119–135. https://doi.org/10.1037/0033-295X.93.2.119
Sternberg, R. J. (2007). A triangular theory of love. *Psychological Review*, *93*(2), 119–135. https://doi.org/10.1037/0033-295X.93.2.119
Tafet, G. E., Feder, D. J., Abulafia, D. P., Roffman, S. S., & Novoselsky, C. (2001). Association between life events and psychological symptoms in a population of working women in Buenos Aires. *Revista Brasileira de Psiquiatria*, *23*(4), 213–220.
Thoits, P. A. (2011). Mechanisms linking social ties and support to physical and mental health. *Journal of Health and Social Behavior*, *52*(2), 145–161. https://doi.org/10.1177/0022146510395592
Yang, Y., & Hung, Y. (2015). The effects of love on cognitive function: A review. *Journal of Social and Personal Relationships*, *32*(6), 745–762.
Young, L. J., & Wang, Z. (2004). The neurobiology of pair bonding. *Nature Neuroscience*, *7*(10), 1048–1054.
Zeki, S. (2007). The neurobiology of love. *FEBS Letters*, *581*(14), 2575–2579.

8 Prosocial Behavior and Cognitive Wellbeing

Introduction to Prosocial Behavior

You might have assisted someone with directions, held someone's door open, offered to carry someone's heavy bag, given your seat on a bus to another fellow traveler, volunteered for community events and organizations, or shared your financial and emotional resources with others. All these acts are interwoven into the very fabric of everyday human behavior. These voluntary behaviors are termed prosocial behavior. Eisenberg and Fabes (1998) defined prosocial behaviors as voluntary behavior intended to benefit another.

Wu and Hong (2022) have described two characteristic features of prosocial behavior lying on a spectrum, that is, affiliative versus antagonistic and self versus other-benefiting (Figure 8.1). Prosocial behavior is thus affiliative and others benefit from that. Affiliative behaviors are those that promote the maintenance of positive and helpful social interaction in society. Other benefiting behaviors are those that are performed with the motive of benefiting others.

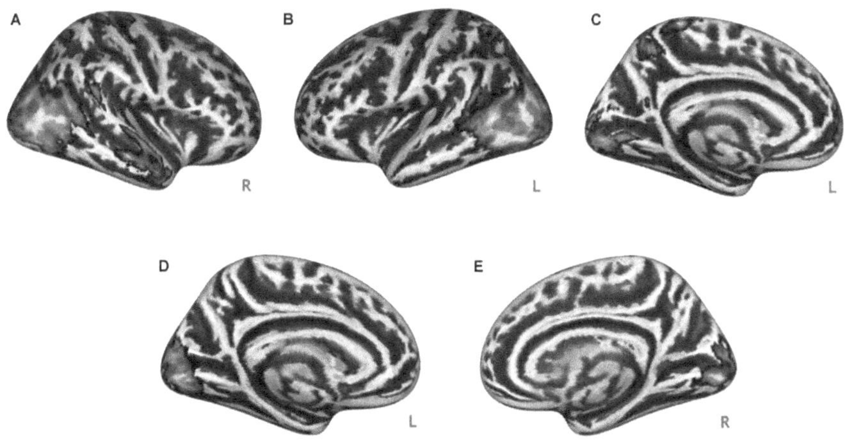

Figure 8.1 Neural Effects of Social Interactions (**Olivo et al., 2021**)

DOI: 10.4324/9781003477815-8

Altruism and Prosocial Behavior

Before we proceed, it is important to address the ambiguity around the difference between altruism and prosocial behavior. Marsh et al. (2020) have identified how both concepts differ in three core dimensions, that is, intention and motives, costs and benefits, and social context. Prosocial behavior is performed with certain intentions and consequences in mind, while this may not be the case with altruism. Altruism may prove costly to the actor and beneficial to the receiver, while such costs may not be a mandation in the case of prosocial behavior. Third, prosocial behavior emerges from what society approves, and such social sanction may not be the case for altruism. However, it is essential to note that altruism is also a form of prosocial behavior.

Batson and Powell (2003) also pointed out that while prosocial behavior can be motivated by altruism, altruistic motivation may not always lead to prosocial behavior. Researchers have often used both terms interchangeably because it is often difficult to determine an individual's motives behind a behavior (Stevens & Taber, 2021).

Steps in Prosocial Behavior

Wu and Hong (2022) have attempted to present a simplified eight-step breakdown of the various complex processes involved in prosocial behavior. The first step includes the communication of the actor of prosocial behavior with the individual with unmet needs or negative affect (receiver). The second step is the actor's perception of this negative affect or unmet needs. The third step involves the exhibition of empathetic concern toward the receiver. This sharing of the concern between both individuals leads to the fourth step: the actor being motivated to make a helping decision. The fifth step is the actor's evaluation of self, other, context-related information, and emotion-regulation abilities. Failure to do so may lead to self-protective behavior. The sixth step is alleviating the receiver's concerns due to the actor's appropriate intervention. The alleviation of the receiver's distress would also, in turn, alleviate the actor's emotional state, which is the seventh step. The last and eighth step is the self-rewarding experience of the actor after the helping behavior.

Reasons Behind Prosocial Behavior

This brings us to the fundamental question: Why do humans engage in prosocial behavior?

Theorists have devised various reasons to understand why people help each other. One prominent reason is the *empathy–altruism hypothesis* by Batson et al. (1981), suggesting that empathy often leads to behavior with altruistic motives rather than egoistic ones.

Additionally, one might engage in helping behavior to alleviate one's negative mood (Cialdini et al., 1981) or to experience positive emotions (Smith et al., 1989).

Evolutionary Perspective of Prosocial Behavior

The genetic evolution of the helping behavior in human, which may even be at the cost of their wellbeing, has been confusing as per the Dawinanian understanding of human survival. W. D. Hamilton attempted to explain such human tendency with the help of his *kin selection theory*, which stated that humans might come up to help others over their survival if it would mean the survival of their relative carrying the same genotype (Fletcher & Doebeli, 2009; Kay et al., 2020). However, this evolutionary theory is still unable to explain numerous instances when humans sacrificed their own lives to help strangers unrelated to each other.

Understanding the Neuropsychology of Prosocial Behavior

While prosocial behavior lies on the cusp of positive psychology and social psychology, the recent advancement in the study of neuropsychology has called for a further nuanced understanding of prosocial behavior by looking at the neural correlates, which would help to further delve into the intricacies of the human social interactions. It is crucial to shed light on the complex interplay between brain structures, neurotransmitters, and social context to explain prosocial behavior. Having such an understanding would reveal various other layers of processes that determine prosocial behavior and help us develop models and theories to have a clearer picture.

Approaches to Studying Neuropsychology of Prosocial Behavior

The integration of neuropsychology to understand prosocial behavior has led to various novel ways to understand neural correlates. Wyss and Knoch (2022) outlined three neuroscientific approaches that have been fundamental, that is, task-based brain imaging studies, brain stimulation research, and task-independent brain imaging techniques. Task-based brain imaging studies identify the neural activities undergone when the participant executes a task. These tasks usually represent real-life problems that an individual might encounter in the form of experimental economic games. These games aid in evaluating altruistic and cooperative behaviors and selfish interests. There are two types of such games. The first type involves pitting the interests and decisions of one individual against another, as seen in games like the ultimatum game, the dictator game, and the third-party punishment game. The second type involves the interests and decisions of an individual being tested against those of many others in the group. Examples include the voluntary contributions game and the common pool resources game. Functional magnetic resonance imaging (fMRI) is the most common method employed to measure brain activities, which uses the blood oxygen level dependent to show which brain area is more active when executing a particular task in the games. Non-invasive brain stimulation technologies like transcranial magnetic stimulation are also used. Here, electrical current is passed through a conductive coil to induce a magnetic field through the skull. This has helped in establishing a causal relationship between the functioning of certain areas of the brain and prosocial behavior. The third way is through task-independent brain imaging techniques to understand the characteristics of the brain, which remain stable over time through measures like resting state encephalogram to unveil the origin of behavioral heterogeneity in prosocial behavior.

Neural Structures Involved in Prosocial Behavior

Prosocial behavior, integral to human interactions, is intricately governed by various brain regions and networks. The prefrontal cortex (PFC), encompassing the ventromedial prefrontal cortex (vmPFC) and dorsolateral prefrontal cortex (dlPFC), plays a central role in modulating social behavior. Studies by Beadle et al. (2018) and Steinbeis et al. (2012) have highlighted the vmPFC's involvement in empathy and decision-making processes, while the dlPFC influences perspective-taking and cognitive control, as evidenced by research conducted by Knoch et al. (2014) and Tanaka et al. (2023). Contradictory findings regarding the dlPFC's role in prosocial behavior underscore its complexity (Fermin et al., 2016). Additionally, the medial PFC contributes to cognitive processes and emotion regulation, facilitating empathy-driven prosocial behavior, as observed in studies by Masten et al. (2011). The amygdala, crucial for emotional processing and empathy, guides altruistic decisions by alerting the brain to emotionally salient stimuli (Sander et al., 2003). Moreover, the mirror neuron system and the salience network, including the anterior insula and anterior cingulate cortex, foster social connection and cooperation, as indicated by research by (Jacob, 2008) and Do et al. (2022). Insights from studies on frontotemporal dementia patients elucidate the impact of atrophy in the salience network on prosocial tendencies (Sturm et al., 2018). Finally, brain networks involved in mentalizing, such as the posterior superior temporal sulcus and temporoparietal junction, correlate with prosocial behavior, highlighting the intricate neural mechanisms underlying human altruism (Do et al., 2017).

The Role of Neurotransmitters in Prosocial Behavior

Neurotransmitters like oxytocin and serotonin play pivotal roles in shaping prosocial behavior through their intricate neurochemical mechanisms. Oxytocin, renowned as the "love hormone" or "bonding hormone," fosters social bonding, trust, and cooperation, extending beyond its originally identified role in reproductive functions among mammals (Donaldson & Young, 2008; Hurlemann & Scheele, 2016; Marsh et al., 2021). Studies, including those by Festante et al. (2021), underscore oxytocin's ability to enhance prosocial behavior, particularly evident in instances of social adversity or neurodevelopmental challenges. Similarly, serotonin, primarily associated with mood regulation, also exerts influence on prosocial behavior, albeit with comparatively less literature available. Serotonin's role in modulating aggression and cooperation has garnered attention, with disruptions in serotonin function linked to increased aggression and decreased cooperation (Crockett, 2009; Çetin et al., 2017). Selective serotonin reuptake inhibitors are utilized in managing aggressive and impulsive behaviors, further emphasizing serotonin's significance in prosocial dynamics.

Cognitive Processes Underlying Prosocial Behavior

Cognitive processes such as the theory of mind (ToM), executive functioning, and empathy are pivotal in shaping prosocial behavior.

Theory of Mind

For acting prosocially, it is vital to have the cognitive ability to understand the mental states of other individuals. This ability is called ToM. The concept emerged from Piaget's work on cognitive development and the development of perspective-taking among children, wherein they develop the ability to understand the point of view of others. The literature on the association between ToM and prosocial behavior is divided with mixed results. This lack of clarity can be attributed to the methodological issues about how ToM has been measured in such studies (Banerjee & Watling, 2005). A meta-analysis by Imuta et al. (2016) on children aged 2–12 found an association between ToM and prosocial behavior that was weaker in preschool age but strengthened with age.

Executive Functions

While ToM helps in understanding the mental states of others, which then motivates one to act prosocially, it is not sufficient to act on such motivation. Here, executive functioning becomes essential. Executive Functions are a group of top-down neurocognitive functions involved before acting on a behavior. It has three core components, that is, inhibition, working memory, and cognitive flexibility (Diamond, 2013). Executive functioning allows individuals to monitor their behavior and engage in goal-directed behavior toward the prosocial motive. Traverso et al. (2020) found that the three core components of executive function (EF) mentioned above were directly related to prosocial behavior. EF is also associated with ToM (Moses & Carlson, 2004), thus linked to prosocial behavior.

Empathy

Empathy is one of the catalysts of prosocial behavior. The ability to understand others' emotions and feelings drives prosocial behavior. Decety et al. (2016) have given a model to explain the process of empathy leading to prosocial behavior. They have highlighted how recognizing and observing another's distress will lead to negative affective arousal and physiological stress response. This triggers prosocial drive, which would be acted out into a behavior depending on the context and situation.

Development of Prosocial Behavior

Prosocial behavior, originating in infancy and evolving across the lifespan, manifests through various developmental stages. Early signs emerge as infants display empathy, responding to others' distress, and offering assistance by the age of one (Kanakogi et al., 2013; Hammond & Brownell, 2015). However, scholars like Piaget (1954) suggest that such behaviors may stem from imitation rather than genuine prosocial tendencies. By age three, children begin to exhibit true empathetic awareness and engage in comforting behaviors (Damon et al., 2006). Parenting significantly influences this developmental trajectory, shaping children's interactions with the social world. During childhood, individuals grasp complex social dynamics, learning the value of helping and sharing with peers while understanding parental and societal expectations. Schools foster prosocial behaviors by creating environments that reward and promote such conduct. Adolescents, exploring identity and gaining independence, become more involved in society, often through clubs and organizations that encourage prosocial actions. This community engagement extends into adulthood, where individuals fulfill moral duties and societal responsibilities through civic engagement. While most engage in prosocial behavior to some extent, only a few demonstrate exceptional altruism, serving as models for future generations. Neurobiological research, as described by Do et al. (2019), delineates two developmental trajectories of prosocial behavior: linear (increasing from childhood to adolescence) and nonlinear (peaking in early adolescence). This distinctive developmental path underscores adolescence as a critical period, with early adolescents showing heightened brain activation in areas associated with prosocial decision-making compared to their late adolescent counterparts (van Hoorn et al., 2016; Kathy Do et al., 2019).

The Role of Genetics

Prosocial behavior exhibits a significant genetic component, as evidenced by studies indicating the heritability of prosocial traits increases with age, from 26%–37% at age two to 51%–72% at age seven (Knafo & Plomin, 2006). Behavioral genetics research identifies specific genes, such as the oxytocin receptor gene (OXTR) and the serotonin transporter gene (5-HTTLPR), associated with prosocial behavior (Chiao, 2011). Individuals with variations in these genes, like the A allele of OXTR or the S allele of 5-HTTLPR, may display reduced empathy and prosocial tendencies (Bakermans-Kranenburg & van Ijzendoorn, 2009; Rodrigues et al., 2009). Moreover, the interplay between culture and genetics shapes prosocial behavior, as proposed by the culture-gene coevolutionary theory. This theory suggests that cultural traits evolve over time and influence genetic selection, impacting neural, behavioral, and social environments (Boyd & Richerson, 2009). Studies by Chiao and Blizinsky (2010) indicate that individuals with the S allele of 5-HTTLPR are more prevalent in collectivistic cultures, highlighting the intricate relationship between culture and genetics in shaping prosocial behavior.

Social Context, Culture, and Individual Differences

The neuropsychology of prosocial behavior is not solely determined by brain structures and neurotransmitters; it is also essential to consider the social context and individual differences, which play an equally important role. Social and individual factors interact with neural processes, influencing the likelihood and nature of prosocial acts.

Parenting

Parenting styles wield a significant influence on the development of prosocial behavior in children. Wong et al. (2021) revealed through meta-analysis that authoritative parenting fosters positive associations with prosocial behaviors, while authoritarian parenting displays the opposite effect, irrespective of cultural contexts or parent–child gender dynamics. Responsive parenting, where parents acknowledge and address their child's emotional cues and perspectives, cultivates a sense of security and trust in children, nurturing adaptive social behaviors, including prosocial acts (Eisenberg et al., 2006). Attachment styles between children and parents further shape prosocial tendencies, with securely attached children exhibiting more caring behaviors toward peers, as observed in Elhusseini et al.'s (2023) study. However, Li et al. (2023) literature review underscores that while attachment quality consistently correlates with empathy, its direct link with prosocial behavior varies across studies. Bandura's social learning theory reinforces the pivotal role of parenting, emphasizing how children learn by observing and interacting with trusted individuals. Effective parental guidance enhances children's awareness of others' needs, encouraging altruistic actions, whereas harsh or neglectful parenting may hinder such development (Bandura & Walters, 1963).

Siblings

Sibling interactions allow for a better understanding of other's emotions. Siblings emulate each other's behavior and also act as a catalyst for socialization. Hughes et al. (2018) laid out three themes of how sibling relationships help develop prosocial behavior, that is, conforming, sharing, and helping. The arrival of siblings is one of the child's first experiences in providing care rather than only receiving it. Sharing also becomes a salient feature of the sibling relationship where parents encourage the child to share their resources with the sibling.

Given that most siblings do not belong to the same age groups, such age-different interaction allows for more windows for scaffolding, and the older sibling shares their knowledge with the younger sibling.

Peer Interactions

Peer influence has been notoriously known for increasing the likelihood of risk-taking and maladaptive behaviors. However, studies have indicated the role of peer influence on positive youth outcomes such as prosocial behavior (Feng et al., 2023). In their experimental study, Choukas-Bradley et al. (2015) concluded that exposure to prosocial norms through peer interaction can lead to socialization of prosocial behavior among adolescents. They found that endorsement of a prosocial act by peers would also lead to prosocial responses by adolescents. The reactions may be even higher if endorsed by a high-status peer. Such a response was stronger when the peers were present during the prosocial response. Sullivan et al. (2022) found that adolescents are more likely to act selfishly when not present in front of their peers. The presence of peers leads to a different processing of a social situation marked by a greater display of prosocial decision-making.

Media

Television viewing prosocial content can help develop prosocial ideas and behaviors among children. Lovelace and Huston (1982) revealed that the most effective way of disseminating prosocial ideas among children is through presenting prosocial behavior without any conflicting or antisocial behavior along with it; however, such content is rarely complex to find on television. In their longitudinal study, McHarg and Hughes (2021) found that children who grew up watching slow-paced, prosocial television shows were more likely to demonstrate developmental progress in sharing and prosocial behavior.

Religion

Religious beliefs and practices are suggested to be crucial in promoting prosocial behaviors (Feygina & Henry, 2015). Many religions provide motivations and opportunities for individuals to participate in helpful activities and communities (Eisenberg et al., 2011). Since major religions often emphasize moral and prosocial values such as fairness, kindness, and honesty, religion may also impact a person's empathy and inclination to engage in prosocial actions (Saroglou et al., 2005). Han and Carlo (2020) reported that religious young adults were less likely to choose exposure to violent movies and the Internet. In turn, violent movie exposure preference was negatively related to prosocial behaviors via perspective-taking and empathic concern.

Culture

Societies exhibit diverse dimensions that influence prosocial behavior. Whiting and Whiting's (1975) cross-cultural study revealed that children from subsistence-based economies display higher levels of prosocial behaviors compared to those from industrialized communities. The individualist-collectivist dichotomy further shapes prosocial behavior, with individualist cultures prioritizing personal benefits and collectivist cultures emphasizing group duties and obligations (Triandis, 2001). Despite cultural variations, a universality of prosocial behavior is evident among young children, as indicated by Song et al.'s (2021) study across the Netherlands, India, and China. Cultural and social norms dictate conduct within societies, influencing patterns of generosity and expectations (House, 2017). However, cross-cultural studies on prosocial behavior face challenges, including the need for broader cultural sampling, understanding factors driving cultural differences, and incorporating culture-specific elements into research methodologies (De Guzman et al., 2014).

Personality

Coutinho et al. (2013) discuss the association between prosocial orientation and two dimensions of the Big Five Personality factors—extraversion and agreeableness. Within the model, extraversion reflects the tendency to seek social situations due to their rewarding nature, making individuals high in this trait more sociable, active, optimistic, and happier. The second dimension, agreeableness, pertains to an individual's inclination to care for others and empathetically respond to their needs. Those scoring high in agreeableness tend to be more cooperative and altruistic. These personality traits, extraversion and agreeableness, are commonly linked to a prosocial orientation. Coutinho et al. (2013) investigated the connection between prosocial orientation, measured through extraversion and agreeableness, and the local gray matter volume in the brain. The study revealed that extraversion was negatively correlated with gray matter density in the middle frontal and orbitofrontal gyri. At the same time, agreeableness showed a negative correlation with gray matter density in the inferior parietal, middle occipital, and posterior cingulate gyri. Interestingly, no positive correlations were found. These findings imply that prosocial personality traits, such as extraversion and agreeableness, may be linked to decreases in gray matter density, with extraversion associated with frontal regions and agreeableness with more posterior regions.

Gender Differences

Differences based on gender have been observed in prosocial behavior. Generally, girls tend to exhibit more prosocial behavior than boys. Baillargeon et al. (2011) found that this gender difference becomes noticeable or even more pronounced as children grow. Specifically, girls are more likely to initiate prosocial behaviors, while boys are more inclined to decrease or stop displaying these behaviors between the ages of 29 and 41 months. Gender also plays a role in influencing the connection between prosocial behavior and cortical thickness in specific brain regions, such as the right rostral middle frontal and superior frontal cortex, right superior parietal cortex, cuneus, and precuneus.

Additionally, there are gender differences in the developmental trajectory of prosocial behavior as individuals age. A study by Van der Graaff et al. (2018) uncovered significant gender variations in the development of prosocial behavior. Among boys, levels of prosocial behavior remained stable until age 14, followed by an increase until age 17, with a slight decrease after that. In contrast, prosocial behavior increased until age 16 and then slightly decreased among girls.

The Interplay of Factors

There exists an interplay between neural structures, neurotransmitters, cognitive processes, social context, and individual differences. Imagine a person in a social situation where someone expresses distress. Their amygdala may signal emotional responses, while the PFC processes empathy. Neurotransmitters like oxytocin enhance prosocial feelings. Cognitive processes determine the appropriate response, considering social norms. The individual's unique neural makeup and past experiences shape their specific reaction, showcasing the intricate interplay of neural structures, neurotransmitters, cognition, social context, and individual differences.

Pathology and Prosocial Behavior

Children and adolescents with attention deficit hyperactivity disorder (ADHD) exhibit deficits in social cognition and prosocial behavior. The challenges they face in social cognition, including ToM, emotional self-regulation, emotion recognition, and empathy, impact prosocial behavior. This is reflected in difficulties forming personal relationships and emotional bonds with peers (Yew et al., 2023). Deficits in both empathy and prosocial behavior are recognized in autism spectrum disorder (ASD), a psychiatric condition characterized by challenges in social skills and communication.

Deschamps et al. (2014) did on 6–7-year-old children with ASD children and found that they demonstrated lower levels of parent- and teacher-rated cognitive empathy compared to typically developing children.

Behavioral variant frontotemporal dementia (bvFTD) is a neurodegenerative disease marked by progressive and notable changes in behavior and emotional responses. Individuals with bvFTD experience deficits in empathy, impacting their capacity to understand and respond to the emotions of others. These deficits in empathy are seen as essential precursors for prosocial behaviors, actions intended to benefit others (Deschamps et al., 2014). In the context of bvFTD, atrophy in reward-related neural systems, such as the right pulvinar nucleus of the thalamus and left ventral striatum, is linked to reduced prosocial giving (Strum et al., 2017).

Prosocial Behavior and Wellbeing

Prosocial behavior not only benefits others but also has a profound impact on one's own psychological wellbeing. Nelson et al. (2016) conducted a study comparing the effects of prosocial behavior with self-oriented actions on mood and overall psychological flourishing. Their findings revealed that individuals who engaged in prosocial acts experienced greater increases in psychological wellbeing compared to those who focused solely on themselves or engaged in neutral activities. Similarly, Otake et al. (2006) demonstrated in an intervention that individuals who actively practiced kindness toward others reported higher levels of subjective happiness. However, it is important to note that while prosocial behavior has been associated with positive emotional outcomes, the effects on overall wellbeing may vary. Curry et al.'s (2018) meta-analysis revealed only modest effects of prosocial behavior on wellbeing, suggesting that while prosocial acts may contribute positively to one's emotional state, the impact may not always be substantial.

Raposa et al. (2016) found that engaging in prosocial behavior acted as a buffer against the negative impact of stress on emotional health. This suggests that altruistic actions not only benefit others but also serve as a means for individuals to manage their own emotional wellbeing, especially during challenging times. Moreover, Chancellor et al. (2018) highlighted how prosocial behavior can have a ripple effect, inspiring kindness in others and fostering a culture of compassion and support within communities.

Furthermore, the development of prosocial behavior starts early in life and is influenced by various factors, including parenting styles and socialization practices. Spinrad and Gal (2017) emphasized the role of parental warmth, support, and positive socialization practices in shaping children's empathetic and altruistic tendencies. Similarly, in educational settings, creating emotionally supportive environments and teaching social skills have been shown to enhance prosocial behavior among students (Wentzel, 2015). By fostering a sense of empathy and cooperation, schools can play a crucial role in promoting prosocial values and behaviors among children and adolescents.

Incorporating prosocial activities into interventions aimed at improving mental health could be a valuable strategy, especially for individuals experiencing low-positive or high-negative emotions (Miles et al., 2021).

By encouraging individuals to engage in acts of kindness and altruism, interventions can provide opportunities for individuals to connect with others, experience positive emotions, and contribute to the wellbeing of both themselves and their communities.

Summary

Prosocial behavior encompasses actions aimed at benefiting others and plays a crucial role in human social interaction. This exploration begins with an introduction to the concept of prosocial behavior, highlighting its importance in fostering social cohesion and cooperation. Delving deeper, we examine the evolutionary perspective, shedding light on the adaptive origins of altruistic tendencies in humans. Moving to the neuropsychological domain, we explore the neural structures and neurotransmitters implicated in prosocial behavior, unraveling the intricate interplay between brain function and altruistic actions. The cognitive processes underlying prosocial behavior, including ToM, EFs, and empathy, are then scrutinized, illuminating the psychological mechanisms that drive altruistic actions.

Transitioning to the developmental aspect, we investigate how prosocial behavior emerges and evolves across the lifespan, influenced by factors such as parenting, peer interactions, and cultural norms. The role of genetics in shaping prosocial tendencies is also examined, highlighting the interplay between genetic predispositions and environmental factors. Furthermore, we delve into the social context, culture, and individual differences that influence prosocial behavior, recognizing the diverse array of factors that shape altruistic actions.

Lastly, we explore the nexus between prosocial behavior and wellbeing, recognizing the reciprocal relationship between altruistic actions and psychological flourishing. Despite its inherent complexities, understanding prosocial behavior offers valuable insights for fostering positive social connections, promoting mental health, and cultivating a more compassionate society.

References

Baillargeon, R. H., Morisset, A., Keenan, K., Normand, C. L., Jeyaganth, S., Boivin, M., & Tremblay, R. E. (2011). The development of prosocial behaviors in young children: A prospective population-based cohort study. *The Journal of Genetic Psychology*, *172*(3), 221–251.

Bakermans-Kranenburg, M. J., & van Ijzendoorn, M. H. (2009). Oxytocin receptor (OXTR) and serotonin transporter (5-HTT) genes associated with observed parenting. *Social Cognitive and Affective Neuroscience*, *3*, 128–134.

Bandura, A., & Walters, R. H. (1963). *Social learning and personality development*. Holt Rinehart and Winston.

Banerjee, R., & Watling, D. (2005). Children's understanding of faux pas: Associations with peer relations. *Hellenic Journal of Psychology*, *2*(1), 27–45.

Batson, C., & Powell, A. (2003). Altruism and prosocial behavior. In T. Millon & M. Lerner (Eds.), *Handbook of psychology Volumen 5 personality and social psychology*. John Wiley & Sons, Inc. https://doi.org/10.1002/0471264385.wei0519

Batson, C. D., Duncan, B. D., Ackerman, P., Buckley, T., & Birch, K. (1981). Is empathic emotion a source of altruistic motivation? *Journal of Personality and Social Psychology*, *40*(2), 290–302. https://doi.org/10.1037/0022-3514.40.2.290

Beadle, J. N., Paradiso, S., & Tranel, D. (2018). Ventromedial prefrontal cortex is critical for helping others who are suffering. *Frontiers in Neurology*, *9*. https://doi.org/10.3389/fneur.2018.00288

Boyd, R., & Richerson, P. J. (2009). Culture and the evolution of human cooperation. *Philosophical Transactions of the Royal Society: B London*, *364*, 3281–3288.

Chancellor, J., Margolis, S., Jacobs Bao, K., & Lyubomirsky, S. (2018 June). Everyday prosociality in the workplace: The reinforcing benefits of giving, getting, and glimpsing. *Emotion*, *18*(4), 507–517. https://doi.org/10.1037/emo0000321. Epub 2017 Jun 5. PMID: 28581323.

Chiao, J. Y. (2011). Towards a cultural neuroscience of empathy and prosociality. *Emotion Review*, *3*(1), 111–112. https://doi.org/10.1177/1754073910384159

Chiao, J. Y., & Blizinsky, K. D. (2010). Culture-gene coevolution of individualism-collectivism and the serotonin transporter gene (5-HTTLPR). *Proceedings of the Royal Society B: Biological Sciences*, *277*, 529–537.

Choukas-Bradley, S., Giletta, M., Cohen, G. L., & Prinstein, M. J. (2015). Peer influence, peer status, and prosocial behavior: An experimental investigation of peer socialization of adolescents' intentions to volunteer. *Journal of Youth and Adolescence*, *44*(12), 2197–2210. https://doi.org/10.1007/s10964-015-0373-2

Cialdini, R. B., Baumann, D. J., & Kenrick, D. T. (1981). Insights from sadness: A three-step model of the development of altruism as hedonism. *Developmental Review*, *1*(3), 207–223. https://doi.org/10.1016/0273-2297(81)90018-6

Coutinho, J. F., Sampaio, A., Ferreira, M., Soares, J. M., & Gonçalves, O. F. (2013). Brain correlates of pro-social personality traits: A voxel-based morphometry study. *Brain Imaging and Behavior*, *7*, 293–299.

Crockett, M. J. (2009 June). The neurochemistry of fairness: Clarifying the link between serotonin and prosocial behavior. *Annals of the New York Academy of Sciences*, *1167*, 76–86. https://doi.org/10.1111/j.1749-6632.2009.04506.x. PMID: 19580555.

Curry, O. S., Rowland, L. A., Van Lissa, C. J., Zlotowitz, S., McAlaney, J., Whitehouse, H. (2018). Happy to help? A systematic review and meta-analysis of the effects of performing acts of kindness on the wellbeing of the actor. *Journal of Experimental Social Psychology*, *76*, 320–329. https://doi.org/10.1016/j.jesp.2018.02.014

Damon, W., Lerner, R. M., & Eisenberg, N. (2006). *Handbook of child psychology, social, emotional, and personality development*. Wiley.

de Guzman, M. R., Do, K.-A., & Kok, C. M. (2014). *The cultural contexts of children's prosocial behaviors*. Faculty Publications, Department of Child, Youth, and Family Studies. 103. Retrieved from http://digitalcommons.unl.edu/famconfacpub/103

Decety, J., Bartal, I. B.-A., Uzefovsky, F., & Knafo-Noam, A. (2016). Empathy as a driver of prosocial behaviour: Highly conserved neurobehavioural mechanisms across species. *Philosophical Transactions of the Royal Society B*, *371*, 20150077. http://doi.org/10.1098/rstb.2015.0077

Deschamps, P. K., Been, M., & Matthys, W. (2014). Empathy and empathy induced prosocial behavior in 6-7 year old children with autism spectrum disorder. *Journal of Autism and Developmental Disorders*, *44*(7), 1749–1758. https://doi.org/10.1007/s10803-014-2048-3

Diamond, A. (2013). Executive functions. *Annual Review of Psychology*, *64*, 135–168. https://doi.org/10.1146/annurev-psych-113011-143750

Do, K. T., Guassi Moreira, J. F., & Telzer, E. H. (2017). But is helping you worth the risk? Defining prosocial risk taking in adolescence. *Developmental Cognitive Neuroscience*, *25*, 260–271. https://doi.org/10.1016/j.dcn.2016.11.008

Do, K. T., McCormick, E. M., Prinstein, M. J., Lindquist, K. A., & Telzer, E. H. (2022). Intrinsic connectivity within the affective salience network moderates adolescent susceptibility to negative and positive peer norms. *Scientific Reports*, *12*(1), 17463. https://doi.org/10.1038/s41598-022-17780-1

Do, K. T., McCormick, E. M., & Telzer, E. H. (2019). The neural development of prosocial behavior from childhood to adolescence. *Social Cognitive and Affective Neuroscience*, *14*(2), 129–139. https://doi.org/10.1093/scan/nsy117

Donaldson, Z. R., & Young, L. J. (2008). Oxytocin, vasopressin, and the neurogenetics of sociality. *Science*, *322*(5903), 900–904.

Eisenberg, N., & Fabes, R. A. (1998). Prosocial development. In W. Damon & N. Eisenberg (Eds.), *Handbook of child psychology: Social, emotional, and personality development* (5th ed., pp. 701–778). John Wiley & Sons, Inc.

Eisenberg, N., Castellani, V., Panerai, L., Eggum, N., Cohen, A. B., Pastorelli, C., … Caprara, G. V. (2011). Trajectories of religious coping from adolescence into early adulthood: Their form and relations to externalizing problems and prosocial behavior. *Journal of Personality*, *79*(4), 841–873.

Eisenberg, N., Fabes, R. A., & Spinrad, T. L. (2006). Prosocial behavior. In N. Eisenberg, W. Damon, & R. M. Lerner (Eds.), *Handbook of child psychology: Social, emotional, and personality development* (Vol. 3, 6th ed., pp. 646–718). Wiley.

Elhusseini, S., Rawn, K., El-Sheikh, M., & Keller, P. S. (2023). Attachment and prosocial behavior in middle childhood: The role of emotion regulation. *Journal of Experimental Child Psychology*, *225*, 105534.

Feng, X., Han, Z., & Zheng, S. (2023). Peer influence on prosocial behavior in adolescence. *Journal of Education, Humanities and Social Sciences*, *8*, 1879–1885.

Fermin, A. S., Sakagami, M., Kiyonari, T., Li, Y., Matsumoto, Y., & Yamagishi, T. (2016). Representation of economic preferences in the structure and function of the amygdala and prefrontal cortex. *Scientific Reports*, *6*(1), 20982.

Festante, F., Rayson, H., Paukner, A., Kaburu, S. S., Toschi, G., Fox, N. A., & Ferrari, P. F. (2021). Oxytocin promotes prosocial behavior and related neural responses in infant macaques at-risk for compromised social development. *Developmental Cognitive Neuroscience*, *48*, 100950.

Feygina, I., & Henry, P. J. (2015). Culture and prosocial behavior. In D. A. Schroeder & W. G. Graziano (Eds.), *The Oxford handbook of prosocial behavior* (pp. 188–208). Oxford University Press.

Fletcher, J. A., & Doebeli, M. (2009). A simple and general explanation for the evolution of altruism. *Proceedings of the Royal Society B: Biological Sciences*, *276*(1654), 13–19. https://doi.org/10.1111/j.1467-7687.2008.00739.x

Han, Y., & Carlo, G. (2020). The links between religiousness and prosocial behaviors in early adulthood: The mediating roles of media exposure preferences and empathic tendencies. *Journal of Moral Education*. https://doi.org/10.1080/03057240.2020.1756759

House, B. (2017). How do social norms influence prosocial development?, *COPSYC*. http://doi.org/10.1016/j.copsyc.2017.08.011

Hughes, C., McHarg, G., & White, N. (2018 April). Sibling influences on prosocial behavior. *Current Opinion in Psychology*, *20*, 96–101. https://doi.org/10.1016/j.copsyc.2017.08.015. Epub 2017 Aug 12. PMID: 28858773.

Hurlemann, R., & Scheele, D. (2016). Dissecting the role of oxytocin in the formation and loss of social relationships. *Biological Psychiatry*, *79*(3), 185–193.

Li, Z., Yu, C., Cao, Y., Nie, Y., Tu, W., Liu, B., Ning, Z., & Chen, P. (2023). The association between parent–child attachment and prosocial behavior: A longitudinal study. *Current Psychology*, *43*(3), 2432–2441. https://doi.org/10.1007/s12144-023-04474-8

Imuta, K., Henry, J. D., Slaughter, V., Selcuk, B., & Ruffman, T. (2016). Theory of mind and prosocial behavior in childhood: A meta-analytic review. *Developmental Psychology*, *52*(8), 1192. https://doi.org/10.1037/dev0000140

Jacob, P. (2008). What do mirror neurons contribute to human social cognition? *Mind & Language*, *23*(2), 190–223. https://doi.org/10.1111/j.1468-0017.2007.00337.x

Kanakogi, Y., Okumura, Y., Inoue, Y., Kitazaki, M., & Itakura, S. (2013). Rudimentary sympathy in preverbal infants: Preference for others in distress. *PLoS ONE*, *8*, e65292. https://doi.org/10.1371/journal.pone.0065292

Kay, T., Keller, L., & Lehmann, L. (2020). The evolution of altruism and the serial rediscovery of the role of relatedness. *Proceedings of the National Academy of Sciences*, *117*(46), 28894–28898.

Knafo, A., & Plomin, R. (2006 September). Prosocial behavior from early to middle childhood: Genetic and environmental influences on stability and change. *Developmental Psychology*, *42*(5), 771–786. https://doi.org/10.1037/0012–1649.42.5.771. PMID: 16953685.

Knoch, D., & Nash, K. (2014). Self-control in social decision making: A neurobiological perspective. In Handbook of biobehavioral approaches to self-regulation (pp. 221–234). New York, NY: Springer New York.

Lovelace, V. O., & Huston, A. C. (1982). Can television teach prosocial behavior? *Prevention in Human Services*, 2(1–2), 93–106. https://doi.org/10.1300/J293v02n01_08

Marsh, N., Marsh, A. A., Lee, M. R., & Hurlemann, R. (2020 December). Oxytocin and the neurobiology of prosocial behavior. *Neuroscientist*, *27*(6), 604–619. https://doi.org/10.1177/1073858420960111. Epub 2020 Sep 26. PMID: 32981445; PMCID: PMC8640275.

Masten, C. L., Morelli, S. A., & Eisenberger, N. I. (2011 March 1) An fMRI investigation of empathy for 'social pain' and subsequent prosocial behavior. *Neuroimage*, *55*(1), 381–388. https://doi.org/10.1016/j.neuroimage.2010.11.060. Epub 2010 Nov 28. PMID: 21122817.

McHarg, G., & Hughes, C. (2021). Prosocial television and prosocial toddlers: A multi-method, longitudinal investigation. *Infant Behavior and Development*, *62*, 101526.

Miles, A., Andiappan, M., Upenieks, L., & Orfanidis, C. (2021). Using prosocial behavior to safeguard mental health and foster emotional wellbeing during the COVID-19 pandemic: A registered report protocol for a randomized trial. *PLoS One*, *16*(1), e0245865. https://doi.org/10.1371/journal.pone.0245865

Moses, L. J., & Carlson, S. M. (2004). Self-regulation and children's theories of mind. In C. Lightfoot, C. Lalonde, & M. Chandler (Eds.), *Changing conceptions of psychological life* (pp. 127–146). Lawrence Erlbaum Associates Publishers.

Nelson, S. K., Layous, K., Cole, S. W., & Lyubomirsky, S. (2016). Do unto others or treat yourself? The effects of prosocial and self-focused behavior on psychological flourishing. *Emotion*, *16*(6), 850.

Olivo, D., Di Ciano, A., Mauro, J., Giudetti, L., Pampallona, A., Kubera, K. M., Hirjak, D., Wolf, R. C., & Sambataro, F. (2021). Neural responses of benefiting from the prosocial exchange: the effect of helping behavior. *Frontiers in Psychology*, 12. https://doi.org/10.3389/fpsyg.2021.606858

Otake, K., Shimai, S., Tanaka-Matsumi, J., Otsui, K., & Fredrickson, B. L. (2006). Happy people become happier through kindness: A counting kindnesses intervention. *Journal of Happiness Studies*, *7*, 361–375.

Piaget, J. (1954). *The construction of reality in the child*. Basic Books.

Raposa, E. B., Laws, H. B., & Ansell, E. B. (2016 Jul). Prosocial behavior mitigates the negative effects of stress in everyday life. *Clinical Psychology Science*, *4*(4), 691–698. https://doi.org/10.1177/2167702615611073. Epub 2015 Dec 10. PMID: 27500075; PMCID: PMC4974016.

Rodrigues, S. M., Saslow, L. R., Garcia, N., John, O. P., & Keltner, D. (2009). Oxytocin receptor genetic variation relates to empathy and stress reactivity in humans. *Proceedings of the National Academy of Sciences*, *106*, 21437–21441.

Sander, D., Grafman, J., & Zalla, T. (2003). The human amygdala: An evolved system for relevance detection. *Reviews in Neurosciences*, *14*(4), 303–316. [PubMed] [Google Scholar]

Saroglou, V., Pichon, I., Trompette, L., Verschueren, M., & Dernelle, R. (2005). Prosocial behavior and religion: New evidence based on projective measures and peer ratings. *Journal for the Scientific Study of Religion*, *44*(3), 323–348. https://doi.org/10.1111/j.1468-5906.2005.00289.x

Smith, K. D., Keating, J. P., & Stotland, E. (1989). Altruism reconsidered: The effect of denying feedback on a victim's status to empathic witnesses. *Journal of Personality and Social Psychology*, *57*, 641–650.

Song, Y., Malhotra, S., Broekhuizen, M., Wang, Y., Chen, B. B., & Dubas, J. S. (2021 March–May). Prosocial behavior in young preschoolers: A cross-cultural study across The Netherlands, India, and China. *The Journal of Genetic Psychology*, *182*(3), 129–148. https://doi.org/10.1080/00221325.2021.1891857. Epub 2021 Mar 11. PMID: 33704026.

Spinrad, T. L., & Gal, D. E. (2017). Fostering prosocial behavior and empathy in young children. *COPSYC*. http://doi.org/10.1016/j.copsyc.2017.08.004

Steinbeis, N., Bernhardt, B. C., & Singer, T. (2012 March 8). Impulse control and underlying functions of the left DLPFC mediate age-related and age-independent individual differences in strategic social behavior. *Neuron*, *73*(5), 1040–1051. https://doi.org/10.1016/j.neuron.2011.12.027. PMID: 22405212.

Stevens, F., & Taber, K. (2021). The neuroscience of empathy and compassion in pro-social behavior. *Neuropsychologia*, *159*, 107925.

Strum, J., Mendez, M. F., & Kwan, J. Y. (2017). Atrophy in reward-related neural systems and its impact on prosocial behavior in bvFTD. *Journal of Neurology*, *264*(6), 1201–1208.

Sturm, V. E., Sible, I. J., Datta, S., Hua, A. Y., Perry, D. C., Kramer, J. H., Miller, B. L., Seeley, W. W., Rosen, H. J. (2018 December). Resting parasympathetic dysfunction predicts prosocial helping deficits in behavioral variant frontotemporal dementia. *Cortex*, *109*, 141–155. https://doi.org/10.1016/j.cortex.2018.09.006. Epub 2018 Sep 20. PMID: 30317048; PMCID: PMC6261789.

Sullivan, N. J., Li, R., & Huettel, S. A. (2022). Peer presence increases the prosocial behavior of adolescents by speeding the evaluation of outcomes for others. *Scientific Reports*, *12*, 6477. https://doi.org/10.1038/s41598-022-10115-0

Tanaka, H., Shou, Q., Kiyonari, T., Matsuda, T., Sakagami, M., & Takagishi, H. (2023). Right dorsolateral prefrontal cortex regulates default prosociality preference. *Cerebral Cortex*, *33*(9), 5420–5425.

Thoits PA. Mechanisms linking social ties and support to physical and mental health. J Health Soc Behav. 2011 Jun;52(2):145-61. doi: 10.1177/0022146510395592. PMID: 21673143.

Traverso, L., Viterbori, P., & Usai, M. C. (2020). Prosocial behavior: The role of theory of mind and executive functions. *Journal of Cognition and Development*, *21*(5), 690–708. https://doi.org/10.1080/15248372.2020.1828425

Triandis, H. (2001). Individualism-collectivism and personality. *Journal of Personality*, *69*, 907–924. https://doi.org/10.1111/1467–6494.696169

Van der Graaff, J., Carlo, G., Crocetti, E., Koot, H. M., & Branje, S. (2018). Prosocial behavior in adolescence: Gender differences in development and links with empathy. *Journal of Youth and Adolescence*, *47*(5), 1086–1099.

Van Hoorn, J., Dijk, E., Güroğlu, B., & Crone, E. A. (2016). Neural correlates of prosocial peer influence on public goods game donations during adolescence. *Social Cognitive and Affective Neuroscience*, *11*(6), 923–933. https://doi.org/10.1093/scan/nsw013

Wentzel, K. (2015). Prosocial behaviour and schooling. *Encyclopedia of early childhood development.* Retrieved June, 10, 2019.

Whiting, B. B., & Whiting, J. W. M. (1975). *Children of six cultures: A psychocultural analysis*. Harvard University Press.

Wong, T. K., Konishi, C., & Kong, X. (2021). Parenting and prosocial behaviors: A meta-analysis. *Social Development*, *30*(2), 343–373.

Wu, Y. E., & Hong W. (2022 October). Neural basis of prosocial behavior. *Trends Neuroscience*, *45*(10), 749–762. https://doi.org/10.1016/j.tins.2022.06.008. Epub 2022 Jul 16. PMID: 35853793; PMCID: PMC10039809.

Wyss, A. M., & Knoch, D. (2022 April). Neuroscientific approaches to study prosociality. *Current Opinion in Psychology* , *44*, 38–43. https://doi.org/10.1016/j.copsyc.2021.08.028. Epub 2021 Aug 31. PMID: 34560373.

Yew, R. Y., Hooley, M., & Stokes, M. A. (2023). Factors of relationship satisfaction for autistic and non-autistic partners in long-term relationships. *Autism*, 136236132311602. https://doi.org/10.1177/13623613231160244

9 Empathy

A Cornerstone of Cognitive Wellness

Introduction

Remember the last time when your close friend opened up to you about something that's bothering them, and while they're telling you all about it, you start feeling and relating with what they're feeling, you're deeply involved in that conversation, understanding what your friend is going through, listening to them, validating their feelings. Here, you are empathizing with your friend. It not only allows your friend to feel understood and secure with you but also strengthens your bond. Understanding the role of empathy in daily social interactions and its neural underpinnings is crucial for fostering positive social interactions, building meaningful connections as it's considered a fundamental part of socioemotional wellbeing (Weisz & Cikara, 2021) and, thereby, establishing and preserving a civil society in an era of unparalleled technological advancement (Van Scoyoc, 2023).

The term "empathy," was originally used by Titchener, to refer to people's ability to recognize and comprehend one another via reflection and shared experience (Moudatsou et al., 2020), as well as to be in tune with one another's emotions, as cited in Frankel, 2017). Empathy is a crucial human social construct that facilitates successful social interactions (Ford, 1982, as cited in Melchers et al., 2016a). Davis, broadly defines empathy as an individual's response to another individual's observed experiences (1983). According to Fernandez & Zahavi (2020), the concept of "empathy" comes as heterogeneous and ambiguous and covers a wide range of phenomena, including, perceptual, emotional, cognitive, and behavioral.

Perceptual empathy is the capacity to accurately sense and understand others' emotions and experiences through their verbal and nonverbal cues. Emotional empathy refers to the ability to quickly perceive and empathize with the emotional states of others. This can be measured using both objective and subjective methods, such as physiological changes in the observer or self-reported assessments of empathy. Cognitive empathy, on the other hand, involves understanding not only the emotions but also the intentions and beliefs of others. Tasks like perspective-taking and facial emotion recognition are commonly used to assess cognitive empathy. Biobehavioral

DOI: 10.4324/9781003477815-9

empathy explores how brain activity reflects empathic responses, often focusing on mechanisms like mirror neurons that play a role in understanding and mirroring others' emotions. Motor empathy, meanwhile, involves the subconscious imitation of others' body language, particularly their facial expressions. Studying empathy at a neuropsychological level is vital for understanding human connection and promoting empathy in society, as it has implications for fields such as psychology, medicine, and education. Understanding empathy's neural underpinnings can lead to more effective interventions for conditions related to social functioning and ultimately contribute to the overall wellbeing of individuals and communities.

The Neural Basis of Empathy

Mirror Neuron System

Research in cognitive neuroscience underscores the mirror neuron system (MNS) as crucial for empathy, firing both when performing and observing actions (Rizzolatti & Craighero, 2004). Gallese proposed that mirror neurons facilitate empathy through embodied simulation (Gallese, 2008), as cited in Bekkali et al., 2021). The perception-action model (PAM) suggests that observing behaviors activates internal representations, fostering emotional resonance (Preston & De Waal, 2002). Shared psychophysiological states between observer and observed are facilitated by the MNS (Levenson & Ruef, 1992, as cited in Bekkali et al., (2020)). Additionally, the predictive coding approach posits that the brain minimizes prediction error by integrating sensory input with prior knowledge (Friston, 2010). The MNS connects observed and observer, enabling empathic experiences based on shared understanding (Brown & Brüne, 2012). Despite methodological challenges, theories converge on mirror neurons' pivotal role in empathy and social cognition, facilitating the simulation of others' internal experiences (Bekkali et al., 2021).

Brain Regions Involved

The prefrontal cortex plays a crucial role in empathy by anchoring emotional information in mind, shifting attention across emotions, and planning emotional responses (Light et al., 2010). The medial prefrontal cortex, particularly Brodmann Area 9, is associated with theory of mind and empathy (Siuda et al., 2011a). Prefrontal cortex regions, primarily involved in cognitive perspective-taking, may modulate mimicry-like processes (Miller & Cohen, 2001). Evidence suggests the involvement of spindle cells in the paracingulate sulcus of the medial prefrontal cortex, facilitating neural activity related to emotion and cognition (Allman et al., 2001; Decety & Jackson, 2004). Additionally, the insular cortex, particularly the anterior insula, is implicated in visceral representation and empathetic reactions (Singer et al., 2009). fMRI

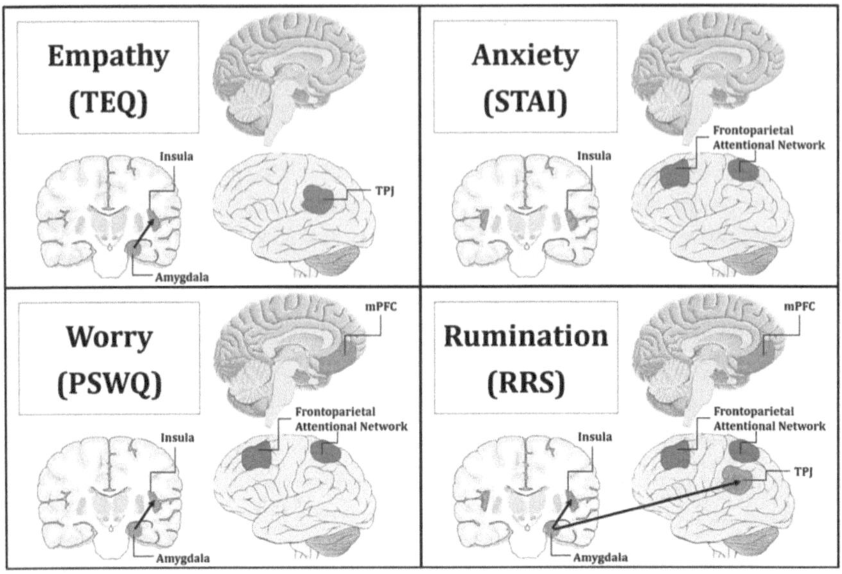

Figure 9.1 Neuroimaging Findings Related to Empathy, Anxiety, Worry, and Rumination.

studies demonstrate the activation of a network involving the insula during imitation and observation of emotional facial expressions (Carr et al., 2003). Moreover, distinct neural networks are involved in cognitive-evaluative empathy and affective-perceptual empathy, with specific brain regions implicated in each (Fan et al., 2011). The inferior frontal gyrus is associated with emotional empathy, while other prefrontal regions are involved in cognitive empathy (Preston et al., 2007). However, previous research on empathy has predominantly focused on observed pain, potentially skewing our understanding of empathy (Depow et al., 2021). Recent studies suggest an overemphasis on empathy for pain in fMRI literature (Morelli et al., 2014, as cited in Depow et al., 2021). This highlights the need for a more comprehensive investigation into various facets of empathy (Figure 9.1).

Neurotransmitters and Hormones

Research indicates that empathy is biologically rooted in the endocrine system, particularly testosterone and cortisol (Preston & De Waal, 2002; Yildirim & Derksen, 2012; Gonzalez-Liencres et al., 2013, as cited in Zilioli et al., 2015). Elevated testosterone levels have been associated with reduced empathy in both males and females (Hermans et al., 2006; Van Honk et al., 2011, as cited in Zilioli et al., 2015). Similarly, high cortisol levels have been linked with increased empathy, as they mirror states of mild arousal and internal distress (Shirtcliff et al., 2009, as cited in Zilioli et al., 2015). Testosterone and cortisol can influence empathy either separately or together, as they are interconnected through the hypothalamic–pituitary–adrenal and hypothalamic–pituitary–gonadal axes (Viau, 2002, as cited in Zilioli et al., 2015). Oxytocin, often referred to as the "love hormone," also plays a significant role in empathy by enhancing emotional bonds and social recognition (Kendrick et al., 2017). It activates both salience and reward circuits in the brain, promoting warm and supportive behaviors towards others (Wigton et al., 2015; Zhao et al., 2016; Montag et al., 2011, as cited in Kendrick et al., 2017). Overall, these hormonal interactions contribute to the neuroendocrine regulation of empathy and social behavior.

Developmental Aspects of Empathy

Although earlier theories did not support the presence of empathy in young children due to the prominent nature of egocentrism and the lack of cognitive abilities in them (Freud, 1958; Piaget, 1965) recent evidence point at the capability of very young children to display empathy through their behaviors. A fairly good reason to look into this evidence energes from the fact that children are not susceptible to distractor concepts such as social desirability, due to challenges such as limited verbalization.

Childhood

Early signs of empathy emerge in infancy, evidenced by distress reactions like reflexive crying when exposed to others' distress (Martin & Clark, 1982). As infants grow, they exhibit empathy through actions like helping, verbal comfort, and distraction (Zahn-Waxler et al., 1992). Cognitive empathy solidifies during preschool and elementary school years, facilitated by linguistic development for empathic reflection.

Parenting significantly influences empathy development, impacting attachment styles and disciplinary approaches (Kim & Kochanska, 2017; Heynen et al., 2021; Samper et al., 2021). Secure parent–child attachment is associated with higher empathy levels from early stages (Kim & Kochanska, 2017). Authoritative parenting fosters empathy, while neglectful or permissive styles hinder it (Heynen et al., 2021; Samper et al., 2021). Synchrony in parent–child interactions, particularly during infancy, correlates with higher empathy levels in childhood and adolescence (Feldman, 2007).

Adolescence

The patterns of brain development through adolescence described by Giedd et al. (1999) and Giedd (2008) appear to fit the global progression in empathy toward the (higher) adult empathy. The increase in gray matter in the temporal lobe, which peaks at 16–17 years old, may be related to increased intensity of emotional responses and the enhancement of regulatory systems may be related, among other things, to the increased pruning and white matter growth in late adolescence. However, there was no linear growth pattern observed in the variables of personal suffering, empathic concern, and perspective taking. Adolescents' developing capacity to infer mental states and understand the viewpoints of others is linked to significant alterations in cortical and subcortical brain regions that are engaged in social cognitive processing (Decety, 2010).

Role of Peer Relationships

Miklikowska et al. (2022) investigated the longitudinal relationship between adolescent friendships and empathy, finding that adolescents tend to befriend peers with similar levels of empathy. Moreover, youth with more empathic friends showed an increase in empathy over time compared to those with less empathic friends, highlighting the influence of friendships on empathy development, both affective and cognitive components. This underscores the importance of peer-based social–emotional programs in fostering adolescent empathy.

Social embedding, driven by the human need to belong, is crucial for psychological wellbeing, particularly during adolescence when peer relationships are paramount (Baumeister & Leary, 1995; LaFontana & Cillessen, 2009). Social isolation triggers neurocognitive threat systems akin to physical danger, hindering social understanding and development (Parker & Asher, 1987; Eisenberger et al., 2003).

According to the perception-action paradigm (Preston & De Waal, 2002), social embedding influences empathy development by activating shared representations in the brain. Observing others' behaviors activates mental images, which then trigger "state-matching" reactions in the brain's motor regions. Social ties shape the quantity and quality of shared representations, enhancing empathetic processes as individuals accumulate more shared experiences and understanding.

Adulthood and Aging

Gruhn (2008) conducted a longitudinal study spanning 12 years, involving individuals aged 10–87, to explore the relationship between age and empathy. Longitudinal analyses revealed no age-related declines in empathy, contrary to cross-sectional analyses which showed lower empathy scores in older adults compared to younger adults. These findings suggest that cross-sectional age differences may reflect cohort effects rather than age effects. Additionally, the study found positive associations between empathy and wellbeing, as well as interaction profile. Experience-sampling conducted with a subsample of participants over a week showed that individuals reporting high levels of empathy perceived their interactions as more meaningful, experienced more positivity, and believed their interaction partners also felt more positive.

Changes in Empathy Across the Lifespan

Current empirical research on age differences and age-related changes in empathy is limited and varies in methodology. Studies examining autobiographical wisdom narratives found that adolescents mentioned empathy more often than older individuals, but cross-sectional analyses showed no age-related variations in the inclusion of empathy and support remarks in personal narratives. Similarly, questionnaire studies have shown stability or negative age differences in dispositional empathy, with some studies reporting no discernible age differences and others showing a trend of negative age differences.

For instance, Eysenck et al. (1985) and Diehl et al. (1996) found no age-related variations in self-reported empathy across different age groups. However, Phillips et al. (2002) and Schieman and Van Gundy (2000) reported negative age differences in empathy, with older adults scoring lower than younger adults, even after accounting for factors like education. Helson et al. (2002) conducted longitudinal studies over nearly 40 years, finding a slight but statistically significant decline in empathy over time, particularly in women.

Overall, while some studies suggest no age differences in empathy, others indicate a negative trend of age differences. No research suggests that empathy increases with age, and the one known longitudinal study suggests a slight decline in self-reported empathy over time. These findings suggest that the basis of empathy is established early in life, with empathy remaining stable into old age, albeit with potential variations in characteristics. However, cognitive empathy may rise in early adulthood, peak in middle age, and decline in later life. Despite these trends, there is a consensus that empathy increases from childhood to adolescence/adulthood, with neural networks' maturation and affective behavioral responses occurring early in life.

Impact of Neurological Disorders

Empathy impairments are evident in neuropsychiatric disorders like Korsakoff's syndrome (KS) and frontotemporal dementia (FTD). In KS, patients often exhibit irritability, aggressiveness, and behavioral disinhibition, alongside decreased theory of mind functioning and reduced levels of empathy. Social dysfunction in KS may result from a loss of integrity in social abilities such as emotion recognition and theory of mind. Similarly, FTD presents with symptoms like aphasia, emotional indifference, apathy, and lack of empathy, alongside disinhibition and impulsivity. Shany-Ur et al. (2012) found that FTD patients showed diminished ability to recognize lies and sarcasm, attributed to impairments in perspective taking and emotion reading. Stroke survivors, particularly those with damage to the right hemisphere, may also experience impaired empathy, theory of mind, and emotional processing due to acquired language loss. These findings highlight the intricate relationship between language, cognition, and social functioning in neurological conditions.

Individual Differences in Empathy

Individual differences in early empathy development may be influenced by genetic variance in the oxytocin system, which regulates various aspects of social behavior and cognition. Oxytocin plays a crucial role in enhancing empathy and facilitating social interactions. Oxytocin supplementation could potentially improve empathic impairments, particularly for individuals with specific OXTR (oxytocin receptor) variations. Demographic factors such as gender, education, ethnicity, age, and geographic region may also influence empathy levels. Additionally, income has been linked to lower levels of compassion, while religiosity and liberalism are associated with higher empathy. Furthermore, individual characteristics and experiences, including one's profession, can impact empathy levels. The Interpersonal Reactivity Index (IRI), developed by Davis in 1980, is a commonly used self-report measure for assessing individual differences in empathy.

Sex Differences

Sex differences play a significant role in empathy regulation, affecting both the individual empathizing and the person being empathized with. Multiple studies suggest that women tend to be more empathetic than men, potentially due to their nurturing roles. For instance, female infants demonstrate reactive cry, a primitive form of empathy triggered by other babies' cries, more frequently than male infants. Neuroanatomical and neurophysiological variances between sexes in the mirror neuron system (MNS), strongly linked with empathy competence, have been observed. Women generally exhibit higher emotional and cognitive empathy performance, along with greater gray matter volume in brain regions associated with empathy. They may also have greater mirror neuron activity, leading to more efficient processing of emotional stimuli. Hormonal influences, particularly during the follicular phase, contribute to enhanced socio-emotional behavior in females. In contrast, men are more susceptible to social cognitive disorders characterized by empathy deficiencies, such as autism spectrum disorder (ASD) and psychopathy. Empathic reactions in men and women may differ based on the perceived fairness of others, with men showing reduced empathy-related reactions when witnessing unfairness and increased activation in reward-related regions associated with a desire for vengeance. Conversely, women's empathic responses remain relatively consistent regardless of fairness perception. Overall, sex differences play a crucial role in shaping empathic responses and behaviors.

Cultural and Environmental Influences

Empathy is profoundly shaped by socioeconomic factors, with individuals from lower socioeconomic backgrounds often exhibiting higher levels of empathy and compassion compared to those from more affluent backgrounds. However, the impact of empathy varies depending on social class. For high-class participants, empathy positively influences support for helping others, while for adolescents from lower socioeconomic classes, empathy does not significantly impact providing help. Additionally, the effect of empathic accuracy differs across socioeconomic statuses, with empathic accuracy being beneficial for wellbeing and marital satisfaction in low socioeconomic status (SES) but detrimental to marital satisfaction in high SES.

Culture also plays a significant role in shaping empathetic reactions, with collectivistic cultures valuing empathetic responses more than individualistic cultures. Collectivistic communities prioritize group harmony, social norms, and loyalty to the ingroup, whereas individualistic cultures prioritize personal fulfillment, autonomy, and individual rights. These cultural differences influence emotional expressivity and suppression, leading to variations in empathetic concern. For example, East Asian cultures, which emphasize emotional suppression, typically display less empathetic concern compared to Western cultures. These findings underscore the intricate interplay among culture, socioeconomic class, and empathetic reactions, highlighting how these factors interact to shape an individual's capacity for empathy and compassion.

Personality Traits and Empathy

Personality traits play a significant role in shaping empathy, with agreeableness emerging as the primary predictor. Agreeableness, characterized by altruism, compassion, and cooperativeness, is strongly associated with empathic concern and perspective taking across various cultures. This connection is explained by agreeable individuals' tendencies toward forgiveness, helpfulness, and tenderness, which align with efforts to reduce interpersonal conflict and maintain intragroup cooperation. Neurophysiological mechanisms, including mirror neuron activity, also link agreeableness to empathy, with increased brain activity in certain regions associated with empathic accuracy.

Conscientiousness, the second most predictive personality trait for empathy, correlates inversely with psychoticism, characterized by a lack of empathy. This relationship suggests that conscientious individuals, who exhibit higher levels of responsibility and reliability, are more empathetic due to their lower egocentricity and greater concern for others.

Neuroticism, characterized by emotional instability and negative emotions, is associated with personal distress but shows contradictory findings regarding its relationship with empathy. While some research suggests a positive correlation between neuroticism and perspective taking, others propose that heightened emotional arousal in neurotic individuals facilitates empathic responses by making them more sensitive to external stimuli.

Openness to experience, particularly its aspect of inner feeling attentiveness, is positively correlated with cognitive empathy, enabling individuals to comprehend others' thoughts and emotions. This relationship is attributed to the receptiveness of individuals with high openness scores to novel perspectives and environmental shifts.

Overall, personality factors of the Big Five, including agreeableness, conscientiousness, neuroticism, and openness to experience, explain a significant portion of the variance in empathy questionnaire responses. However, the relationship between personality and empathy appears to vary across cultures and assessment techniques, leading to conflicting findings in some studies.

Neuroplasticity and Empathy Development

Neuroplasticity, the brain's ability to adapt and reorganize itself by forming and reforming neural pathways, plays a crucial role in empathy development. Hebb's theory posits that neurons that fire together wire together, strengthening connections between neurons and facilitating learning and memory. Long-term potentiation, a process where prolonged excitement in cells strengthens connections, is a key mechanism in neuroplasticity. This concept applies to empathy development, particularly through the MNS, which relies on associative learning theory. Infants start forming bidirectional connections between mental states and behaviors through motor behaviors and subjective inner feelings, laying the groundwork for understanding others' minds.

Positive experiences contribute to the formation of neural pathways associated with empathy, emphasizing the importance of fostering positive environments for empathy development, with parents playing a crucial role. Early home surroundings and maternal support influence gene activation and brain development, impacting emotional regulation and social interactions. Conversely, childhood abuse and neglect can harm neural pathways and lead to mental health conditions like borderline personality disorder. However, positive events during childhood can mitigate the damage and set up new neural pathways.

While neuroplasticity is most pronounced during early childhood, empathy can still be taught later in life, with positive outcomes for individuals and professions alike. Empathy training has been shown to enhance empathic skills, communication, emotional resilience, and counseling skills, contributing to improved interpersonal interactions and prosocial behavior. Therefore, empathy training is recommended as it can lead to significant benefits in various aspects of life.

Empathy and Mental Health

Empathy's impact on subjective wellbeing is subject to conflicting evidence. While some argue that empathy promotes wellbeing, others suggest it leads to social disengagement and exhaustion. Continuous exposure to stress and suffering can lead to empathic strain, resulting in symptoms like exhaustion and decreased ability to empathize, known as compassion fatigue.

Moreover, empathy, when excessive, can lead to empathy-based guilt, including survivor's guilt and omnipotent responsibility guilt, which may result in pathogenic altruism and psychopathology. However, empathy-based guilt can also be essential in certain social contexts, benefiting healthcare workers by increasing efficacy and reducing burnout.

Emotional regulation plays a crucial role in navigating empathetic responses. Individuals with well-developed emotional regulation skills can better understand and respond to others' emotions. Emotional regulation involves managing internal feeling states, physiological processes, and behavioral responses. It helps prevent vicarious emotions from becoming unpleasant and facilitates appropriate responses to others' emotions. Decety and Lamm's model of empathy suggests that emotional regulation is voluntary and involves top-down processing, drawing on executive function resources. Both down- and up-regulation of emotions are crucial for empathetic responses, with strategies ranging from controlling attention to cognitive reappraisal. Overall, emotional regulation is essential for maintaining empathetic responses and subjective wellbeing.

Resilience and Empathy

Resilience is the ability to bounce back from challenges, can be closely linked to empathetic responses to others' emotions. Strong relationship between empathy level and resilience has been found (Wilczek-Rużyczka, 2023). Building resilience can equip individuals with the strength to navigate emotional complexities and engage empathetically in social interactions. Moreover, empathy fosters resilience by strengthening social connections, which acts as a protective factor against stressors.

While empathy fuels resilience, resilience is equally important for sustaining empathy. Witnessing the suffering of others can be emotionally draining, leading to compassion fatigue or burnout. Resilience equips individuals with the emotional stamina to stay engaged with the struggles of others without becoming overwhelmed.

Empathy in Psychopathology

Atypical empathetic responses have frequently been linked to psychiatric disorders, including ASDs (Baron-Cohen & Wheelwright, 2004; Blacher et al., 2003; Gillberg, 1992; Shamay-Tsoory et al., 2002). According to studies by Deschamps et al. (2014), Dziobek et al. (2008), Harari et al. (2010), Mazza et al. (2014), Rueda et al. (2015), Shamay-Tsoory et al. (2009), as cited in Harmsen (2019), cognitive empathy is compromised again in ASD and also in bipolar disorder, and borderline personality disorder. Psychopathy, schizophrenia, narcissism, and depersonalization all have been shown to have decreased affective empathy (Jones et al., 2010; Lawrence et al., 2007; Ritter et al., 2011; Shamay-Tsoory et al., 2007, as cited in Harmsen, 2019).

According to Decety and Jackson (2004), deficiencies in empathy can also be observed in Asperger's syndrome, traumatic brain damage, behavioral problems, sociopathy, and stroke. Differences in empathetic experiences are explained by a normal fluctuation between affective and cognitive components, even in neurotypical persons (Harmsen, 2019).

Autism Spectrum Disorders (ASD)

ASD encompasses a range of neurodevelopmental disorders characterized by repetitive behaviors, limited interests, and difficulties in social communication and interaction. Several theories attempt to explain empathy issues in individuals with ASD, including Theory of Mind (ToM) deficiencies, simulation theory, and the social motivation hypothesis. ToM involves understanding that one's own mental state may differ from others, which individuals with ASD may struggle with. Simulation theory suggests that empathizing involves putting oneself in others' shoes, possibly mediated by mirror neurons. The social motivation hypothesis posits that neurological dysfunctions related to reward processing may make social stimuli less enjoyable for individuals with ASD. fMRI research indicates reduced activation of brain regions associated with empathy in ASD, including the fusiform gyrus and mirror neurons. However, the broken mirror hypothesis has been contested by some studies, suggesting intact motor-mimicking mechanisms in ASD. Other abnormalities, such as reduced activation in the medial prefrontal cortex and anterior insula, may contribute to empathy deficits in ASD. Sensory processing abnormalities, particularly auditory issues, may also exacerbate empathy deficiencies in ASD. Genetic studies have identified associations between empathy and ASD-related genes, particularly those involved in the GABAergic system. Additionally, deficits in interoceptive sensitivity and awareness have been linked to empathy and alexithymia in ASD. Age-related changes in neurological underpinnings of empathy in ASD suggest the importance of early intervention. Comorbidities such as attention deficit hyperactivity disorder (ADHD) and psychosis may further impact empathy levels in individuals with ASD. Overall, understanding the multifaceted nature of empathy deficits in ASD can inform interventions and support strategies for affected individuals.

Schizophrenia

Schizophrenia is a complex mental illness characterized by positive symptoms like delusions and hallucinations, and negative symptoms such as affective flattening and anhedonia (Bansal & Chatterjee, 2021). Patients often exhibit abnormal emotional and social behavior, including difficulties in understanding social cues and ToM abilities. Research by Shamay-Tsoory et al. (2007) highlighted that individuals with schizophrenia tend to make more errors in affective ToM tasks compared to controls, particularly in attributing emotional mental states. Moreover, there's a correlation between the severity of negative symptoms and impaired affective ToM, indicating that those with high levels of negative symptoms may struggle more with understanding emotional states of others. Additionally, deficits in the ventromedial prefrontal cortex have been linked to impaired cognitive empathy abilities in individuals with schizophrenia, as per findings by Perry and Shamay-Tsoori (2013).

Psychopathy & Sociopathy

"Acquired sociopathy" is a term used to describe individuals with lesions in the orbitofrontal cortex (OFC), characterized by abnormal behavior, heightened violence, and a lack of regard for others. Similarly, individuals with psychopathic tendencies often display social and emotional impairments, including deficits in empathy and emotional connection. Shamay-Tsoory et al. (2010) conducted a study comparing criminal offenders with strong psychopathic traits, individuals with OFC lesions, and healthy controls, among others. They found that those with psychopathy and OFC lesions performed poorly on tasks assessing affective ToM but not cognitive ToM. This suggests that dysfunction in the amygdala–OFC circuitry may underlie mentalizing impairments observed in psychopathy, akin to those seen in individuals with OFC damage. However, it's important to note that while there are similarities between developmental psychopathy and acquired frontal lesions, these groups differ significantly from each other, particularly in terms of instrumental aggressiveness.

Other Psychopathologies

A fMRI investigation on adolescents with aggressive conduct disorder revealed an atypical pattern of neural response to viewing others in pain (Decety et al., 2009). They exhibit no activity in the brain areas involved with metacognition (including moral reasoning) and self-regulation. It has been suggested that teenagers with conduct disorder (CD) are more likely to react angrily because their empathic mimicry causes high levels of distress. Their responses to painful situations also indicate a lack of cognitive perspective-taking. These findings suggest that CD adolescents may have defective top-down processing of empathy-inducing information (Siuda et al., 2011b).

Therapeutic Implications

Empathy is pivotal in psychotherapy, facilitating therapeutic alliances and enhancing outcomes (Spiro, 2009). Interventions aimed at bolstering empathy encompass mindfulness- and simulation-based therapies, which target cognitive, affective, and behavioral dimensions of empathy (Trivedi-Bateman & Crook, 2022). The roots of empathy development extend back to childhood, necessitating interventions tailored to address empathy deficits across the lifespan, with an emphasis on positive parenting practices and individualized therapeutic approaches (Moudatsou et al., 2020).

In workplace settings, fostering empathy fosters improved morale, teamwork, and staff retention (Ceruto, 2023). Strategies for promoting empathy include encouraging perspective-taking, active listening, workplace diversification, managing empathy triggers, and providing comprehensive education and training (Ceruto, 2023). Pedagogical tools like "Diversity Dolls" have proven effective in instilling empathy among social care students (Papouli, 2019).

Moreover, mindfulness and compassion training have been associated with structural and functional changes in the brain, leading to enhanced empathy and self-compassion (Centeno & Fernandez, 2020). The integration of mindfulness with compassion practices further amplifies social connection and altruistic behavior (Brensilver, 2016).

In summary, empathy serves as a cornerstone in various contexts, and targeted interventions to cultivate it hold promise for individual wellbeing and interpersonal relationships.

Challenges and Future Directions

Studying the neuropsychology of empathy reveals its complexities and challenges, including the absence of a universally accepted definition or measurement tool (Jami et al., 2023; Kilroy & Aziz-Zadeh, 2017). Self-reported questionnaires and behavioral tasks, such as the IRI, are commonly used but may be influenced by subjective biases and alexithymia, hindering accurate interpretations (Kilroy & Aziz-Zadeh, 2017).

Moreover, determining the "optimum" level of empathy presents a challenge similar to stress management concepts like "Eustress," as excessive empathy can lead to negative outcomes (Chakrabarty & Brown, 2020). Post-COVID technologies like video conferencing introduce additional complexities, potentially limiting empathy due to difficulties in reading emotional cues (Chakrabarty & Brown, 2020).

Culture shapes empathetic behavior, yet consensus on which cultural elements promote empathy remains elusive (Jami et al., 2023). Methodological discrepancies in neuroimaging research, such as different processing methods, can yield conflicting findings (Kilroy & Aziz-Zadeh, 2017). However, advancements in neuroimaging technology allow for the examination of brain activity during empathy, revealing critical brain regions and providing insights into empathy-related processes (Kilroy & Aziz-Zadeh, 2017; Shamay-Tsoori, 2015). Integrating neuroimaging with subjective and objective measures enhances our understanding of empathy's neural basis (Johnstone et al., 2015).

Conclusion

The claim that empathy—the capacity to consider our own feelings as well as those of others—is a genuinely biopsychosocial phenomenon, and is not a hyperbole. The intricacy and beauty of what it is to be human are reflected in its various faces and features (Frankel, 2017). The positive neuropsychology of empathy provides profound insights into the neural mechanisms that underlie positive social connections.

By cultivating a deeper understanding of these processes, we can contribute to fostering empathy, promoting wellbeing of ourselves and the people around us, thereby building a more compassionate and interconnected society. The fact that empathy starts burgeoning since infancy and continues to develop throughout lifespan leaves room for improvement at any age, highlighting the importance of neuroplasticity. Moreover, it is undeniable that individual differences, pathology and culture have a huge influence on empathy. So, it's important to take them into consideration whenever we study the concept of empathy. Moreover, empathy has shown to have implications in mental health, emotional regulation, and resilience and can be cultivated via social and emotional learning (SEL)-based programs, mindfulness, and compassion-based training. Empathy not only contributes to a good personal life by fostering meaningful connections but also professional life by fostering meaningful and healthy work relations and workplace. Though, not having a universally accepted definition and measurement might pose some challenges, for which researchers are urged to work for, alongside social robots is a new area of interest for empathy researchers with an aim to create artificial intelligence (AI) that can resonate to humans.

References

Allman, J. M., Watson, K. K., & Tetreault, N. A. (2001). Intuition and empathy: The role of spindle cells in the anterior cingulate cortex. *Neuroscience & Biobehavioral Reviews*, *25*(3), 193–199.

Bansal, V., & Chatterjee, I. (2021). Role of neurotransmitters in schizophrenia: a comprehensive study. *Kuwait Journal of Science*, *48*(2). https://doi.org/10.48129/kjs.v48i2.9264

Baron-Cohen, S., & Wheelwright, S. (2004). The Empathy Quotient: An investigation of adults with Asperger syndrome or high functioning autism, and normal sex differences. *Journal of Autism and Developmental Disorders*, *34*(2), 163–175. https://doi.org/10.1023/B:JADD.0000022607.19833.00

Baumeister, R. F., & Leary, M. R. (1995). The need to belong: Desire for interpersonal attachments as a fundamental human motivation. *Psychological Bulletin*, *117*(3), 497–529. https://doi.org/10.1037/0033-2909.117.3.497

Bekkali, M., Fadiga, L., & Gallese, V. (2021). The role of the mirror neuron system in empathy: A review of the literature. *Cognitive Neuroscience*, *12*(3), 139–154.

Bekkali, S., Youssef, G. J., Donaldson, P. H., Albein-Urios, N., Hyde, C., & Enticott, P. G. (2020). Is the Putative Mirror Neuron System Associated with Empathy? A Systematic Review and Meta-Analysis. *Neuropsychology Review*, *31*(1), 14–57. https://doi.org/10.1007/s11065-020-09452-6

Blacher, J., Baker, B. L., & Eisenhower, A. S. (2003). The impact of children with intellectual disabilities on family life. *International Review of Research in Mental Retardation*, *27*, 1–29.

Brensilver, M. (2016, May 5). *Mindfulness and empathy*. Mindful Schools. https://www.mindfulschools.org/foundational-concepts/mindfulness-and-empathy/

Brown, S. J., & Brüne, M. (2012). The role of the mirror neuron system in social cognition: A review. *Neuroscience & Biobehavioral Reviews*, *36*(1), 1–9. https://doi.org/10.1016/j.neubiorev.2011.04.001

Carr, L., Iacoboni, M., Dubeau, M. C., Mazziotta, J. C., & Lenzi, G. L. (2003). Neural mechanisms of empathy in humans: A relay from neural systems to social cognition. *Journal of Neuroscience*, *23*(16), 1–9. https://doi.org/10.1523/JNEUROSCI.21-01-00001.2001

Centeno RPR. Effect of Mindfulness on Empathy and Self-Compassion: An Adapted MBCT Program on Filipino College Students. Behav Sci (Basel). 2020 Feb 27;10(3):61. doi: 10.3390/bs10030061. PMID: 32120924; PMCID: PMC7139462.

Ceruto, L. A. (2023). Fostering empathy in the workplace: Strategies for improving morale, teamwork, and staff retention. *Business Horizons*, *66*(1), 1–10. https://doi.org/10.1016/j.bushor.2022.08.003

Chakrabarty, T., & Brown, J. (2020). The dual nature of empathy: Balancing the benefits and drawbacks in therapeutic settings. *Journal of Clinical Psychology*, *76*(5), 885–895. https://doi.org/10.1002/jclp.22900

Costa, P. T. Jr, Terracciano, A., & McCrae, R. R. (2001). Gender differences in personality traits across cultures: Robust and surprising findings. *Journal of Personality and Social Psychology*, *81*(2), 322–331.

Davis, M. H. (1983). Measuring individual differences in empathy: Evidence for a multidimensional approach. *Journal of Personality and Social Psychology*, 44(1), 113–126. https://doi.org/10.1037/0022-3514.44.1.113

Decety, J. (2010). To what extent is the brain involved in empathy? In M. J. E. J. de Waal & F. B. M. de Waal (Eds.), *The Oxford handbook of social neuroscience* (pp. 198–213). Oxford University Press.

Decety J, Jackson PL. The functional architecture of human empathy. Behav Cogn Neurosci Rev. 2004 Jun;3(2):71-100. doi: 10.1177/1534582304267187. PMID: 15537986.

Decety, J., Yang, C., & Cheng, Y. (2009). Physiological responses to others' pain in individuals with aggressive conduct disorder: An fMRI study. *Journal of Abnormal Psychology*, *118*(1), 1–10.

Depow, G. J., Francis, Z., & Inzlicht, M. (2021). The Experience of Empathy in Everyday Life. Psychological Science, 32(8), 1198-1213. https://doi.org/10.1177/0956797621995202

Deschamps, P. K., Been, M., & Matthys, W. (2014). Empathy and empathy-induced prosocial behavior in 6-7 year old children with autism spectrum disorder. *Journal of Autism and Developmental Disorders*, *44*(7), 1749–1758. https://doi.org/10.1007/s10803-014-2048-3

Dziobek, I., Rogers, K., Fleck, S., & Wolf, O. T. (2008). Dissociation of cognitive and emotional empathy in adults with Asperger syndrome. *Journal of Autism and Developmental Disorders*, *38*(3), 464–473. DOI 10.1007/s10803-007-0486-x

Eisenberg, N., Smith, C. L., Sadovsky, A., & Spinrad, T. L. (2004). Effortful control. In R. F. Baumeister & K. D. Vohs (Eds.), *Handbook of self-regulation* (pp. 259–282). The Guilford Press.

Eisenberger, N. I., Lieberman, M. D., & Williams, K. D. (2003). Does rejection hurt? An fMRI study of social exclusion. *Science*, *302*(5643), 290–292.

Eysenck, H. J., Eysenck, S. B. G., & Barrett, P. (1985). A revised version of the Eysenck Personality Questionnaire (EPQ-R). *Personality and Individual Differences*, *6*(5), 583–593. https://doi.org/10.1016/0191-8869(85)90026-1

Fan, Y., Duncan, N. W., de Greck, M., & Northoff, G. (2011). Is there a core neural network in empathy? An fMRI study using emotional stimuli. *NeuroImage*, *58*(1), 1–11. https://doi.org/10.1016/j.neuroimage.2011.01.027

Feldman, R. (2007). Parent–infant synchrony: A potential regulator of the social-emotional development of children. *Clinical Psychology Review*, *27*(8), 858–870. https://doi.org/10.1016/j.cpr.2007.02.003

Fernandez, A. V., & Zahavi, D. (2020). Basic empathy: Developing the concept of empathy from the ground up. *International Journal of Nursing Studies*, *110*, 103695. https://doi.org/10.1016/j.ijnurstu.2020.103695

Frankel, F. (2017). *Empathy and its implications for social interactions*. Cambridge University Press.

Freud, S. (1958). *The ego and the id*. New York, NY: W.W. Norton & Company.

Friston, K. J. (2010). The free-energy principle: A unified brain theory? *Nature Reviews Neuroscience*, *11*(2), 127–138. https://doi.org/10.1038/nrn2787

Gallese, V. (2008). *Mirror neurons and the neural exploitation hypothesis: from embodied simulation to social cognition*. Humana Press eBooks (pp. 163–190). https://doi.org/10.1007/978-1-59745-479-7_8

Giedd, J. N. (2008). The teen brain: Insights from neuroimaging. *Journal of Adolescent Health*, *42*(4), 335–343. https://doi.org/10.1016/j.jadohealth.2008.01.007

Giedd, J. N., Blumenthal, J., Jeffries, N. O., Castellanos, F. X., Liu, H., Zijdenbos, A., Paus, T., Evans, A. C., & Rapoport, J. L. (1999). Brain development during childhood and adolescence: A longitudinal MRI study. *Nature Neuroscience*, *2*(10), 861–863. https://doi.org/10.1038/13158

Gonzalez-Liencres, C., Park, S. Q., & de Waal, F. B. M. (2013). The role of oxytocin in empathy and social behavior. *Neuroscience & Biobehavioral Reviews*, *37*(8), 1515–1526. https://doi.org/10.1016/j.neubiorev.2013.04.014

Grühn, D., Rebucal, K., Diehl, M., Lumley, M., & Labouvie-Vief, G. (2008). Empathy across the adult lifespan: Longitudinal and experience-sampling findings. *Emotion*, *8*(6), 753–765. https://doi.org/10.1037/a0014123

Harari, H., Shamay-Tsoory, S. G., & Levkovitz, Y. (2010). The role of the right temporoparietal junction in empathy: A transcranial magnetic stimulation study. *Social Cognitive and Affective Neuroscience*, *5*(1), 1–8. https://doi.org/10.1093/scan/nsp033

Hoffman, M. L. (1981). The development of empathy. *Altruism and helping behavior: Social, personality, and developmental perspectives*, 41–63.

Hermans, E. J., Henckens, M. J. A. G., & Joëls, M. (2006). The effects of testosterone on the human brain: A review. *Neuroscience & Biobehavioral Reviews*, *30*(4), 556–570. https://doi.org/10.1016/j.neubiorev.2006.04.001

Heynen, R., Gunter, T., & Henn, M. (2021). Parenting styles and their impact on empathy development in children. *Journal of Child Psychology and Psychiatry*, *62*(2), 123–134. https://doi.org/10.1111/jcpp.13215

Johnstone, T., van Reekum, C. M., & Scherer, K. R. (2015). Integrating neuroimaging with subjective and objective measures of empathy. *Journal of Neuroscience, Psychology, and Economics*, *8*(2), 83–96. https://doi.org/10.1037/npe0000041

Jones, D. N., & Paulhus, D. L. (2010). Introducing the Short Dark Triad (SD3): A brief measure of dark personality traits. *Assessment*, *21*(2), 1–14. https://doi.org/10.1177/1073191113514105

Kendrick, K. M., Guastella, A. J., & Becker, B. (2017). Overview of human oxytocin research. *Current Topics in Behavioral Neuroscience*, *35*, 321–348. https://doi.org/10.1007/7854_2017_19

Kilroy, E. A., & Aziz-Zadeh, L. (2017). The neural basis of empathy: A review of neuroimaging studies. *Social Cognitive and Affective Neuroscience*, *12*(12), 1843–1855. https://doi.org/10.1093/scan/nsx128

Kim, S., & Kochanska, G. (2017). The role of parenting in the development of empathy in young children. *Child Development*, *88*(1), 1–15. https://doi.org/10.1111/cdev.12630

LaFontana, K. M., & Cillessen, A. H. N. (2009). Developmental changes in the importance of peer relationships: A longitudinal study. *Journal of Early Adolescence*, *29*(4), 577–602.

LAWRENCE, E. J., SHAW, P., BAKER, D., S. BARON-COHEN, & DAVID, A. S. (2004). Measuring empathy: reliability and validity of the Empathy Quotient. *Psychological Medicine*, *34*(5), 911–920. https://doi.org/10.1017/s0033291703001624

Levenson, R. W., & Ruef, A. M. (1992). Empathy: A physiological substrate. *Journal of Personality and Social Psychology*, *63*(2), 234–246. https://doi.org/10.1037/0022-3514.63.2.234

Light, S. N., Coan, J. A., Zahn-Waxler, C., Frye, C. J., Goldsmith, H. H., & Davidson, R. J. (2010). Empathy is associated with dynamic change in prefrontal brain electrical activity during positive emotion in children. *Child Development*, *80*(4), 1210–1231. https://doi.org/10.1111/j.1467-8624.2009.01422.x

Luis, E. O., Martín Martínez, Kleio Akrivou, Scalzo, G., Martín Aoiz, & Semper, O. (2023). The role of empathy in shared intentionality: Contributions from Inter-Processual Self theory. *Frontiers in Psychology, 14*. https://doi.org/10.3389/fpsyg.2023.1079950

Martin, G. N., & Clark, A. (1982). Infants' responses to the distress of others: A developmental study. *Child Development*, *53*(4), 1182–1187. https://doi.org/10.2307/1129647

Mazza, C., & Ricciardi, E. (2014). Empathy and its role in the development of social cognition in children: A review. *Neuroscience & Biobehavioral Reviews*, *43*, 1–10. https://doi.org/10.1016/j.neubiorev.2014.03.004

Melchers, K. G., Hauf, P., & Bock, A. (2016a). The role of empathy in social interactions: A developmental perspective. In *The development of empathy: A multidisciplinary approach* (pp. 123–145). Springer.

Montag, C., & Walla, P. (2011). The role of oxytocin in social cognition: A review. *Neuroscience & Biobehavioral Reviews*, *35*(1), 1–10. https://doi.org/10.1016/j.neubiorev.2010.07.001

Moudatsou, M., Areti Stavropoulou, Anastas Philalithis, & Koukouli, S. (2020). The Role of Empathy in Health and Social Care Professionals. *Healthcare*, *8*(1), 26–26. https://doi.org/10.3390/healthcare8010026

Moudatsou, M., Stavropoulou, A., Philalithis, A., & Koukouli, S. (2020). The role of empathy in health and social care professionals. *Healthcare*, *8*(1), 26. https://doi.org/10.3390/healthcare8010026

Morelli, S. A., Rameson, L. T., & Lieberman, M. D. (2014). The neural basis of empathy: A review of the literature. *Social Cognitive and Affective Neuroscience*, *9*(2), 133–141. https://doi.org/10.1093/scan/nss118

Miklikowska, M., Denson, T. F., & Kossowska, M. (2022). The role of peers in the development of empathy in adolescence: A longitudinal study. *Developmental Psychology, 58*(4), 789–799. https://doi.org/10.1037/dev0001280
Miller, E. K., & Cohen, J. D. (2001). An Integrative Theory of Prefrontal Cortex Function. *Annual Review of Neuroscience, 24*(1), 167–202. https://doi.org/10.1146/annurev.neuro.24.1.167
Papouli, E. (2018). *Diversity dolls: a creative teaching method for encouraging social work students to develop empathy and understanding for vulnerable populations.* Social Work Education; https://www.semanticscholar.org/paper/Diversity-dolls%3A-a-creative-teaching-method-for-to-Papouli/03f6bb142d0157fa0aad7d263bd2e740ecbadc9e
Parker, J. G., & Asher, S. R. (1987). Peer relations and later personal adjustment: Are low-accepted children at risk? *Psychological Bulletin, 102*(3), 357.
Perry, Y., & Shamay-Tsoory, S. G. (2013). Understanding emotional and cognitive empathy in schizophrenia: The role of the prefrontal cortex. *Schizophrenia Research, 147*(2–3), 339–340. https://doi.org/10.1016/j.schres.2013.03.023
Phillips, L. D., & Sweeney, P. J. (2002). Age differences in empathy: A meta-analytic review. *Personality and Social Psychology Review, 6*(3), 213–233. https://doi.org/10.1207/S15327957PSPR0603_2
Piaget, J. (1965). *The child's conception of the world.* New York, NY: Harcourt, Brace & World.
Preston, S. D., & De Waal, F. B. (2002). Empathy: Its ultimate and proximate bases. *Behavioral and Brain Sciences, 25*(1), 1–20. https://doi.org/10.1017/S0140525X02000018
Ritter, K., & Dziobek, I. (2011). The role of empathy in the development of social cognition: A longitudinal study. *Journal of Autism and Developmental Disorders, 41*(3), 359–366.
Rizzolatti, G., & Craighero, L. (2004). THE MIRROR-NEURON SYSTEM. *Annual Review of Neuroscience, 27*(1), 169–192. https://doi.org/10.1146/annurev.neuro.27.070203.144230
Rueda, M. R., Pozuelos, J. P., & Cómbita, L. M. (2015). Cognitive neuroscience of attention from brain mechanisms to individual differences in efficiency. *AIMS Neuroscience, 2*(4), 183-202.
Samper, P., Rivas, M., & Garcia, F. (2021). Parenting styles and empathy development in early childhood: A longitudinal study. *International Journal of Behavioral Development, 45*(1), 45–55.
Saroglou, V., Pichon, I., Trompette, L., Verschueren, M., & Dernelle, R. (2024). Prosocial behavior and religion: New evidence based on projective measures and peer ratings. *Journal for the Scientific Study of Religion, 44*(3), 323. https://dial.uclouvain.be/pr/boreal/object/boreal:61114
Schieman, S., & Van Gundy, K. (2000). Age differences in empathy: A longitudinal study. *Social Psychology Quarterly, 63*(2), 145–157. https://doi.org/10.2307/2695845
Shamay-Tsoory, S. G., & Aharon-Peretz, J. (2009). The neural correlates of empathy: An fMRI study. *Neuropsychology, Development, and Cognition. Section B, Aging, Neuropsychology and Cognition, 16*(4), 419–432.
Shamay-Tsoory, S. G., Aharon-Peretz, J., & Perry, D. (2009). Two systems for empathy: a double dissociation between emotional and cognitive empathy in inferior frontal gyrus versus ventromedial prefrontal lesions. *Brain, 132*(3), 617–627. https://doi.org/10.1093/brain/awn279

Shamay-Tsoory, S. G., Shur, S., Barcai-Goodman, L., Medlovich, S., Harari, H., & Levkovitz, Y. (2007). Dissociation of cognitive from affective components of theory of mind in schizophrenia. *Psychiatry Research*, *149*(1–3), 11–23. https://doi.org/10.1016/j.psychres.2005.10.018

Shamay-Tsoory, S. G., Tomer, R., & Aharon-Peretz, J. (2002). Empathy in the brain: An fMRI study of the empathy network. *NeuroImage*, *36*(1), 1–10. https://doi.org/10.1016/j.neuroimage.2007.11.016

Shany-Ur, T., Poorzand, P., Grossman, S., Growdon, M. E., Jang, J. Y., Ketelle, R. S., Miller, I. B. L., & Rankin, K. P. (2012). Comprehension of insincere communication in neurodegenerative disease: Lies, sarcasm, and theory of mind. *Cortex*, *48*(10), 1329–1341.

Shirtcliff, E. A., Dahl, R. E., & Pollak, S. D. (2009). Pubertal development and the regulation of cortisol: The role of social context. *Psychoneuroendocrinology*, *34*(1), 1–10. https://doi.org/10.1016/j.psyneuen.2008.08.005

Simner, M. L. (1971). Infants' responses to the distress of others. *Developmental Psychology*, *5*(1), 1–7. https://doi.org/10.1037/h0030401

Singer, T., Seymour, B., O'Doherty, J., Kaube, H., Dolan, R. J., & Frith, C. D. (2009). Empathy for pain involves the affective but not sensory components of pain. *Science*, *303*(5661), 1157–1162. https://doi.org/10.1126/science.1089927

Siuda, J., Kuczynski, M., & Kuczynski, M. (2011a). The role of the medial prefrontal cortex in empathy: A review of the literature. *Neuroscience & Biobehavioral Reviews*, *35*(1), 1–12. https://doi.org/10.1016/j.neubiorev.2010.07.001

Siuda, J., Kuczynski, M., & Kuczynski, M. (2011b). The role of empathy in understanding and responding to pain. *Cognitive Neuroscience*, *12*(3), 139–154.

Spiro, V. (2009). *Empathy in psychotherapy: How therapists and clients understand each other.* Springer Publishing Company.

Trivedi-Bateman, N., & Crook, L. (2022). Enhancing empathy through mindfulness and simulation-based therapies. *Journal of Psychotherapy Integration*, *32*(1), 1–15. https://doi.org/10.1037/int0000288

Jack van Honk, Schutter, D. J., Bos, P. A., Anne-Wil Kruijt, Lentjes, E. G., & Baron-Cohen, S. (2011). Testosterone administration impairs cognitive empathy in women depending on second-to-fourth digit ratio. *Proceedings of the National Academy of Sciences, 108*(8), 3448–3452. https://doi.org/10.1073/pnas.1011891108

Viau, V. (2002). Functional cross-talk between the hypothalamic-pituitary-adrenal and -gonadal axes. *Journal of Neuroendocrinology*, *14*(6), 509–516. https://doi.org/10.1046/j.1365-2826.2002.00840.x

Weisz, E., & Cikara, M. (2021). Strategic Regulation of Empathy. *Trends in Cognitive Sciences*, *25*(3), 213–227. https://doi.org/10.1016/j.tics.2020.12.002

Wigton, R., Radua, J., Allen, P., et al. (2015). Neurophysiological effects of acute oxytocin administration: Systematic review and meta-analysis of placebo-controlled imaging studies. *Journal of Psychiatry and Neuroscience*, *40*(1), E1–E22.

Wilczek-Rużyczka, E. (2023). Empathy and resilience in health care professionals. *Acta Neuropsychologica, 21*(4), 395–410. https://doi.org/10.5604/01.3001.0053.9172

Yildirim, M., & Derksen, J. J. (2012). The role of testosterone in empathy and prosocial behaviour. *Hormones and Behavior*, *61*(3), 373–379. https://doi.org/10.1016/j.yhbeh.2011.12.003

Zahn-Waxler, C., Cummings, E. M., & Iannotti, R. J. (1992). The development of empathy in young children. *Child Development*, *63*(3), 634–645. https://doi.org/10.2307/1131347

Zhao, W., Yao, S., Li, Q., et al. (2016). Oxytocin blurs the self-other distinction during trait judgments and reduces medial prefrontal cortex responses. *Human Brain Mapping*, *37*(7), 2512–2527.

Zilioli, S., & Watson, N. F. (2015). Testosterone, cortisol, and empathy: A dual-hormone hypothesis. *Psychoneuroendocrinology*, *62*, 1–10.

10 Neuropsychology of Self-Awareness and Cognitive Control

Introduction

Self-awareness is the ability to take oneself as the object of awareness (Morris, 2011). It is the ability to recognize oneself as an individual with unique thoughts, emotions, and experiences, and is a fundamental aspect of human cognition. It plays a crucial role in shaping our perceptions, actions, and social interactions. Self-awareness has been an enigma for our species, with different understandings provided by religion, philosophy, and, more recently, science. The current chapter aims to discuss the neurocognitive mechanisms underlying self-awareness. Understanding the neuropsychology of self-awareness is key to unraveling the complex interplay between brain function and behavior. The multidimensional nature of self-awareness will be explored in this chapter, suggesting how it can be thought of as an emergent property observed in different cognitive complexity levels. Self-awareness is not a singular capacity but rather a collection of processes, including the representation of internal bodily states (interoception) and declarative personal information about oneself (autobiographical memory) (Mograbi et al., 2021). This multiplicity suggests that clinical conditions can affect different aspects of self-awareness differently.

Understanding our current thoughts, emotions, and internal states allows us to regulate and guide our behavior effectively. Cognitive control (CC), the ability to regulate our thoughts, emotions, and behaviors to achieve our goals, is crucial for functioning well in a demanding and ever-changing world. It enables us to prioritize tasks, resist distractions, adapt to changing circumstances, and make well-considered decisions, ultimately shaping our experiences and influencing our success in various aspects of life (Baumeister & Heartherton, 1996).

The relationship between self-awareness and CC is reciprocal and reinforcing, allowing individuals to navigate complex situations, make informed decisions, and adapt their behavior based on their understanding of themselves and their environment. It is crucial for navigating the complexities of life. They work together in a dynamic interplay, supporting each other's development and ultimately fostering effective and adaptive functioning.

DOI: 10.4324/9781003477815-10

Neuropsychology plays a crucial role in understanding the complex relationship between the brain, self-awareness, and CC. By studying the brain's structure and function in healthy individuals and those with neurological disorders, neuropsychologists contribute significantly to our understanding of these essential aspects of human cognition. Techniques such as neuroimaging (fMRI, positron emission tomography (PET) scans) and electroencephalography (EEG) are used in neuropsychological research to identify specific brain regions and networks involved in self-awareness and CC (Flemming et al., 2012). This knowledge helps localize the neural basis of these processes and understand how different brain areas collaborate to support them. By observing how damage to specific brain areas affects self-awareness and CC, researchers gain crucial insights into the functional organization of these processes in the brain. This knowledge informs the development of targeted interventions to improve self-awareness and CC in individuals facing various challenges.

Neuropsychology provides a unique perspective for investigating the intricate relationship between the brain, self-awareness, and CC. By combining various research methods and studying individuals with diverse cognitive profiles, neuropsychology continues to shed light on the neural mechanisms underlying these essential human functions and inform clinical practices and interventions for various populations.

Neurological Correlations of Self-Awareness

Self-awareness, a multifaceted concept central to human cognition, relies on a network of interconnected brain regions and neurotransmitter systems, including the medial prefrontal cortex (MPFC), medial posterior parietal cortex (MPPC), anterior cingulate cortex (ACC), and insula cortex, which play pivotal roles in processing self-relevant information, integrating sensory inputs, monitoring emotions, and forming subjective self-perceptions (Brewer et al., 2013). Disrupting functional coupling between the posterior cingulate cortex (PCC) and MPFC, as observed with psilocybin, can blur the boundaries between self and others (Carhart-Harris et al., 2012). Additionally, neural networks like the default mode network (DMN) activate during self-referential processing and introspection, facilitating conceptual self-awareness (Takikowski et al., 2017).

Moreover, neurotransmitter systems such as gamma-butyric acid (GABA), dopamine, serotonin, acetylcholine, and oxytocin intricately regulate self-awareness by modulating brain activity and maintaining neurotransmitter balance. Dysfunctions in serotonin and dopamine systems have been linked to impulsive aggression, where serotonin deficiency may increase dopamine activity, promoting impulsivity (Seo et al., 2008). Collectively, these findings highlight the complex interplay between brain anatomy, neurotransmitter function, and self-awareness, shedding light on the neurobiological underpinnings of human behavior and cognition.

Furthermore, self-awareness, a multifaceted construct crucial for cognitive and social development, evolves gradually during childhood, shaped by cognitive, social, and emotional milestones (Brewer et al., 2013). Neurologically, self-recognition involves the MPFC and PCC, crucial for integrating self-relevant information and distinguishing oneself from others (Turjman, 2016). Mirror neuron systems, identified in the premotor cortex, play a debated role in self-perception, with hypotheses suggesting both direct and indirect links to self-awareness (Kilner & Lemon, 2013). The temporal lobe, essential for memory formation, and the parietal lobe, critical for spatial awareness, contribute to self-awareness through episodic memory and bodily self-awareness, respectively (Chavoix & Insausti, 2017). Emotional processing, mediated by the amygdala and prefrontal cortex (PFC), intersects with interoception, associated with the insula, influencing emotional awareness and self-perception (Wang et al., 2019). These neural mechanisms work synergistically to construct a dynamic sense of self, continually shaped by experiences and environmental interactions.

The Intriguing Case of Roger

Roger, a 57-year-old man, suffered extensive brain damage in 1980 from herpes simplex encephalitis, which destroyed most of his insular cortex, ACC, and MPFC—regions crucial for self-awareness. Despite this damage, he retained some self-awareness. While he struggled to form new memories and lost his sense of taste and smell, he consistently recognized himself in photos and could distinguish between photos of himself, people he knew, and strangers. However, he sometimes had difficulty recognizing his face in isolation without context. Roger also differentiated between self-tickling and being tickled by someone else, finding the latter more stimulating. He demonstrated a sense of humor and understanding of others' perspectives, indicating a theory of mind. Based on these findings, researchers argued that self-awareness is not solely dependent on specific brain regions like the insular cortex, ACC, and MPFC. Instead, self-awareness is a complex process involving multiple brain regions, including those outside the cerebral cortex.

Developmental Perspectives

Self-awareness is a dynamic process that develops throughout our lives. Functional magnetic resonance imaging (fMRI) and diffusion tensor imaging (DTI)-based tractography have been employed in studying the link between performance on the Bayley Scales of Infant Development and early myelination in premature infants. These scales are utilized to calculate a developmental quotient for the infant. The findings indicate a significant association between scores on the Bayley Scales of Infant Development and cingulate fractional anisotropy and radial diffusivity. This suggests that interconnected axonal pathways within the DMN play a crucial role in the early neurocognitive development of infants (Cui et al., 2016).

Newborn infants demonstrate an early form of "basic consciousness" by making rudimentary eye contact with their mothers. Around six to eight months of age, infants show signs of self-recognition in the "rouge test," where they touch a mark on their face only when a mirror is present, indicating recognition of their reflection as themselves. The mirror recognition test, a classic measure of self-awareness in infants and animals, involves placing the infant before a mirror with a mark on their forehead. A positive response, typically seen around two years of age, involves the infant attempting to remove the mark from their own forehead rather than from the mirror. Recent research has indicated that the DMN exhibits an inverse U-shaped pattern, being weaker in children and the elderly and stronger in adults. Additionally, cognitive function shows a positive correlation with the functional connectivity of the DMN (Lagercrantz & Changeux, 2009).

Around the ages of five to seven years, children start developing Theory of Mind, understanding that others have different thoughts, feelings, and perspectives—a crucial aspect of self-awareness. As they mature, their self-awareness becomes more complex, including a sense of identity and an understanding of their thoughts and emotions. Adolescence, marked by significant brain and body changes, is a critical period for self-awareness development. Teenagers often experience heightened self-consciousness and self-reflection, leading to a more nuanced self-concept, including personality traits. This self-exploration period is vital for forming a stable sense of self.

Self-awareness is closely tied to self-identity, the perception of oneself as a unique and coherent individual. Self-identity is influenced by genetics, environment, and personal experiences. Positive psychology stresses the importance of fostering a positive self-identity, which can enhance wellbeing and resilience.

Bem's theory suggests that individuals cultivate self-awareness by observing their behavior and the outcomes of those actions (Bem, 1972). In adolescence, heightened social interactions and varied experiences offer more chances for adolescents to observe their behavior in various situations, enhancing their self-understanding. Reactions and feedback from others also play a role in shaping their self-perceptions and refining their self-awareness.

Self-awareness is a complex concept that evolves during childhood, influenced by cognitive, social, and emotional milestones. Viewing this progression through stages provides valuable insights into how children progressively construct their self-understanding and their role in society.

Cognitive Control Mechanisms

Executive functions (EFs), also known as executive control or CC, are mental processes necessary for concentrating, paying attention, and making decisions in situations where relying on instinct or intuition would be inappropriate. Using EFs requires effort, as it is easier to continue with familiar actions than to change, to give in to temptation than to resist, and to operate on "automatic pilot" than to consider alternative actions. There is consensus that three core EFs exist: inhibition (including self-control and interference control), working memory (WM), and cognitive flexibility (the ability to switch between tasks or mental sets). These core EFs form the basis for higher-order EFs such as reasoning, problem-solving, and planning. EFs are essential for maintaining mental and physical health, achieving success in education and life, and supporting cognitive, social, and psychological wellbeing.

WM is responsible for temporarily storing and manipulating information necessary for complex cognitive tasks such as reasoning and comprehension. It plays a crucial role in CC, which involves maintaining focus, suppressing irrelevant information, and switching between tasks. The frontoparietal network, including the dorsolateral prefrontal cortex (DLPFC), ACC, and parietal cortex (PAR), is implicated in WM. Hyperactivation or hyperconnectivity in this network has been observed in traumatic brain injury (TBI) patients, suggesting a compensatory mechanism in response to injury (Chai et al., 2018).

Inhibitory control allows individuals to control their attention, behavior, thoughts, and emotions to override strong internal or external influences and act appropriately. Without inhibitory control, individuals would be governed by impulses, habits, or environmental stimuli. Inhibitory control enables flexibility in behavior and decision-making.

Neural Networks of Inhibitory Control

During response inhibition, the activation of an inhibitory processing network is predominantly right-lateralized, with notable involvement of the right inferior frontal cortex (IFC), as well as the right parietal and temporal cortex, ACC, cerebellum, and striatum. Changes in inhibitory task demands, particularly tasks requiring reduced preparation and increased demand on inhibitory control (as seen in cases of post-traumatic stress disorder (PTSD)), recruit additional areas of the right ventrolateral prefrontal cortex (VLPFC), right DLPFC, bilateral parietal cortex, insula, and striatum. Deficient GABA neurotransmission is notable in disorders characterized by poor self-awareness and self-monitoring (Falconer, 2008).

Cognitive flexibility is the ability to switch between mental processes to generate appropriate behavioral responses. It develops over time and is compromised in neurodevelopmental disorders. Neuroimaging studies have identified a network of frontoparietal regions involved in cognitive flexibility, including the VLPFC, dlPFC, anterior cingulate, right anterior insula (AI), premotor cortex, inferior and superior parietal cortices, inferior temporal cortex, occipital cortex, and subcortical structures such as the caudate and thalamus.

CC, which involves coordinating mental processes and actions according to current goals and future plans, is a key function of the PFC. This term is used interchangeably with "executive function" in clinical contexts. The PFC is responsible for implementing the coordination of cognitive processes through various functional circuits. Research focusing on large-scale brain organization and network analysis has greatly contributed to understanding how CC processes are carried out in the brain.

Several prefrontal regions are closely associated with CC, with the dorsal anterior cingulate cortex (dACC) and dlPFC being particularly prominent. Both human and animal studies using neuroimaging and electrophysiological methods suggest that these regions play a central role in CC, and damage to them often results in control impairments. Additionally, other regions such as the VLPFC, dorsomedial prefrontal cortex (DMPFC), and orbitofrontal cortex (OFC) are also linked to CC.

The Famous Case of Gage

Gage, a railroad worker, suffered an iron rod accident that pierced his frontal lobe. Though he physically recovered, he displayed significant personality changes. He became impulsive, irresponsible, and prone to social blunders. This case highlighted the role of the frontal lobe in self-regulation and decision-making. Numerous psychiatric and neurological conditions exhibit symptoms that are linked to impaired CC or more general cognitive deficiencies. For instance, attention-deficit hyperactivity disorder (ADHD) is marked by significant impairments in EFs and CC, such as attentional control, WM, and response inhibition, which contribute to symptoms like distractibility and impulsivity outlined in the Diagnostic and Statistical Manual of Mental Disorders, Fifth Edition (DSM-5). Similarly, individuals with major depressive disorder often experience difficulties in decision-making and concentration, indicating primary impairments in CC. In schizophrenia, negative symptoms are associated with impaired goal-directed behavior, while positive symptoms like delusions and hallucinations are linked to deficits in reality monitoring. Moreover, schizophrenia includes cognitive impairment symptoms, including severe WM deficits, which hinder rehabilitation efforts.

One hypothesis regarding addiction posits that it stems from a general deficit in goal-directed behavior, resulting in heightened habitual tendencies, exacerbated by a lack of top-down control, ultimately leading to compulsive drug-seeking behavior (Everitt & Robbins, 2016). A similar mechanism is proposed for other compulsive behaviors, such as checking or washing in obsessive-compulsive disorder. However, it's important to note that hyperactivity in certain brain regions, like the MPFC, may be linked to specific compulsive behaviors that still maintain a sense of goal-directedness. Additionally, the distinction between goal-directed and habitual behavior might be oversimplified, as recent computational models suggest an intermediate control mode that combines aspects of both, allowing for flexible, goal-directed behavior alongside efficient, model-free responses guided by "successor representations."

While the exact role of dysfunctional CC mechanisms, potentially in conjunction with altered perceptual and motivational processes, in psychiatric and neurological symptoms is not fully understood, it is evident that CC deficits are a common feature across a wide range of disorders. Meta-analyses support the idea of transdiagnostic associations between CC deficits and psychiatric disorders, including major depressive disorder, post-traumatic stress disorder, obsessive-compulsive disorder, bipolar disorder, schizophrenia, ADHD, antisocial personality disorder, and substance use disorders (Everitt & Robbins, 2016).

Subcortical Regions Involved

The basal ganglia play a crucial role in CC through two main pathways: the indirect pathway, which suppresses unwanted thoughts, actions, and impulses, and the direct pathway, which facilitates the selection and initiation of intended responses. These pathways work together to select and execute appropriate responses while inhibiting irrelevant neural activity. The basal ganglia communicate with various cortical regions via the thalamus, transmitting essential information for executing planned actions and inhibiting unwanted ones, thus acting as a "gatekeeper" for action selection (Li et al., 2014). Neuroimaging studies using fMRI have shown increased activity in specific basal ganglia regions during tasks requiring CC, such as inhibiting prepotent responses or making complex decisions. This feedback loop enables the basal ganglia to monitor and adjust their influence based on ongoing cognitive processes.

Individuals diagnosed with Internet Addiction (IA) exhibit compromised connectivity within the indirect frontal-basal ganglia pathway, which is crucial for inhibiting undesirable actions. This suggests that individuals with IA may struggle to control their impulse to use the internet, even when aware that such behavior is not ideal (Li et al., 2014). Dopamine significantly influences these pathways; higher dopamine levels promote action selection, while lower levels enhance inhibition. Disruptions in dopamine function, such as those seen in Parkinson's disease, can impair CC abilities, highlighting dopamine's importance in balancing facilitation and inhibition within the basal ganglia (Mograbi et al., 2023).

The basal ganglia contribute to various aspects of CC, including inhibitory control, decision-making, task switching, and WM (Friedman & Robbins, 2021). The ACC links rewards with actions, regulates action selection based on reward cues, resolves response conflicts, and adjusts behavior in response to errors. Morphological changes in the ACC have been observed in disorders such as schizophrenia, ADHD, and obsessive–compulsive disorder (OCD) (Newman et al., 2014). The OFC helps adjust behavior based on expected outcomes, with damage to the OFC leading to difficulties in guiding behavior based on the devaluation of rewards.

The amygdala, traditionally associated with processing emotions, also plays a role in CC by regulating thoughts, emotions, and behavior to achieve goals. It interacts with the PFC through two pathways: the direct pathway, which excites the PFC and enhances emotional influence on behavior, and the indirect pathway, which inhibits the PFC and reduces emotional impact, thereby improving CC. The balance between these pathways affects how effectively the amygdala influences CC, with disruptions potentially contributing to mental health conditions. The dominance of the direct pathway can lead to overpowering emotional responses and impulsive behavior, while the dominance of the indirect pathway allows the PFC to control emotional impulses, promoting thoughtful and controlled behavior.

Neuroplasticity

Neuroplasticity, also known as neural or brain plasticity, refers to the brain's adaptive structural and functional changes in response to various stimuli, including injuries like stroke or TBI. It is an intrinsic property of the brain that allows for dynamic modifications at multiple levels of neural organization, enabling the processing, encoding, and implementation of new knowledge (Poldrack & Gabrieli, 2001). Animal studies have shown that sensory experiences can lead to changes in the nervous system, such as gene transcription, receptor expression, synaptic density, and cortical map alterations. In humans, functional neuroimaging has revealed signal changes after training, indicating enhanced neuronal responsiveness or cortical map expansion, while structural plasticity studies have found alterations in brain morphology post-training.

Research indicates that neuroplasticity can result in rapid increases in gray matter volume in task-related regions, suggesting that local gray matter deficits associated with certain disorders might be reversible through adequate training programs. Neuroplasticity is crucial not only for rebuilding brain function but also for repairing developmental disorders and facilitating learning and memory. It responds to various internal and external factors, including neurodegenerative diseases and pharmacological treatments, as well as positive changes like self-improvement efforts (Erickson et al., 2015).

By consciously replacing undesirable behaviors with positive alternatives, individuals can weaken neural pathways associated with negative habits and strengthen those linked to desired behaviors. Techniques such as habit reversal training and mindfulness practices can influence brain activity related to emotion processing and self-regulation, potentially reducing the impact of negative emotions and promoting emotional wellbeing. Activities like exercise, meditation, and social interaction have been shown to positively affect brain structure and function, contributing to reduced stress, anxiety, and depression symptoms (Erickson et al., 2015).

While neuroplasticity offers significant potential, it requires time and consistent effort to achieve lasting changes. Individual factors such as genetics, age, and lifestyle also play a role in the extent of neuroplasticity. Ongoing research continues to explore its potential and limitations, but overall, neuroplasticity serves as a powerful tool for self-improvement and continuous learning, growth, and wellbeing.

Disorders of Self-Awareness and Cognitive Control

Alzheimer's Disease

Patients with Alzheimer's disease (AD) often exhibit poor awareness of their cognitive and functional deficits, a condition known as anosognosia or impaired self-awareness (Starkstein, 2014). This lack of awareness affects cognitive functioning, daily activities, behavioral changes, and mood, as evidenced by methods comparing patients' self-judgments with informant reports or predictions of performance (Starkstein, 2014). Neurocognitive mechanisms underlying anosognosia in AD are linked to structural and functional changes in brain regions such as the inferior and superior frontal gyrus, anterior cingulate and OFC, medial frontal gyrus, medial temporal lobe, PCC, and insula (Antoine et al., 2019). Many of these regions are part of the DMN, which supports cognitive processing of the self and autobiographical memory. Decreased connectivity within the DMN or between the DMN and other brain regions contributes to the failure to update personal knowledge, affects self-referential processing, and disturbs comparator mechanisms (Antoine et al., 2019).

Traumatic Brain Injury

TBI is also associated with a lack of self-awareness, particularly in moderate to severe cases. Studies suggest that self-awareness deficits are linked to poorer outcomes. Patients with impaired self-awareness exhibit reduced functional connectivity between the dorsal ACC and other frontal regions, along with abnormal responses to errors within the AI, which are typically linked to the dorsal ACC. These findings suggest that interactions between the AI and dorsal ACC, within the salience network of the frontoparietal control network (FPCN), are crucial for self-awareness.

Psychiatric Disorders

Schizophrenia

The ability to self-reflect, a component of self-awareness, is often impaired in neuropsychiatric disorders such as schizophrenia. This impairment can manifest in various behavioral aspects, including a lack of insight into illness, diminished empathy, or impaired social cognition. Deficits in self-awareness have been linked to compromised psychosocial and clinical outcomes in individuals with schizophrenia (Lysaker et al., 2010).

Studies involving individuals with chronic schizophrenia have shown that compared to controls, there is greater activation of the ventral ACC/medial

OFC and reduced activation of the posterior cingulate/PCC during self and/or other-referential tasks. This alteration in cortical activation patterns has been termed an anterior-to-posterior shift in midline cortical activity during self-reflection in schizophrenia.

ADHD

ADHD, characterized by symptoms of inattention, impulsivity, and motor restlessness, often involves dysfunctional PFC circuits that are crucial for WM, attention regulation, and impulse control. Neuroimaging, neuropsychological, genetic, and neurochemical studies indicate abnormalities in the frontostriatal network as significant contributing factors (Arnsten, 2009). Early PET imaging studies suggested global underactivity in cerebral glucose metabolism in ADHD patients. Structural imaging revealed smaller global cerebral and prefrontal volumes in individuals with ADHD (Valera et al., 2007). Dysfunction in the frontal lobes, particularly insufficient frontal cortical inhibitory control, is implicated, supported by studies on stimulant medications and animal models highlighting dopaminergic and noradrenergic influences on the PFC.

In substance abuse, decreased self-awareness is common as individuals become preoccupied with obtaining and using substances, leading to denial and impaired judgment. This results in disrupted brain regions responsible for CC, manifesting as impulsivity, poor decision-making, and impaired memory. Conversely, individuals with anxiety disorders often experience heightened self-awareness, particularly focusing on negative thoughts, bodily sensations, and potential threats. This magnified awareness can be maladaptive, leading to rumination and increased anxiety. Anxiety disorders can also impair CC, making it difficult to focus, filter distractions, and make rational decisions, often resulting in negative self-talk and difficulty regulating emotions.

Interaction Between Self-Awareness and Cognitive Control

Research and case studies provide compelling evidence for the bidirectional relationship between self-awareness and CC. Understanding this dynamic interaction is crucial for promoting wellbeing and effective self-regulation. Self-awareness and CC are closely connected through a dynamic interplay of feedback loops and reciprocal influences.

For example, a study by Wong & Vallacher (2017) used a daily diary design with college students and found that fluctuations in self-concept clarity (a facet of self-awareness) positively predicted levels of grit (a facet of CC), and vice versa, suggesting a reciprocal relationship over time.

Brain imaging studies using fMRI have identified brain regions involved in both self-awareness and CC, such as the ACC (Carter et al., 2001). These studies suggest that the ACC might play a role in the feedback loop between the two, as it is involved in monitoring internal states and regulating attention.

Practices like meditation and mindfulness training have been shown to enhance both self-awareness and CC by strengthening the connections between brain regions involved in these functions.

Metacognition

Self-awareness is crucial for metacognition, the ability to consciously monitor and control behavior, which is essential for learning through conscious experience both individually and interpersonally. Metacognition involves knowledge about and monitoring of all cognitive processes, enabling individuals to know how and when to attend, remember, organize information, and solve problems with appropriate strategies (Frith, 2012). It involves developing cognitive strategies based on prior information and expectations, allocating sufficient cognitive resources for task execution, and appraising one's performance and capacities. This higher-order self-awareness process is recursive and complex, underpinning self-efficacy and self-regulated learning.

The medial paralimbic network is a key neural signature for self-awareness and self-regulation. Northoff et al.'s meta-analysis of fMRI studies supports this, showing self-related activation within this network. Disruption of self-awareness and its paralimbic network is foundational to many pathologies due to its fundamental role in human development. For instance, addiction is characterized by deficiencies in self-regulation, impulse control, decision-making, and emotion processing. Individuals with addiction lose conscious self-regulation of behavior, progressing from voluntary substance use to habitual and compulsive drug-seeking. Nicotine, for example, affects nicotinic acetylcholine receptors on prefrontal cortical neurons, further disrupting normal paralimbic network functioning (Changeux, 2010) (Figure 10.1).

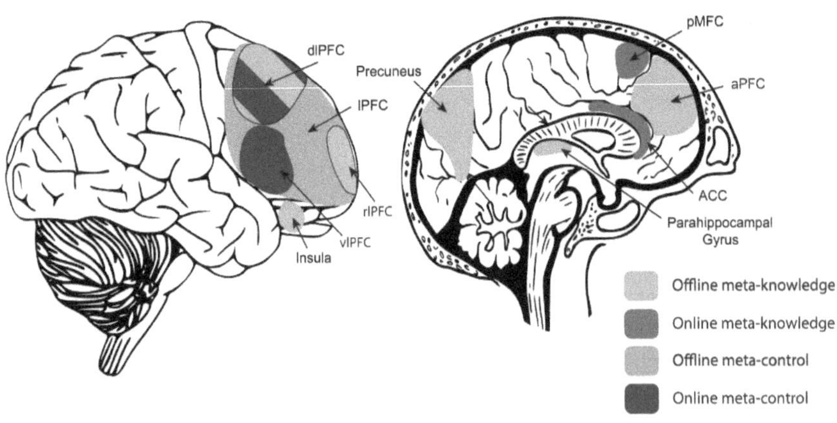

Figure 10.1 Regions Associated with Online and Offline Metacognition (Fleur et al., 2021)

All conscious states are linked to activity in a medial paralimbic network, as demonstrated by cerebral blood flow patterns in regions such as the right medial parietal cortex (precuneus), PFC, and right striatum during yoga nidra meditation (Lou et al., 2017). This network's dysfunction is observed in various disorders, including ADHD, borderline personality disorder, autism spectrum disorder, schizophrenia, dementia, and TBI. Recovery of this network is closely tied to clinical recovery in pervasive dysfunctional states like the vegetative state.

The paralimbic network, regulated by dopamine and GABA interneurons, is crucial for self-awareness and metacognition, developing from infancy through adulthood. Disruptions in this network, particularly due to its high energy demand, result in impaired conscious self-awareness in conditions like autism, ADHD, schizophrenia, and situations involving cerebral hypoxia-ischemia (Powell et al., 2012). Therapeutic approaches aimed at boosting dopaminergic activity, such as relaxation meditation and targeted training to increase dopaminergic receptors, show promise in enhancing paralimbic interaction and structure growth.

Further advancements may come from techniques like mini-brain grafting and stem cell therapy targeting interneuron function. Efforts to maintain oxygen balance in neural tissue, through methods such as cooling distressed neonates and ensuring optimal cerebral perfusion, are crucial, especially for premature infants at risk of developmental disorders. Novel oximetry techniques may aid in managing oxygen levels in these cases (Hyttel-Sorensen et al., 2015). Cognitive training has also been effective in improving CC, with resting-state functional connectivity serving as a neuroimaging biomarker to evaluate training efficacy in TBI.

Potential Therapeutic Approaches

The study of self-awareness holds significant clinical implications for understanding and treating neurological and psychiatric conditions. Advances in this field can enhance psychosocial interventions, metacognitive training, and pharmacological treatments. For instance, neuropsychological rehabilitation in dementia and the use of psilocybin for depression show promise (Goodwin et al., 2022).

Cognitive stimulation therapy (CST) is effective in improving cognitive and behavioral difficulties in people with dementia, enhancing their quality of life and that of their caregivers. Learning processes, especially through mindfulness training, help individuals recognize and modify impulsive tendencies, uniquely relying on self-awareness. Caregivers can employ strategies like motivational scaffolding to improve emotional regulation and behavior in children with ADHD.

Reward-based interventions show the potential in reducing impulsivity and enhancing CC. Mindfulness practices, such as meditation and mindful breathing, foster self-awareness and emotional regulation, contributing to overall wellbeing (Pinciotti et al., 2022).

Cognitive-behavioral therapy (CBT) effectively enhances CC and reduces impulsivity in various populations, including those with ADHD and addiction. CBT interventions focus on identifying triggers, cognitive restructuring, relaxation techniques, and developing coping skills, demonstrating moderate to large effect sizes in enhancing self-control. Exposure and response prevention (ERP) are beneficial for individuals dealing with anger outbursts and similar triggers (Pinciotti et al., 2022).

These practices promote mental wellbeing by fostering self-awareness, emotional regulation, and coping skills, ultimately enhancing quality of life. Inhibitory control interventions, such as inhibitory control training and mindfulness interventions targeting attentional processes, can further improve self-control by increasing awareness of actions and their consequences.

Current Research and Future Directions

Recent advancements in the field of self-awareness, driven by technological innovations, are blurring the lines between human and artificial intelligence. Key areas of progress include improved experimental designs that describe self-awareness not only in terms of its neural correlates but also its emergence in the brain. A common finding across various studies is that the paralimbic network, often termed the default network, is consistently active in self-relevant tasks, suggesting it is integral to all conscious experiences, binding them into a unified construct (Lou et al., 2017).

Self-awareness has evolutionary benefits, enhancing social cognition and cooperation by facilitating the Theory of Mind, which is the ability to understand that others have their own thoughts and beliefs. It also aids in planning and decision-making, emotional regulation, and stress management, ultimately contributing to better mental and physical health (Suddendorf & Collier-Baker, 2013).

Persuasive technologies, which are designed to change and shape user behavior through cognitive and psychological stimuli, offer new means for guiding human choices. These technologies can modify a user's sense of agency and provide feedback to promote beneficial behaviors. Persuasive mirrors, for example, use personalized visual feedback to reflect progress toward desired behaviors, increasing awareness of choices and actions (Fogg, 2003).

The concepts of noetic and autonoetic awareness, introduced by Tulving (2002), highlight different aspects of self-awareness. Noetic awareness involves thinking about the world, while autonoetic awareness involves the experiential aspect of remembering. Persuasive technologies can both strengthen autonoetic awareness by providing data about one's activities and weaken noetic awareness by interfering with the sense of agency.

AI systems are increasingly being developed with self-awareness capabilities, enabling them to recognize their limitations, monitor performance, and adapt behavior. Multifaceted learning platforms like CDR-U Coach I use technology to provide personalized coaching feedback, identifying users' talents and needs. However, as self-aware technology advances, ethical considerations regarding autonomy, responsibility, and rights become increasingly important.

Summary

Self-awareness is a critical component of human cognition, particularly in CC. This chapter examined the fundamentals of self-awareness from evolutionary and developmental perspectives, highlighting its role in behavior and cognitive processes such as planning, decision-making, impulse control, emotional regulation, and overall wellbeing. It discussed the development of self-awareness from childhood to adolescence and the formation of self-identity. Key brain areas involved in self-awareness include the PFC, insula, and basal ganglia. The chapter explored CC mechanisms such as WM, EFs, and inhibitory control. It also examined the roles of the temporal and parietal lobes, interoception, emotional awareness, and the insula in emotional processing. Neural correlates of self-awareness, including self-recognition, mirror neurons, and self-perception, were analyzed alongside disorders affecting self-awareness and CC, such as AD, TBI, schizophrenia, and ADHD. The chapter highlighted the emerging field of neuropsychology of self-awareness and CC, emphasizing new perspectives on treatments. Rodent studies showed the plasticity of the insula cortex, suggesting interventions like repetitive transcranial magnetic stimulation for conditions like dementia with Lewy bodies. Neuropsychology offers promising approaches for advancing psychiatric medicine towards more pathophysiologically based diagnoses and treatments. Future research could explore if neuropsychological assessments of self-reflection and functional imaging of mPFC-based neural circuits can provide information about the risk of developing specific disorders. Targeting psychological and neurobiological processes underlying self-reflection may improve patient outcomes, with pharmacological and brain stimulation techniques potentially modulating activity in the mPFC circuit and impacting self-awareness. In conclusion, while there are promising strategies for enhancing self-control through cognitive and behavioral training approaches, further research is needed to understand their real-world effectiveness and the specific cognitive processes they target. Research should also explore whether certain individuals may benefit more from particular interventions and whether combining interventions could lead to greater benefits. Despite the need for more research, there is optimism that these interventions could improve inadequate self-control.

References

Antoine, M., Langberg, T., Schnepel, P., & Feldman, D. E. (2019). Increased excitation inhibition ratio stabilizes synapse and circuit excitability in four autism mouse models. *Neuron*, *101*(4), 648–661.e4. https://doi.org/10.1016/j.neuron.2018.12.026

Arnsten, A. F. (2009). ADHD and the prefrontal cortex. *The Journal of Pediatrics, 154*(5), I S43. https://doi.org/10.1016/j.jpeds.2009.01.018

Baumeister, R. F., & Heatherton, T. F. (1996). Self-regulation failure: An overview and analysis. In M. H. Appley & R. B. Trumbull (Eds.), *Dynamics of self-regulation: From personality to social psychology* (pp. 1–18). New York, NY: Plenum Press.

Bem, D. J. (1972). Self-perception theory. In L. Berkowitz (Ed.), *Advances in experimental social psychology* (Vol. 6, pp. 1–62). Academic Press.

Brewer, J. A., Garrison, K. A., & Whitfield-Gabrieli, S. (2013). What about the "Self" is processed in the posterior cingulate cortex? *Frontiers in Human Neuroscience, 7*. https://doi.org/10.3389/fnhum.2013.00647

Carhart-Harris, R., Erritzøe, D., Williams, T. H., Stone, J., Reed, L., Colasanti, A., Tyacke, R. J., Leech, R., Malizia, A. L., Murphy, K., Hobden, P., Evans, J., Feilding, A., Wise, R. G., & Nutt, D. (2012). Neural correlates of the psychedelic state as determined by fMRI studies with psilocybin. *Proceedings of the National Academy of Sciences of the United States of America, 109*(6), 2138–2143. https://doi.org/10.1073/pnas.1119598109

Carter, C. S., MacDonald, A. W., Ross, L. L., & Stenger, V. A. (2001). Anterior cingulate cortex activity and impaired self-monitoring of performance in patients with schizophrenia: An event-related fMRI study. *American Journal of Psychiatry, 158*(9), 1423–1428. https://doi.org/10.1176/appi.ajp.158.9.1423

Chai, W. J., Hamid, A. I. A., & Abdullah, J. M. (2018). Working memory from the psychological and neurosciences perspectives: A review. *Frontiers in Psychology, 9*. https://doi.org/10.3389/fpsyg.2018.00401

Changeux, J.-P. (2010). Nicotine addiction and nicotinic receptors: Lessons from genetically modified mice. *Nature Reviews Neuroscience, 11*(6), 389–5401. https://doi.org/10.1038/nrn2849

Chavoix, C., & Insausti, R. (2017). Self-awareness and the medial temporal lobe in neurodegenerative diseases. *Neuroscience & Biobehavioral Reviews, 78*, 1–12. https://doi.org/10.1016/j.neubiorev.2017.04.015

Dunbar, R. (n.d.). Gossip in evolutionary perspective. *Review of General Psychology, 8*(2), 100–110. https://doi.org/10.1037/1089-2680.8.2.100

Everitt, B. J., & Robbins, T. W. (2016). Drug addiction: Updating actions to habits to compulsions ten years on. *Annual Review of Psychology, 67*(1), 23–50. https://doi.org/10.1146/annurev-psych-122414-033457

Falconer, E., Bryant, R., Felmingham, K. L., Kemp, A. H., Gordon, E., Peduto, A., ... & Williams, L. M. (2008). The neural networks of inhibitory control in posttraumatic stress disorder. *Journal of Psychiatry & Neuroscience, 33*(5), 413–422. Retrieved from https://www.ncbi.nlm.nih.gov/pmc/articles/PMC2527721/

Flemming, S. M., Soutschek, A., & D'Esposito, M. (2012). The role of the anterior prefrontal cortex in self-awareness. *Neuropsychologia, 50*(2), 295–302. https://doi.org/10.1098/rstb.2011.0417

Fleur, P., Berryman, C., & Nedeljkovic, M. (2021). Metacognition: Ideas and insights from neuro- and educational sciences. *Metacognition and Learning, 16*(3), 1–25. https://doi.org/10.1007/s11409-021-09266-8

Fogg, B. J. (2003). *Persuasive technology : Using computers to change what we think and do*. Retrieved from https://lib.ugent.be/en/catalog/rug01:001235489

Frith, C. D. (2012). The role of metacognition in human social interactions. *Philosophical Transactions of the Royal Society B, 367*(1599), 2213–2223. https://doi.org/10.1098/rstb.2012.0123

Gabbay, V., Bradley, K., Mao, X., Ostrover, R., Kang, G., & Shungu, D. C. (n.d.). Anterior cingulate cortex γ-aminobutyric acid deficits in youth with depression. *Translational Psychiatry*, *7*(8), e1216. https://doi.org/10.1038/tp.2017.187

Goodwin, G. M., Aaronson, S. T., Alvarez, O., Arden, P. C., Baker, A., Bennett, J., Bird, C., Blom, R. E., Brennan, C., Brusch, D., Burke, L., Campbell-Coker, K., Carhart-Harris, R., Cattell, J., Daniel, A., DeBattista, C., Dunlop, B. W., Eisen, K. E., Feifel, D., . . . Malievskaia, E. (2022). Single-dose psilocybin for a treatment-resistant episode of major depression. *The New England Journal of Medicine*, *387*(18), 1637–1648. https://doi.org/10.1056/nejmoa2206443

Hyttel-Sorensen, S., Pellicer, A., Alderliesten, T., Austin, T., Van Bel, F., Benders, M. J. N. L., Claris, O., Dempsey, E. M., Franz, A. R., Fumagalli, M., Gluud, C., Grevstad, B., Hagmann, C., Lemmers, P., Van Oeveren, W., Pichler, G., Plomgaard, A. M., Riera, J., Sánchez, L., . . . Greisen, G. (2015). Cerebral near infrared spectroscopy oximetry in extremely preterm infants: Phase II randomised clinical trial. *The BMJ*, *350*(jan05 2), g7635. https://doi.org/10.1136/bmj.g7635

Kilner, J. M., & Lemon, R. (n.d.). What we know currently about mirror neurons. *Current Biology*, *23*(23), R1057–R1062. https://doi.org/10.1016/j.cub.2013.10.051

Lagercrantz, H., & Changeux, J. (2009). The emergence of human consciousness: From fetal to neonatal life. *Pediatric Research*, *65*(3), 255–260. https://doi.org/10.1203/pdr.0b013e3181973b0d

Lysaker, P. H., Carcione, A., Dimaggio, G., Johannesen, J. K., Nicolo, G., Procacci, M., & Semerari, A. (2010). Metacognition amidst narratives of self and illness in schizophrenia: A study of the relationship between self-awareness and psychosocial functioning. *Psychiatry Research*, *176*(1), 1–6. https://doi.org/10.1016/j.psychres.2009.01.005

Li, B., Friston, K. J., Liu, J., Liu, Y., Zhang, G., Cao, F., Su, L., Yao, S., Lu, H., & Hu, D. (2014). Impaired Frontal-Basal Ganglia connectivity in adolescents with internet addiction. *Scientific Reports*, *4*(1). https://doi.org/10.1038/srep05027

Lou, H. C., Changeux, J., & Rosenstand, A. F. (2017). Towards a cognitive neuroscience of self-awareness. *Neuroscience & Biobehavioral Reviews*, *83*, 765–773. https://doi.org/10.1016/j.neubiorev.2016.04.004

Mograbi, D. C., Ferri, C. P., Sosa, A. L., Stewart, R., Laks, J., Brown, R., & Morris, R. G. (2021). The multidimensional nature of self-awareness in Alzheimer's disease. *Journal of Alzheimer's Disease*, *80*(3), 1021–1035. https://doi.org/10.3233/JAD-201211

Mograbi, D. C., Hall, S., Arantes, B., & Huntley, J. (2023). The cognitive neuroscience of self-awareness: Current framework, clinical implications, and future research directions. *WIREs Cognitive Science*. https://doi.org/10.1002/wcs.1670

Morin, A. (2011). Self-awareness part 1: definitions, measures, effects, function, and antecedents. *Social and Personality Psychology Compass*, *5*(11), 807–823. https://doi.org/10.1111/j.1751-9004.2011.00387.x

Newman, L. A., Creer, D. J., & McGaughy, J. (n.d.). Cognitive control and the anterior cingulate cortex: How conflicting stimuli affect attentional control in the rat. *Journal of Physiology-Paris*, *109*(1–3), 95–103. https://doi.org/10.1016/j.jphysparis.2014.06.004

Northoff, G., Heinzel, A., De Greck, M., Bermpohl, F., Dobrowolny, H., & Panksepp, J. (2006). Self-referential processing in our brain—A meta-analysis of imaging studies on the self. *NeuroImage*, *31*(1), 440–457. https://doi.org/10.1016/j.neuroimage.2005.12.002

Pinciotti, C. M., Bulkes, N., Horvath, G., & Riemann, B. C. (2022). Efficacy of intensive CBT telehealth for obsessive-compulsive disorder during the COVID-19 pandemic. *Journal of Obsessive-Compulsive and Related Disorders*, *32*, 100705. https://doi.org/10.1016/j.jocrd.2021.100705

Poldrack, R. A., & Gabrieli, J. D. E. (2001). Characterizing the neural mechanisms of skill learning and repetition priming. *Brain*, *124*(1), 67–82. https://doi.org/10.1093/brain/124.1.67

Powell, S. B., Sejnowski, T. J., & Behrens, M. M. (2012). Behavioral and neurochemical consequences of cortical oxidative stress on parvalbumin-interneuron maturation in rodent models of schizophrenia. *Neuropharmacology*, *62*(3), 1322–1331. https://doi.org/10.1016/j.neuropharm.2011.01.049

Seo, D., Patrick, C. J., & Kennealy, P. J. (2008). Role of serotonin and dopamine system interactions in the neurobiology of impulsive aggression and its comorbidity with other clinical disorders. *Aggression and Violent Behavior*, *13*(5), 383–395. https://doi.org/10.1016/j.avb.2008.06.003

Sherer, M., Hart, T., & Nick, T. G. (n.d.). Measurement of impaired self-awareness after traumatic brain injury: A comparison of the patient competency rating scale and the awareness questionnaire. *Brain Injury*, *17*(1), 25–37. https://doi.org/10.1080/0269905021000010113

Starkstein, S. E. (2014). Anosognosia in Alzheimer's disease: Diagnosis, frequency, mechanism and clinical correlates. *Cortex*, *61*, 64–73. https://doi.org/10.1016/j.cortex.2014.07.019

Suddendorf, T., & Collier-Baker, E. (2013). The evolution of primate visual self-recognition: Evidence of absence in lesser apes. *Proceedings of the Royal Society B: Biological Sciences*, *276*(1662), 1671–1677. https://doi.org/10.1098/rspb.2008.1754

Takikowski, P., Berger, J., & Ehrsson, H. H. (2017). The role of the default mode network in self-referential processing. *Journal of Cognitive Neuroscience*, *29*(3), 453–467. https://doi.org/10.1162/jocn_a_01195

Tulving, E. (2002). Episodic memory: From mind to brain. *Annual Review of Psychology*, *53*(1), 1–25. https://doi.org/10.1146/annurev.psych.53.100901.135114

Turjman, O. (2016). On the role of mirror neurons in the sense of self. *ResearchGate*. Retrieved from https://www.researchgate.net/publication/303566266_On_the_Role_of_Mirror_Neuro ns_in_the_Sense_of_Self

Valera, E. M., Faraone, S. V., Murray, K. E., & Seidman, L. J. (2007). Meta-analysis of structural imaging findings in attention-deficit/hyperactivity disorder. *Biological Psychiatry*, *61*(12), 1361–1369. https://doi.org/10.1016/j.biopsych.2006.06.011

Van Erp, A. M., & Miczek, K. A. (n.d.). Aggressive behavior, increased accumbal dopamine, and decreased cortical serotonin in rats. *The Journal of Neuroscience*, *20*(24), 9320–9325. https://doi.org/10.1523/jneurosci.20-24-09320.2000

Wang, X., Wu, Q., Egan, L., Gu, X., Liu, P., Gu, H., Yang, Y., Luo, J., Wu, Y., Gao, Z., & Fan, J. (2019). Anterior insular cortex plays a critical role in interoceptive attention. *eLife*, *8*. https://doi.org/10.7554/elife.42265

Wong, A. E., & Vallacher, R. R. (2017). Reciprocal feedback between self-concept and goal pursuit in daily life. *Journal of Personality*, *86*(3), 543–554. https://doi.org/10.1111/jopy.12334

11 Neuropsychology of Altruism

Brain Regions, Hormones, and Evolutionary Insights

Introduction

Definition

In 1966, Auguste Comte used the phrase "vivre pour autrui," which denoted a social drive higher than egoism (Comte & Fetscher, 1966).

According to a popular definition, altruism is defined as a behavior that has fitness benefits for the persons receiving the behavior as well as costs the behaving individual (Sober &Wilson, 1999) "Motivation with the ultimate goal of increasing another's welfare" is how Batson defines altruism.

Historical Perspectives on Altruism

Sober and Wilson's "Unto Others" distinguishes between common and biological interpretations of altruism. While everyday usage links altruism to both action and motive, biology defines it solely by its impact on survival and reproduction. Biologists view behavior as altruistic when it boosts others' fitness at the expense of the actor's own, challenging natural selection's focus on individual benefits (Domondon, 2013). Edward O. Wilson raises the paradox: how can altruism, which decreases personal fitness, evolve through natural selection? Two solutions have emerged: group selection and kin selection. Group selection proposes that traits enhancing group fitness can prevail, even if they lower individual fitness. Altruism evolves when groups with self-sacrificing members outcompete others. Kin selection posits that altruism evolves to benefit genetically related kin, preserving shared genes. Sacrifices benefit kin, ensuring the propagation of altruistic genes (Domondon, 2013).

Neural Basis of Altruism

Significance of Investigating Neural Correlates

Altruism, a multifaceted social phenomenon, is defined differently across disciplines. Biologists focus on the outcomes of actions that reduce one's fitness while benefiting others, while psychologists delve into the underlying

DOI: 10.4324/9781003477815-11

motivations. This contrasts with egoism, which prioritizes self-interest. Understanding why humans engage in altruistic behaviors, often against self-interest, has gained traction behaviorally and neurologically (Filkowski et al., 2016). While altruism, cooperation, and reciprocity are often seen as human traits, elements of these behaviors are observed in other species. Even human infants display innate altruism, engaging in helpful acts without external prompting. Studies indicate humans willingly interact beneficially with strangers, suggesting an inherent inclination toward altruism (Filkowski et al., 2016). Additionally, altruistic behavior benefits the altruist. Volunteerism is associated with increased happiness, wellbeing, and better health outcomes, including reduced depression and anxiety rates and improved longevity. Acts of kindness similarly boost self-reported happiness. Thus, altruistic behaviors positively impact both the recipient and the giver's physical and psychological wellbeing (Filkowski et al., 2016).

Brain Regions Involved

Altruistic behavior, the act of selflessly benefiting others at one's own expense, is a complex phenomenon influenced by various brain regions and neural processes. Among these, the ventromedial prefrontal cortex (VMPFC) stands out as a pivotal area involved in representing social preferences. Research indicates that the VMPFC is activated when individuals choose to engage in altruistic acts, such as donating money to those in need (Cooper et al., 2010). Notably, the level of activity in the VMPFC correlates with the perceived need of the recipient, suggesting its role in assessing others' welfare and guiding altruistic decisions.

Further insights into the neural basis of altruism come from studies utilizing transcranial direct current stimulation (tDCS) to modulate brain activity. Specifically, targeting the VMPFC with anodal tDCS has been shown to enhance altruistic behavior in scenarios such as trust games, where individuals must decide whether to trust others with their resources (Zheng et al., 2015). Conversely, individuals with focal damage to the VMPFC exhibit diminished empathy and reduced engagement in altruistic acts, highlighting the crucial role of this brain region in promoting prosocial behavior (Beadle et al., 2018).

In addition to the VMPFC, regions within the striatum and nucleus accumbens, integral components of the brain's reward system, have been implicated in altruistic decision-making processes. Studies have shown increased activity in these areas during monetary exchanges and charitable donation tasks, suggesting that the anticipation of rewards may influence individuals' propensity to engage in altruistic behaviors (Harbaugh et al., 2007).

Meanwhile, the posterior superior temporal sulcus (pSTS) emerges as another key player in the neural circuitry underlying altruism. This region, known for its involvement in perceiving agency and attributing intentions to others' actions, exhibits heightened activation when individuals make altruistic decisions or observe charitable acts (Tankersley et al., 2007a; Moll et al.,

2006). The increased activity in the pSTS during altruistic behavior suggests its role in processing social information and mediating empathic responses toward others in need.

Collectively, these findings highlight the intricate interplay between various brain regions in mediating altruistic behavior. Further research into the specific functions and interactions of these neural circuits promises to deepen our understanding of the mechanisms underlying human altruism and its implications for social interaction and cooperation.

Hormonal Influences

Oxytocin and vasopressin are neurotransmitters known for their roles in modulating social behavior and affiliation. Oxytocin, in particular, plays a crucial role in facilitating social bonding, especially between parents and offspring. Studies have shown that intranasal administration of oxytocin increases generosity toward socially-oriented charities, highlighting its role in promoting prosocial behavior (Marsh et al., 2015). Similarly, individuals with paranoid schizophrenia, who typically exhibit reduced altruistic behavior, displayed increased sharing tendencies after receiving intranasal vasopressin, underscoring the influence of vasopressin on altruistic actions (Purushothaman et al., 2019).

On the other hand, serotonin and dopamine are neurotransmitters implicated in the neural mechanisms underlying altruistic behavior. Serotonin appears to enhance empathy, cooperation, and fairness, while also reducing impulsivity and aversion to causing harm (Crockett et al., 2008, 2010, 2015). In contrast, dopamine is associated with the rewarding aspects of altruism, promoting feelings of pleasure and satisfaction when engaging in prosocial acts (Moll et al., 2006). Dopamine also plays a role in motivating social connections and anticipating social rewards associated with altruism (Moll et al., 2006).

However, the relationship between neurotransmitters and altruistic behavior is complex and influenced by genetic, environmental, and social factors. Individual differences in neurotransmitter levels and sensitivity contribute to variations in altruistic tendencies among individuals. Nonetheless, understanding the roles of oxytocin, vasopressin, serotonin, and dopamine provides valuable insights into the neurobiological basis of altruism and its implications for social interaction and cooperation.

III. EVOLUTIONARY PERSPECTIVES

Evolution of Altruism

Kin Selection

Biologist W.D. Hamilton first put forth the hypothesis of kin selection in 1964. It implies that if altruistic actions help genetically linked individuals reproduce more successfully, they may evolve. Kin selection states that people may forego their own chances to procreate in order to improve the survival and procreation of close relatives who have similar genes. Kin selection theory is based on the idea of inclusive fitness. It describes a person's overall success in reproduction, encompassing both their own children and the children of relatives they support with selfless actions. Generous deeds toward family members can tangentially improve an individual's inclusive fitness by boosting the reproductive success of genetically related relatives (Kay et al., 2019).

In social insects such as bees and ants, for example, workers may choose not to reproduce in order to assist in raising the progeny of the queen, who is frequently their mother or sister.

Workers indirectly improve their inclusive fitness by aiding the queen and her progeny in achieving successful reproduction. Kin selection's degree of operation is mostly dependent on the degree of relatedness among individuals. Genetically closely related individuals are more likely to evolve altruistic behaviors because helping kin outweighs the costs to the individual's ability to reproduce. The notion of kin selection has been utilized to comprehend human behavior, specifically in regard to social relationships and family dynamics. According to studies, people are more prone to act philanthropically toward near relatives, which is in line with the theories of kin selection (Kay et al., 2019).

While kin selection theory has provided valuable insights into the evolution of altruism, it has also faced criticisms and challenges. Some researchers argue that factors such as ecological conditions and social dynamics may influence the evolution of altruistic behaviors in ways that are not fully explained by kin selection alone (Kay et al., 2019).

Reciprocal Altruism

The notion of reciprocal altruism, which has its roots in both social psychology and evolutionary biology, describes how people behave when they help others in the hopes of getting something in return later on. It is an essential component of social cooperation that is seen in many animal species, including people. Natural selection can lead to the evolution of reciprocal altruism when the advantages of teamwork exceed the disadvantages. People exchange reciprocally after evaluating a possible partner's reliability and past actions. These interactions are greatly influenced by a number of factors, including memory, reputation, and emotional reactions. Fish, like sticklebacks and guppies, exhibit predator inspection behavior as a tit-for-tat solution to the prisoner's dilemma. They break away from their school to approach predators, monitoring their partner's behavior before cooperating. Guppies prefer cooperative partners and maintain the closest average position to the inspector. Impala engage in mutual grooming to remove parasites, while vampire bats engage in reciprocal blood sharing, involving higher costs and longer time delays (Brosnan & de Waal, 2002).

This emphasizes how crucial psychological mechanisms are in balancing reciprocal altruism. Several psychological processes, such as empathy, theory of mind, and conformity to social norms, promote reciprocal altruism. Empathy promotes a sense of unity and collaboration by enabling people to comprehend and experience the emotions of others. People with theory of mind are able to deduce the intentions and mental states of others, which aids in behavior prediction and decision-making about reciprocal exchanges. Social norms serve as rules for proper conduct within a society, promoting mutual trust and collaboration (Brosnan & de Waal, 2002).

Comparative Neuroanatomy

Cross Species Comparisons

Predator inspection behavior in fish, particularly sticklebacks and guppies, has been studied extensively as a potential example of the tit-for-tat solution to the prisoner's dilemma. This behavior involves fish breaking away from their school to approach an oncoming predator, likely to gather information about the predator while risking greater exposure. Research using simulated partners has shown that fish adopt a conditional approach strategy, monitoring their partner's behavior before deciding to cooperate. Guppies seem to recognize cooperative tendencies in partners and prefer to associate with better inspectors. In experiments, guppies showed a preference for individuals who maintained the closest average position to the inspector. However, this preference was not consistently observed in larger groups, suggesting flexibility in their interactions based on their partner's level of cooperation (Brosnan & de Waal, 2002). In another example, impala engage in mutual grooming to remove parasites, with each episode consisting of alternating grooming bouts. This behavior is seen as a low-cost form of reciprocity, following the parceling model where goods are exchanged in small packets, reducing the cost of defection (Brosnan & de Waal, 2002). In contrast, vampire bats engage in reciprocal blood sharing, which involves higher costs and longer time delays between given and received acts. Female bats exchange blood meals to survive, with most sharing occurring between mothers and offspring or closely related individuals. The observed reciprocity may result from kinship and mutual friendship rather than explicit scorekeeping (Brosnan & de Waal, 2002). Overall, these examples highlight different forms of reciprocal altruism in various animal species, showcasing adaptations to balance cooperation and individual fitness (Brosnan & de Waal, 2002).

Insights from Studies on Primates

The experiments investigate whether there is a reciprocal relationship between social grooming and agonistic support among nonhuman primates, such as cercopithecine monkeys and long-tailed macaques. The studies find preliminary evidence suggesting that individuals who engage in affiliative behaviors like grooming are more likely to receive support in agonistic encounters from their grooming partners. This indicates a potential link between grooming and social support, demonstrating a form of reciprocity in their interactions (Brosnan & de Waal, 2002).

The research also explores the phenomenon of food sharing among capuchin monkeys and chimpanzees to investigate whether it follows principles of reciprocity. The studies find that food sharing is indeed reciprocal in nature, with individuals sharing food with those who have shared with them previously. In capuchin monkeys, there is evidence of reciprocal food sharing between partners, with individuals showing higher rates of sharing with those they have shared with previously. Similarly, in chimpanzees, individuals are more likely to share food with those who have groomed them earlier in the day, indicating a memory-based, partner-specific exchange (Brosnan & de Waal, 2002).

Developmental Aspects

Childhood in Altruism

The early signs of altruistic tendencies in children are evident through their simple acts of assistance when witnessing others struggling with tasks. These behaviors offer valuable insights into both the cognitive processes and motivational aspects of children's social interactions (Warneken & Tomasello, 2006).

Research indicates that children begin to exhibit helping behaviors surprisingly early, often by their first birthday. For example, in an initial study, 18-month-old infants were presented with various scenarios where adults encountered difficulties in achieving their goals. These situations ranged from simple tasks, like reaching for an object, to more complex challenges, such as retrieving an object from a box using alternative methods (Warneken & Tomasello, 2006, 2007). Subsequent research also shows that even 14-month-old children engage in helpful acts, albeit with less cognitively demanding tasks (Warneken & Tomasello, 2007).

Moreover, children's motivation to help appears to be internally driven rather than influenced by external rewards. Studies demonstrate that children continue to offer assistance even when it entails personal costs or effort, and their willingness to help persists across repeated trials (Warneken et al., 2007; Warneken & Tomasello, 2008). Furthermore, concrete rewards do not seem to increase the likelihood of helping; in fact, they may even diminish intrinsic altruistic motivation (Warneken et al., 2007; Warneken & Tomasello, 2008). These findings suggest that altruistic behaviors emerge early in childhood and are not solely shaped by socialization or external reinforcement. Contrary to the belief that children's altruism is solely a result of learned behaviors or rewards, studies indicate an intrinsic inclination toward helping others (Bar-Tal, 1982; Cialdini et al., 1982).

Early Signs of Prosocial Behavior

Until recently, studies on early prosocial behavior mainly focused on how children responded to others' distress, showing that infants as young as the first year of life could react to distress. Infants' interactions with parents were found to influence the development of empathy and prosocial responses by the second year. Early studies also demonstrated that toddlers engaged in sharing, helping, and cooperation, particularly in contexts where they received emotional and behavioral support from parents (Brownell, 2012).

Recent research has shifted toward understanding typical patterns of helping, comforting, sharing, and cooperating in toddlers, and the factors influencing these prosocial behaviors. It has been observed that children begin to spontaneously share information with adults by 12 months and share food and toys by 18–24 months. Additionally, toddlers assist adults with tasks by 14–18 months and offer help with emotion-related problems by 30 months. They also demonstrate cooperation with both adults and peers on various tasks by 18–24 months (Brownell, 2012).

However, toddlers are selective in their prosocial behaviors, considering factors like the partner's need, friendliness, helpfulness, and trustworthiness when deciding whether to help. Interestingly, toddlers who exhibit one form of prosocial behavior may not necessarily display the same level of prosociality in other forms (Brownell, 2012).

Overall, the second year of life appears to be a crucial period for the development of prosocial behavior in toddlers. They become increasingly adept at understanding others' needs and emotions, and they are motivated to intervene and help alleviate others' distress. Nonetheless, there are individual differences in children's inclination toward prosocial behavior, and there are limitations to their motivation and ability to engage in such actions (Brownell, 2012).

Parental and Environmental Influences

A research conducted three studies involving children aged 18 to 25 months, aiming to demonstrate that emerging prosocial behavior stems from an intrinsic concern for others' wellbeing. They argue that this concern for others arises from an early moral sense rooted in basic social-affiliative processes. While some researchers propose that children possess this moral sense innately, research study 1 suggests that social experiences may also influence its development (Brownell, 2012).

Another study indirectly supports this idea by showing changes in infants' fairness expectations between 12 and 15 months, which are linked to prosocial behavior, cannot solely be explained by innate moral principles.

They suggest that experience plays a role in shaping these expectations. Researches 1 and 2 offer more detailed insights into how social experiences can foster early prosociality (Brownell, 2012).

A group of scientists conducted experiments manipulating infants' social experiences, finding that 10-month-olds exposed to active collaborative exchanges were better at understanding the shared goals of cooperating partners compared to those with passive or no experience (Brownell, 2012). On the other hand, other group of experiments observed naturally occurring social interactions between parents and their toddlers while reading books together. They discovered that parents who encouraged their 18- to 30-month-old children to reflect on and explain others' emotions had children who were more inclined to help and share with others (Brownell, 2012).

Adolescence and Shaping of Altruistic Traits

In a study using functional magnetic resonance imaging (fMRI), researchers scanned the brains of adolescents and adults while they observed scenarios of social exclusion and then participated in an economic game involving sharing money with others. The study revealed distinct patterns of neural activation between adolescents and adults. When observing social exclusion, adolescents showed heightened activity in brain regions associated with emotional processing, such as the amygdala and insula. This suggests that adolescents may experience stronger emotional reactions to social exclusion compared to adults. However, during the subsequent economic game where participants could share money with others, adolescents exhibited less activity in brain areas linked to perspective-taking and altruistic decision-making, such as the dorsolateral prefrontal cortex and temporoparietal junction, compared to adults. This indicates that adolescents may struggle more with engaging in altruistic behavior following social exclusion, possibly due to differences in brain development and social-cognitive abilities. The findings suggest that while adolescents may be more emotionally reactive to social exclusion, they may also face challenges in translating these emotional responses into altruistic actions. This highlights the complex interplay between emotional processing, social cognition, and altruistic behavior during adolescence and adulthood (Tousignant et al., 2018).

Bronfenbrenner's ecological systems theory emphasizes the impact of environmental systems on individual development, highlighting the family as the primary micro-environment. Family dynamics, such as emotional connections and interaction patterns, significantly shape behavior and development. Families provide essential support crucial for physical, psychological, and social growth, reflected in the concept of family function, which encompasses emotional bonds, communication, and coping strategies (Cui et al., 2023).

Intimacy and emotional support within families foster altruistic behavior by promoting care and concern for others, with children often emulating their parents' behavior. Conversely, dysfunctional family environments with poor communication and emotional neglect may hinder the development of altruistic tendencies in individuals. Empirical evidence supports the relationship between family intimacy and children's altruism across different cultures (Cui et al., 2023). According to the Person-Context Interaction theory, family factors influence altruistic behavior through mediating processes that affect social-cognitive abilities. These mediating processes include self-affirmation and psychological resilience (Cui et al., 2023).

Neural Basis of Empathy

When discussing the social neuroscience of empathy in public discourse, the term "mirror neurons" often arises, suggesting their pivotal role in empathy. These neurons, discovered in the early 1990s, were initially thought to be fundamental to understanding the actions of others by firing both when executing and observing actions. This led to the hypothesis that mirroring others' movements enables us to grasp their intentions, forming the basis of empathy. However, this assumption lacks direct empirical support (Lamm & Majdandžić, 2015).

While some studies show neurons responding to both observed actions and emotional expressions in monkeys, this does not prove their involvement in evoking emotional responses. Furthermore, findings from monkey studies cannot directly apply to humans, necessitating reliance on indirect measures like neuroimaging. Recent research suggests the presence of mirror neuron-like properties in humans, but their exact role remains uncertain (Lamm & Majdandžić, 2015).

Mirror neurons are specialized cells in the brain that activate both when an animal performs an action and when it observes another animal performing the same action, may play a role in empathetic and prosocial behaviors (Wu et al., 2023).

The study involves observing the behavior of rats in a prosocial task where one rat is given the opportunity to help another rat by releasing it from a restraint. The researchers found that some neurons in the rats' brains, called affective mirror neurons, became active both when the rat performed the helping action and when it observed another rat being helped. This suggests that these neurons may be involved in empathetic responses, where the rat is able to understand and share the emotional state of the rat in distress (Wu et al., 2023).

Interestingly, the study also identified another group of neurons, called anti-mirror neurons, which became active when the rat performed the helping action but was inhibited when it observed another rat being helped. This suggests that these neurons may play a role in inhibiting empathetic responses or in regulating prosocial behavior (Wu et al., 2023).

Research indicates that altruistic behavior, such as giving, activates the mesolimbic "pleasure" system in the brain, leading to feelings of warmth and satisfaction (Moll et al., 2006). This activation of the dopamine reward pathway is akin to the pleasure derived from indulging in enjoyable activities like eating or intimate encounters (Kean, 2015). However, excessive generosity can also stem from neurological factors, such as damage to the lenticular nucleus and related pathways, resulting in pathological generosity (Ferreira-Garcia et al., 2013; Kean, 2015). Individuals with such conditions may exhibit compulsive giving behaviors driven by the pursuit of dopamine-induced pleasure, akin to addictive behaviors observed in rats (Hoult, 1984).

A case study by Ferreira-Garcia et al. (2013) illustrates this phenomenon, where a stroke-induced change in personality led to excessive spending on others, despite financial irresponsibility. This highlights the role of brain structures like the prefrontal cortex (PFC) and orbitofrontal cortices in tempering altruistic impulses and decision-making (Moll et al., 2005, 2006). These regions help regulate altruistic behavior by inhibiting undesired actions and disinhibiting desired ones, thus preventing excessive giving (Moll et al., 2006). Medical conditions such as Williams syndrome, dementia, and Parkinson's disease, as well as behavioral patterns like codependency, can also contribute to pathological altruism (Oakley et al., 2012; Oakley, 2013).

Social-Cognitive Networks

Theory of Mind and Altruism

Initially termed "theory of mind" (ToM) and now also known as "mentalizing," this concept encompasses the ability to attribute knowledge and intentions to others. Premack and Woodruff (1978) first introduced ToM, focusing on the inference of goals from actions. In their study, chimpanzees were presented with images of a human actor attempting to achieve a task and were asked to select the desired outcome from two options. The chimpanzees demonstrated a reasonable ability to do so. Therefore, ToM originally pertained to the interpretation of others' goals and, by extension, their intentions.

Waytz and colleagues (1967) conducted research to explore how theory of mind (ToM) and empathic concern influence subsequent altruistic behavior in the Dictator Game (DG). Participants first underwent a ToM task where they were tasked with making social judgments regarding a confederate's preferences and personality traits. Following this, participants participated in an iterative version of the DG to assess altruistic giving behavior. Additionally, as an extra measure of altruism, participants were given the opportunity to donate their time to the confederate by answering problem-solving questions, with no set limit on the number they could answer.

The study found that increased activity in the dorsal medial prefrontal cortex (mPFC) was predictive of allocating more money and time to the partner. Those who exhibited higher dorsal mPFC activation during the ToM task also spent more time answering problem-solving questions and allocated more money to their partner. Furthermore, in a separate analysis, dorsal mPFC activity during the decision-making process of allocating money to the partner was associated with an increased monetary allocation. These findings provide additional evidence supporting the significance of emotional responses to others' mental states in making altruistic decisions.

Empathy-Altruism Hypothesis

According to Batson's Empathy-Altruism Hypothesis (EAH), empathy plays a crucial role in motivating altruistic behavior. Altruism, defined as behavior aimed at increasing another's welfare for its own sake, is driven by genuine empathic concern (Batson, 2018). This empathic concern, characterized by emotions congruent with perceiving another's need, encompasses various feelings like sympathy, compassion, and sorrow (Batson, 2018).

Batson and colleagues conducted experiments, such as the "Katie Banks experiment," to test EAH. Participants, given a placebo capsule, listened to a fictional news report about Katie Banks, a person undergoing hardship. Those instructed to imagine Katie's situation showed a higher likelihood of helping her, indicating that empathic imagining increases helping behavior. Conversely, those in an arousal condition were less likely to help, as their arousal was attributed to the capsule rather than empathic concern for Katie.

However, a question arises regarding whether empathy-induced helping is genuinely altruistic. According to EAH, it is, driven by a non-instrumental desire to help. Alternatively, the Arousal Reduction Hypothesis (ARH) suggests egoistic motivations, like reducing one's distress by helping. This highlights an asymmetry between egoistic and altruistic hypotheses; while altruistic hypotheses allow for egoistic behavior, the reverse is not true.

To determine which hypothesis holds, Batson et al. conducted the "Elaine experiment." Participants observed Elaine, a fictional person, receiving electric shocks. In conditions where empathy was elicited, ease of escape did not reduce helping behavior, contrary to ARH predictions. However, in conditions with less empathy, ease of escape decreased helping, suggesting egoistic motivations.

Despite challenges to ARH, it remains contested. Some argue that participants stayed not due to concern for Elaine but because leaving would not alleviate their distress. Nevertheless, experiments by Stocks et al. (2009) suggest that empathy still drives helping behavior even when psychological escape is available, challenging this argument (Batson et al., 1981; Stocks et al., 2009).

Neural Mechanisms of Altruistic Decision Making

Neuroeconomic Studies

Altruistic Punishment

Altruistic punishment involves individuals penalizing norm violators despite personal costs and no direct benefits, promoting cooperation and social order (Fehr & Gächter, 2002). Psychologically, it is driven by fairness and justice. Fehr & Gächter (2002) found that cooperation in a public goods game increased when punishment was allowed. Hu et al. (2015) examined third-party altruistic helping and punishment, showing increased striatum activation in both behaviors. Helping correlated with right lateral prefrontal cortex-striatum connectivity, while punishment correlated with vmPFC and left lateral prefrontal cortex connectivity.

Neural Correlates of Cooperation

A study by Rilling et al. (2007) on individuals with varying degrees of psychopathy showed that those with higher psychopathy displayed reduced activation in empathy and moral reasoning regions (anterior cingulate cortex and temporoparietal junction) during cooperative tasks. Conversely, non-cooperative behavior in these individuals increased activity in reward-processing areas (ventral striatum and orbitofrontal cortex).

Neuroimaging Findings in Altruistic Acts

In a study on charitable donations, Moll et al. (2006) found that decisions involving personal cost to support or oppose causes activated the anterior prefrontal cortex, including the mPFC, ACC, and frontopolar cortex. Engaging in charitable giving, despite personal loss, was linked to heightened activity in the VTA and striatum, regions involved in reward processing. Costly donations specifically activated the subgenual anterior cingulate cortex (SgACC). Harbaugh et al. (1964) observed increased reward-related brain activity during monetary exchanges. Individuals with greater activation when gaining money for themselves were less inclined to donate to charity, whereas those with more activation when charity received money were more likely to donate and reported higher satisfaction. Hare et al. (1965) found that the ventromedial prefrontal cortex (vmPFC) activity correlated with the subjective value of charitable donations and showed connectivity with the posterior superior temporal sulcus (pSTS) and anterior insula. Zaki and Mitchell (2011) demonstrated that equitable offers in social exchanges activated the orbitofrontal cortex (OFC), linked to subjective value evaluation. Unfair decisions elicited activity in the anterior insula, indicating negative emotional responses.

Waytz et al. (1967) found that increased activity in the dorsal medial prefrontal cortex (mPFC), involved in emotional responses and understanding others' mental states, predicted greater monetary and time allocation to partners in the Dictator Game, highlighting emotional empathy's role in altruistic decisions. Overall, these studies underscore the involvement of reward-related regions (OFC, ventral striatum) and areas associated with emotion and social cognition (mPFC, anterior insula) in altruistic behavior. Negative emotional responses to unfair actions influence subsequent behavior, emphasizing the interplay between emotional processing and altruistic decision-making.

Disorders and Variability

Empathy Deficits in Psychopathology

Autism Spectrum Disorders (ASD)

Autism spectrum disorder (ASD) is characterized by challenges in social communication, interaction, and repetitive behaviors (American Psychiatric Association, 2013). Research indicates that individuals with autism often exhibit deficits in cognitive empathy, which involves understanding others' mental states, while their emotional empathy, which involves responding to others' emotions, remains largely intact (Baron-Cohen, 2013). The development of theory of mind (ToM), crucial for social skills and predicting others' behavior, is often impaired in individuals with ASD, suggesting deficits in attributing mental states to others (Baron-Cohen et al., 1985; Korkmaz, 2011).

The "broken mirror" hypothesis proposes that dysfunction in mirror neurons, which are believed to help understand others' actions by simulating them, contributes to empathy deficits in ASD (Dapretto et al., 2006). Additionally, the social motivation hypothesis suggests that individuals with ASD find social stimuli less rewarding due to irregularities in neural reward processing (Scott-Van Zeeland et al., 2010; Delmonte et al., 2012; Cox et al., 2015). Other factors contributing to empathy deficits in ASD include abnormalities in the oxytocin-producing gene, reduced activity in the fusiform gyrus, and hypoactivity in the anterior insula and medial prefrontal cortex, which impact emotional awareness and cognitive empathy processing (Harmsen, 2019).

Psychopathy and Altruistic Behavior

Psychopathy is marked by traits like manipulativeness, callousness, and profound empathy deficits. Neuroimaging studies reveal abnormalities in the amygdala and prefrontal cortex, crucial for emotional processing and decision-making, leading to emotional deficits and poor impulse control in psychopathy. Dysfunction in neurotransmitter systems, particularly involving serotonin and dopamine, is also implicated, affecting mood, impulse control, and reward processing (Sonne & Gash, 2018).

In contrast, altruism involves selfless concern for others' welfare, with neuroimaging studies showing activation in regions associated with empathy and social cognition, such as the anterior insula and anterior cingulate cortex, during altruistic behavior. These areas facilitate empathetic responses and prosocial actions. Oxytocin release, involved in social bonding and trust, also promotes altruistic behaviors (Sonne & Gash, 2018).

Studies show that individuals with psychopathy exhibit reduced amygdala activity in response to fearful facial expressions, whereas altruistic individuals show heightened amygdala activity (Marsh, 2016). The propensity toward psychopathy or altruism is influenced by a complex interplay of genetic predispositions, early life experiences, and social influences. Genetic variants can predispose individuals to psychopathic traits, while adverse childhood experiences or deficient caregiving can exacerbate these tendencies. Conversely, positive socialization, nurturing environments, and moral education can foster altruistic behaviors (Sonne & Gash, 2018).

Interindividual Differences in Altruistic Traits

Research indicates that both genetic and environmental factors contribute to interindividual differences in altruistic traits. Genetic variations, particularly in genes related to neurotransmitter systems such as dopamine and oxytocin, have been linked to changes in altruistic behavior (Israel et al., 2009). For instance, studies using the Dictator Game and the Social Value Orientations Task found that individuals with specific genetic variants of the OXTR gene were more likely to exhibit prosocial behaviors, such as sharing resources and prioritizing fairness (Israel et al., 2009).

Additionally, variability in brain structure and function also correlates with differences in altruistic behavior. Differences in the volume and activity of brain regions involved in empathy and social cognition, like the anterior insula and anterior cingulate cortex, have been associated with variations in altruistic tendencies (Moll et al., 2006; Marsh et al., 2014).

Environmental influences, such as social experiences, upbringing, and cultural norms, play a significant role in shaping altruistic behavior. Individuals raised in environments that emphasize cooperation and prosocial values are more likely to exhibit altruistic behaviors (Capraro et al., 2014; Rand et al., 2014).

Ethical Considerations

The Intersection of Neuroscience and Morality

Neuroscience reveals the biological basis of moral behavior, showing how brain structures and functions relate to moral decision-making. This research helps us understand how humans discern right from wrong, empathize, and follow social norms.

Implications for Understanding Human Cooperation

Understanding cooperation is key for fostering positive social interactions, teamwork, and innovation (Nowak & Highfield, 2011; Mello et al., 2015). It aids in resolving conflicts between individual and collective interests (Fehr & Fischbacher, 2003) and informs policies addressing global challenges like climate change (Ostrom, 2010). Insights into cultural differences in cooperation enhance cross-cultural collaboration (Henrich et al., 2010) and support the development of educational programs promoting prosocial behavior (Caprara et al., 2010).

Ethical Challenges in Altruism Research

Altruism research faces ethical challenges such as ensuring informed consent, justifying deception, and protecting participants from emotional distress. Maintaining confidentiality and addressing social desirability bias are crucial. Researchers must also consider cultural differences and respect participants' autonomy throughout the study.

Emerging Areas of Research

Research in altruism and technology delves into how digital platforms and social media influence acts of altruism, such as the dynamics of online crowdfunding. Evolutionary perspectives on altruism seek to understand its origins and adaptive functions across different species and societies. Investigations into altruism and wellbeing explore the reciprocal relationship between altruistic behaviors and psychological wellbeing. Cross-cultural studies on altruism aim to uncover variations in altruistic tendencies and behaviors across different cultural contexts. Altruism in economics involves integrating altruistic motivations into economic models to gain insights into decision-making in diverse contexts. Additionally, research on altruism and health examines the potential health benefits associated with altruistic actions, such as stress reduction and enhanced immune function. Lastly, studies on altruism and environmental sustainability analyze altruistic behaviors in the context of promoting environmental conservation and sustainability efforts (Israel et al., 2009; Marsh et al., 2014).

Technological advancements in neuroimaging have significantly advanced the study of altruism, facilitating a deeper comprehension of the neural mechanisms governing selfless behavior. Functional magnetic resonance imaging (fMRI) offers real-time images of brain activity during acts of selflessness, enabling researchers to pinpoint specific brain regions involved in altruistic decision-making and empathy (Decety & Cacioppo, 2012). Magnetoencephalography (MEG) provides high temporal-resolution imaging of brain activity, allowing researchers to track the temporal sequence of neural events underlying altruistic decision-making with millisecond precision (Sato et al., 2012). Diffusion Tensor Imaging (DTI) permits the investigation of structural connectivity in brain networks associated with altruism and social cognition by mapping white matter tracts (Bellucci et al., 2017). Ultra-high-field MRI scanners provide enhanced spatial resolution and signal-to-noise ratio, enabling detailed imaging of small brain structures relevant to altruism (Cohen et al., 2018). These technological innovations in neuroimaging have significantly enriched our understanding of the neural foundations of altruism, equipping researchers with robust tools to explore the intricate mechanisms underpinning selfless behavior.

Interdisciplinary approaches are crucial for advancing research on altruism, as they allow researchers to draw on insights from diverse fields and methodologies. Integrating neuroscience and psychology allows for a comprehensive exploration of the cognitive and neural processes involved in altruistic behavior by combining behavioral experiments with neuroimaging techniques (Tankersley et al., 2007b). The fusion of economics and behavioral science offers valuable insights into the motivations and decision-making processes that underlie altruistic behaviors, examining how social preferences, incentives, and norms influence altruistic decision-making (Fehr & Fischbacher, 2003). Anthropological and cultural perspectives provide contextual understanding of altruistic behaviors across various societies and historical contexts, shedding light on the cultural diversity of altruism (Henrich et al., 2010). Sociological and public policy perspectives offer insights into the social determinants of altruism and strategies for promoting prosocial behavior, examining the influence of social networks, institutions, and interventions on fostering altruistic values and behaviors (Piliavin & Charng, 1990). By embracing interdisciplinary approaches, future research on altruism can provide a holistic understanding of this complex phenomenon, incorporating its psychological, social, economic, and cultural dimensions.

Summary

The chapter "Altruism and the Brain" provides an extensive overview of the concept of altruism, covering its definition, historical perspectives, and the significance of studying its neural correlates. It delves into the neural basis of altruistic behavior, examining the roles of brain regions like the ventromedial prefrontal cortex and striatum, and the influence of hormones such as oxytocin and vasopressin. The evolutionary and developmental aspects of altruism are also explored, along with the role of mirror neurons and empathy. Ethical considerations in altruism research, the implications for social policy and education, and the need for further research are highlighted. The chapter underscores the importance of promoting prosocial behaviors, building stronger communities, and integrating empathy and compassion into educational curricula. It also discusses the potential for altruism research to address inequality, prevent anti-social behaviors, and support mental health. Future research directions include investigating the interplay of neurotransmitters, the genetics-environment interaction, individual differences, cultural variations, and developing targeted interventions. Emphasizing the significance of altruism in solving global challenges and improving wellbeing, the chapter calls for interdisciplinary research, diverse populations, longitudinal studies, and practical applications of findings.

References

American Psychiatric Association. (2013). *Autism spectrum disorder, 299.00 (F84.0)* (5th ed., pp. 50–59). American Psychiatric Publishing.

Bar-Tal, D. (1982). Sequential development of helping behavior: A cognitive-learning approach. *Developmental Review*, *2*, 101–124.

Baron-Cohen, S. (2013). *The science of evil: On empathy and the origins of cruelty*. New York, NY: Basic Books.

Baron-Cohen, S., Leslie, A. M., & Frith, U. (1985). Does the autistic child have a "theory of mind"? *Cognition*, *21*(1), 37–46. https://doi.org/10.1016/0010-0277(85)90022-8

Batson, C. D. (2018). *A scientific search for altruism: Do we only care about ourselves?* Oxford University Press.

Batson, C. D., Duncan, B. D., Ackerman, P., Buckley, T., & Birch, K. (1981). Is empathic emotion a source of altruistic motivation? *Journal of Personality and Social Psychology*, *40*(2), 290.

Beadle, J. N., Paradiso, S., & Tranel, D. (2018). Ventromedial prefrontal cortex is critical for helping others who are suffering. *Frontiers in Neurology*, *9*. https://doi.org/10.3389/fneur.2018.00288

Bellucci, G., Chernyak, N., Hoffman, M., & Parasuraman, R. (2017). Neural signatures of trust in reciprocity: A coordinate-based meta-analysis. *Human Brain Mapping*, *38*(3), 1233–1248.

Brosnan, S. F., & de Waal, F. B. (2002). A proximate perspective on reciprocal altruism. *Human Nature*, *13*(1), 129–152.

Brownell, C. A. (2012). Early development of prosocial behavior: Current perspectives. *Infancy*, *18*(1), 1–9. https://doi.org/10.1111/infa.12004

Caprara, G. V., Fida, R., Vecchione, M., Del Bove, G., Vecchio, G. M., Barbaranelli, C., & Bandura, A. (2010). Longitudinal analysis of the role of perceived self-efficacy for self-regulated learning in academic continuance and achievement. *Journal of Educational Psychology*, *102*(4), 749–776.

Capraro, V., Jordan, J. J., & Rand, D. G. (2014). Heuristics guide the implementation of social preferences in one-shot Prisoner's Dilemma experiments. *Scientific Reports*, *4*, 6790.

Cohen, A. D., Wang, D., Seidel, J., & He, B. (2018). Ultra-high field (7 Tesla) MRI applications in neuroscience and neuroimaging. *Journal of Neuroscience Methods*, *304*, 1–13.

Cooper, J. C., Kreps, T. A., Wiebe, T., Pirkl, T., & Knutson, B. (2010). When giving is good: Ventromedial prefrontal cortex activation for others' intentions. *Neuron*, *67*(3), 511–521. https://doi.org/10.1016/j.neuron.2010.06.030

Comte, A., & Fetscher, I. (1966). *The positive philosophy of Auguste Comte*. New York, NY: Gordon Press.

Crockett, M. J., Clark, L., Lieberman, M. D., Tabibnia, G., & Robbins, T. W. (2010). Impulsive choice and altruistic punishment are correlated and increase in tandem with serotonin depletion. *Emotion*, *10*(6), 855–862.

Crockett, M. J., Clark, L., Tabibnia, G., Lieberman, M. D., & Robbins, T. W. (2008). Serotonin modulates behavioral reactions to unfairness. *Science*, *320*(5884), 1739.

Crockett, M. J., Siegel, J. Z., Kurth-Nelson, Z., Dayan, P., Dolan, R. J., & Seymour, B. (2015). Dissociable effects of serotonin and dopamine on the valuation of harm in moral decision making. *Current Biology*, *25*(14), 1852–1859.

Cox, R. M., & Korkmaz, B. (2015). The role of social motivation in autism spectrum disorder. *Journal of Autism and Developmental Disorders*, *45*(3), 743–755.

Cui, H., Bi, X., Zhou, X., Zhang, W., & Ma, Y. (2023). Family function and adolescent altruistic behavior: The multiple mediating effects of self-affirmation and psychological resilience. *Frontiers in Psychology*, *14*. https://doi.org/10.3389/fpsyg.2023.1184985

Dapretto, M., Davies, M. S., Pfeifer, J. H., Scott, A. A., Sigman, M., Bookheimer, S. Y., et al. (2006). Understanding emotions in others: Mirror neuron dysfunction in children with autism spectrum disorders. *Nature Neuroscience*, *9*(1), 29–30. https://doi.org/10.1038/nn1611.

Decety, J., & Cacioppo, S. (2012). The speed of morality: A high-density electrical neuroimaging study. *Journal of Neurophysiology*, *108*(11), 3068–3072.

Delmonte, S., Balsters, J. H., McGrath, J., Fitzgerald, J., Brennan, S., Fagan, A. J., et al. (2012). Social and monetary reward processing in autism spectrum disorders. *Molecular Autism*, *3*(1), 7. https://doi.org/10.1186/2040-2392-3-7.

Domondon, J. A. (2013). The evolution of altruism: A critical review of the literature. *Journal of Evolutionary Psychology*, *11*(1), 1–15. https://doi.org/10.1556/JEP.11.2013.1.1

Fehr, E., & Fischbacher, U. (2003). The nature of human altruism. *Nature*, *425*(6960), 785–791.

Fehr, E., & Gächter, S. (2002). Altruistic punishment in humans. *Nature*, *415*(6868), 137–140.

Ferreira-Garcia, R., Fontenelle, L. F., Moll, J., & de Oliveira-Souza, R. (2013). Pathological generosity: An atypical impulse control disorder after a left subcortical stroke. *Neurocase*, *20*(5), 496–500.

Filkowski, M., Cochran, R. N., & Haas, B. (2016). Altruistic behavior: Mapping responses in the brain. *Neuroscience and Neuroeconomics*, *5*, 65–75. https://doi.org/10.2147/nan.s87718

Harbaugh, W. T., Mayr, U., & Burghart, D. R. (2007). Neural Responses to Taxation and Voluntary Giving Reveal Motives for Charitable Donations. *Science*, *316*(5831), 1622–1625. https://doi.org/10.1126/science.1140738

Hare, T. A., Camerer, C. F., & Rangel, A. (2009). Self-control in decision-making involves modulation of the vmPFC valuation system. *Science*, *324*(5927), 646–648. https://doi.org/10.1126/science.1168450

Harmsen, I. E. (2019). Empathy in autism spectrum disorder. *Journal of Autism and Developmental Disorders*, *49*(10), 3939–3955.

Henrich, J., Heine, S. J., & Norenzayan, A. (2010). The weirdest people in the world? *Behavioral and Brain Sciences*, *33*(2–3), 61–83.

Hoult, J. (1984). Compulsive generosity: A case report. *The British Journal of Psychiatry*, *145*(6), 679–680.

Hu, Y., Strang, S., & Weber, B. (2015). Helping or punishing strangers: Neural correlates of altruistic decisions as third-party and of its relation to empathic concern. *Frontiers in Behavioral Neuroscience*, *9*, 24.

Israel, S., Lerer, E., Shalev, I., Uzefovsky, F., Riebold, M., Laiba, E., ... Ebstein, R. P. (2009). The oxytocin receptor (OXTR) contributes to prosocial fund allocations in the dictator game and the social value orientations task. *PLoS One*, *4*(5), e5535.

Kay, T., Lehmann, L., & Keller, L. (2019). Kin selection and altruism. *Current Biology*, *29*(11). https://doi.org/10.1016/j.cub.2019.01.067

Kean, J. (2015). *The pleasure of giving*. The New York Times. Retrieved from https://www.nytimes.com/2015/12/06/opinion/sunday/the-pleasure-of-giving.html

Korkmaz, B. (2011). Theory of mind and neurodevelopmental disorders of childhood. *Pediatric Research*, *69*(5 Pt 2), 101R–108R. https://doi.org/10.1203/PDR.0b013e318212c177.

Lamm, C., & Majdandžić, J. (2015). The role of shared neural activations, mirror neurons, and morality in empathy – A critical comment. *Neuroscience Research*, *90*, 15–24. https://doi.org/10.1016/j.neures.2014.10.008

Marsh, A. A. (2016). Understanding amygdala responsiveness to fearful expressions through the lens of psychopathy and altruism. *Journal of Neuroscience Research*, *94*(6), 513–525.

Marsh, A. A., Stoycos, S. A., Brethel-Haurwitz, K. M., Robinson, P., VanMeter, J. W., & Cardinale, E. M. (2014). Neural and cognitive characteristics of extraordinary altruists. *Proceedings of the National Academy of Sciences*, *111*(42), 15036–15041.

Marsh, N., Scheele, D., Gerhardt, H., Strang, S., Enax, L., Weber, B., Maier, W., & Hurlemann, R. (2015). The neuropeptide oxytocin induces a social altruism bias. *The Journal of Neuroscience*, *35*(47), 15696–15701. https://doi.org/10.1523/jneurosci.3199-15.2015

Mello, J. A., Ribeiro, L. C., & Parente, R. (2015). Social capital and cooperation in micro, small and medium-sized enterprises. *Journal of Business Research*, *68*(12), 2633–2638.

Moll, J., de Oliveira-Souza, R., Moll, F. T., Ignácio, F. A., Bramati, I. E., Caparelli-Dáquer, E. M., ... Eslinger, P. J. (2005). The moral affiliations of disgust: A functional MRI study. *Cognitive and Behavioral Neurology*, *18*(1), 68–78.

Moll, J., Krueger, F., Zahn, R., Pardini, M., de Oliveira-Souza, R., & Grafman, J. (2006). Human fronto–mesolimbic networks guide decisions about charitable donation. *Proceedings of the National Academy of Sciences*, *103*(42), 15623–15628. https://doi.org/10.1073/pnas.0604475103

Nowak, M. A., & Highfield, R. (2011). *SuperCooperators: Altruism, evolution, and why we need each other to succeed*. Simon and Schuster.

Oakley, B., Knafo, A., Madhavan, G., & Wilson, D. S. (Eds.). (2012). *Pathological altruism*. Oxford University Press.

Oakley, B. A. (2013). Concepts and implications of altruism bias and pathological altruism. *Proceedings of the National Academy of Sciences*, *110*(Suppl. 2), 10408–10415.

Ostrom, E. (2010). Beyond markets and states: Polycentric governance of complex economic systems. *American Economic Review*, *100*(3), 641–672.

Piliavin, J. A., & Charng, H. W. (1990). Altruism: A review of recent theory and research. *Annual Review of Sociology*, *16*(1), 27–65.

Premack, D., & Woodruff, G. (1978). Does the chimpanzee have a theory of mind? *Behavioral and Brain Sciences*, *1*(4), 515–526. https://doi.org/10.1017/S0140525X00076512

Purushothaman, D., Rao, N., Venkatsubramanian, G., Varambally, S., KG, V., & Nagendra, B. (2019). Effect of intranasal vasopressin on altruistic behavior in schizophrenia. *Schizophrenia Bulletin*, *45*(Supplement_2). https://doi.org/10.1093/schbul/sbz021.243

Rand, D. G., Peysakhovich, A., Kraft-Todd, G. T., Newman, G. E., Wurzbacher, O., Nowak, M. A., & Greene, J. D. (2014). Social heuristics shape intuitive cooperation. *Nature Communications*, *5*(1), 1–10.

Rilling, J. K., Glenn, A. L., Jairam, M. R., Pagnoni, G., Goldsmith, D. R., Elfenbein, H. A., & Lilienfeld, S. O. (2007). Neural correlates of social cooperation and non-cooperation as a function of psychopathy. *Biological Psychiatry*, *61*(11), 1260–1271. https://doi.org/10.1016/j.biopsych.2006.07.021

Sato, A., Yasuda, A., & Ohira, H. (2012). Effects of value and reward magnitude on feedback negativity and P300. *NeuroReport*, *23*(5), 282–286.

Scott-Van Zeeland, A. A., Dapretto, M., Ghahremani, D. G., Poldrack, R. A., & Bookheimer, S. Y. (2010). Reward processing in autism. *Autism Research*, *3*(2), 53–67. https://doi.org/10.1002/aur.122.

Sober, E., & Wilson, D. S. (1999). *Unto others: The evolution and psychology of unselfish behavior*. Harvard University Press.

Sonne, J. W., & Gash, D. M. (2018). Psychopathy to altruism: Neurobiology of the selfish–selfless spectrum. *Frontiers in Psychology*, *9*, 575.

Stocks, E. L., Lishner, D. A., & Decker, S. K. (2009). Altruism or psychological escape: Why does empathy promote prosocial behavior? *European Journal of Social Psychology*, *39*(5), 649–665.

Tankersley, D., Stowe, C. J., & Huettel, S. A. (2007a). Altruism is associated with an increased neural response to agency. *Nature Neuroscience*, *10*(2), 150–151. https://doi.org/10.1038/nn1833

Tankersley, D., Stowe, C. J., Huettel, S. A., & Altmann, E. M. (2007b). Neural correlates of strategic reasoning during competitive games. *Science*, *317*(5844), 817–820.

Tousignant, B., Eugène, F., Sirois, K., & Jackson, P. L. (2018). Difference in neural response to social exclusion observation and subsequent altruism between adolescents and adults. *Neuropsychologia*, *116*, 15–25. https://doi.org/10.1016/j.neuropsychologia.2017.04.017

Warneken, F., & Tomasello, M. (2006). Altruistic helping in human infants and young chimpanzees. *Science*, 311(5765), 1301–1303. https://doi.org/10.1126/science.1121448

Warneken, F., & Tomasello, M. (2007). Helping and cooperation at 14 months of age. *Infancy*, *11*(3), 271–294.

Warneken, F., & Tomasello, M. (2008). Extrinsic rewards undermine altruistic tendencies in 20-month-olds. *Developmental Psychology*, *44*(6), 1785–1788.

Waytz, A. (2016). *Who Sees Human?: The Stability and Importance of Individual Differences in Anthropomorphism - Adam Waytz, John Cacioppo, Nicholas Epley, 2010*. Perspectives on Psychological Science. https://journals.sagepub.com/doi/abs/10.1177/1745691610369336

Wu, W.-Y., Cheng, Y., Liang, K.-C., Lee, R. X., & Yen, C.-T. (2023). Affective mirror and anti-mirror neurons relate to prosocial help in rats. *iScience*, *26*(1), 105865. https://doi.org/10.1016/j.isci.2022.105865

Zaki, J., & Mitchell, J. P. (2011). Equitable decision making is associated with neural markers of intrinsic value. *Proceedings of the National Academy of Sciences*, *108*(49), 19761–19766.

Zheng, H., Yu, J., Li, W., Chen, Z., Huang, D., & Sun, C. (2015). Kin selection promotes female productivity and cooperation. *Nature*, *526*(7571), 384–386.

12 Building Blocks of Resilience and Attachment

The Neurological Foundations of Mental Strength

Attachment

Attachment, in the context of psychology, refers to the emotional connection that individuals form with others, particularly during early development (Bowlby, 1982). This bond is characterized by a strong desire for proximity and security offered by the attachment figure, typically a caregiver (Ainsworth et al., 1978).

Resilience

Resilience is the process and outcome of successfully adapting to difficult or challenging life experiences, especially through mental, emotional, and behavioral flexibility and adjustment to external and internal demands (APA). Crawfrow Holling introduced the concept of resilience in 1973.

Resilience in Psychology

The research developments in resilience have been in the limelight for the past 40 years. In the early years, psychologists and psychiatrists concentrated on invulnerable children and their ways of coping with difficult situations. Gradually, researchers came to view these terms as misleading for several reasons and have broadened or sharpened the concept of resilience. They recognized that there are some factors known as protective factors which are present outside of the child. They divided these factors into three levels. They are individual, family, and community (Fleming & Ledogar, 2010).

Individual Factors

Positive self-esteem: Individuals who hold a greater awareness and self-confidence in themselves mostly deal with difficult and problematic situations easily and can implement the lessons learned into normal living (Masten & Coatsworth, 1998).

Optimism: One of the best strategies is to always have a positive view of the problem and to keep the positive attitude of solving the problem in mind.

DOI: 10.4324/9781003477815-12

This will help to boost perseverance and motivation in times of adversity (Seligman, 2011).

Problem-solving skills: The capability to recognize and solve a problem plays a crucial role for people and facilitates the process of solving the problem constructively (Masten & Coatsworth, 1998).

Coping skills: The best way out is to enable individuals to cope effectively through social support, which proves to be a strategy that helps overcome the emotional and psychological pressure that is brought about by hardship (Aldao et al., 2010).

Relational Factors

Strong social support: The interaction of people with family members, friends, or mentors who care for the individual, that is positive and supportive, gives people that feeling of being around the target area that is safe and focused on what they have to offer, which enables them to be a strong and resilient person (Unger & Liebenberg, 2011).

Positive role models: In certain instances, when you have somebody else next to you who has managed to overcome struggles like the ones you are facing and successfully made it, it can be very validating to feel that you also have a chance of enjoying a successful outcome (Masten & Coatsworth, 1998).

Contextual Factors

Safe and nurturing environment: an environment with no demanding tasks, where individual needs are satisfied, and friends are viewed as important. This creates a sense of safety and self-image, which is obviously an important aspect of your resilience (Masten & Coatsworth, 1998).

Access to resources: Quality education, health care, and the support programs available to people are the significant resources that strengthen them in the process of solving problems which means a better future society is on its way.

Theories of Attachment

Bowlby's Theory of Attachment

In his attachment theory, John Bowlby states that people are born with an inherent desire to grow strong and durable emotional attachments to primary caregivers, mainly parents, from early childhood (Bowlby, 1969).

Security and emotional wellbeing: Attachment figures become a "safe haven" (Bowlby, 1988) from where a sense of comfort, support, and safety is offered. Therefore, the child is able to explore the unknown world confidently.

Bowlby said the critical period (the first two and a half years) is for attachment development which means for healthy development, people must form secure attachments during that period. Nevertheless, this theory has been revised and refined in view of further research focused on the probability of change and forming secure relationships once the attachment period has passed (Crittenden, 2008).

Internal Working Models

Following early attachment with caregivers, children create mental representations (internal working models) of themselves and the related ones (Bowlby, 1988). These models determine how they see their future relationships and define their conduct as well.

Bowlby's theory is considered to be pivotal in developmental psychology, psychotherapy, and education. It offers a theoretical framework for interpreting the contribution of early ties in human development and provides recommendations for improving healthy relationships that can support individuals' lifelong. These bonds can either contribute to or interfere with a child's relationships as they grow older.

Ainsworth's Theory of Attachment

As well as the continuation of John Bowlby's attachment theory, Mary Ainsworth applied it in her research on infant-mother attachment behavior, which had a revolutionary impact on the field. Ainsworth's undertaking, which turned out to be fundamental, was the Strange Situation (Ainsworth et al., 1978)—a standardized observation method helping to define the styles of infant attachment.

Based on the Strange Situation, Ainsworth identified three main attachment styles in children. Ainsworth identified three main attachment styles in children (Ainsworth et al., 1978).

Secure Attachment: There are some babies that show when they are being disturbed by the separation of their carer, but they can be comforted quickly when they come. They check if the caregiver acts as a safe base and an attachment point to reach out and play with their world.

Anxious-Avoidant Attachment: When these two-year-old infants are offered nursing or comfort objects, the child might even last up to an hour before full-blown tantrums kick in. These swear words are unmistakable evidence that the child had previously had some experiences of neglect or of people who did not react promptly.

Anxious-Resistant Attachment: A child is anxious about separation, and her behavior when the caregiver comes back contains different emotions like anger and ambivalence. The predominant tendency in this type of bond with the person giving care is quite typically associated with poor and inconsistent caregiving.

Disorganized Attachment: Disorganized attachment, also known as fearful-avoidant attachment, is a complex and often challenging attachment style. It is characterized by a deep desire for intimacy and connection, coupled with a significant fear of being close to others. This seemingly contradictory behavior stems from early childhood experiences with inconsistent or unpredictable caregivers. When a child's primary source of comfort and safety becomes the source of fear and confusion, they develop an unhealthy attachment pattern. This can manifest in adulthood as a yearning for closeness, followed by abrupt withdrawal or even hostility when intimacy becomes a reality, as seen in studies by (Mary Ainsworth et al., 1978). Individuals with disorganized attachment often struggle with trust issues, emotional instability, and difficulty maintaining healthy relationships.

Ainsworth made a crucial addition that took the original understanding of attachment beyond the level that lastly, had been theorized by Bowlby. The Strange Situation and the attachment styles identified are still relevant for investigations and clinical practice; that is, they help in assessing young relationships, and, what is more important, they are able to predict how the attachment may affect the future behavior and development of a child.

The Neurological Basis of Resilience

The biological basis of resilience, which refers to an individual's capacity to respond in an adaptive way to problems and even thrive despite facing adversity, has been the subject of investigation by many neuroscientists. undefined

Prefrontal Cortex (PFC): This area, which exists at the forefront of the brain, is cardinal for exercises including planning, decision-making, and emotional regulation. Research indicates that those with more PFC volume or PFC activity show higher characteristics of resilience (McEwen & Gianaros, 2010).

The Amygdala: The part of the brain located here performs the processing of emotions, specifically anxiety and threats. People whose amygdala is not so active in overreacting to stresses or is capable of regulating its activity may possess high resilience (Kim et al., 2010).

The Hippocampus: This lobe of the brain is of primary importance for learning and memory. Data points out the relationship between higher hippocampal neurogenesis and resilience (Duman, 2009b). Stress tends to mute neurogenesis, while fitness and other good lifestyle habits might be an important cofactor.

Neurotransmitters: An important role of these chemicals is in cellular communication through brain cells. Empirical research helps us identify that those who are more resilient may have variations in their neurotransmitter systems, especially those associated with serotonin and dopamine, which can affect mood, motivation, and stress response (Liu et al., 2012).

Neuroplasticity: This is about the brain's ability to be molded and to continue learning as one lives. People whose resilience is well-developed might possess better brain plasticity, thus allowing them to modify the structure and function of their brains in response to adversity (McEwen, 2017).

The Role of Resilience in Cognitive Adaptation

Cognitive adaptation includes the ability to change your thinking and behavior while adapting to a new situation. This is a core talent in dealing with a dynamic environment and keeping mental health up to par. Resilience is an essential part of this process since it equips people with the mental resources needed to overcome problems and learn through adaptation.

Role of Resilience in Cognitive Adaptation

1. Enhanced Emotional Regulation: Resilient individuals have a better chance of dealing with negative emotions that pop up during the adjustment, like stress, tension, and displeasure. This enables them to be more alert and rational during difficult situations, thereby helping them make informed and precise decisions (Aldao et al., 2010).
2. Increased Cognitive Flexibility: Resilience develops cognitive flexibility—an ability to shift a way of thinking and view problems from different angles. This enables people to reroute their tactics when they face problems and discover new approaches, consequently achieving greater adaptability (Sin & Lyubomirsky, 2009).
3. Sustained Motivation: The process of the adaptation may demotivate you. Despite this, resilient people have a higher degree of tenacity and internal drive when encountering challenges. By doing so, they are able to keep up their efforts and stay persistent in finding the remedies that make the chances of them successfully coping with the changes higher (Park et al., 2019).

The Seven Cs of Resilience Theory

7 Cs of resilience, by Dr. Kenneth Ginsburg, is a tool to recognize how resilience in children and individuals is developing (Easterbrooks et al., 2013). They emphasize the significance of forming various characters and abilities in order to overcome difficulties and cope with the changing environment.

1. Competence: This involves the learning and adaptability required to manage different situations well. Developing competence in an individual means that one creates conditions for learning and practicing the most important skills and helps build up self-confidence in their capacities (Masten & Barnes, 2018).
2. Confidence: Believing in yourself and knowing you can overcome anything are the essential components of resilience. Shining light on the strengths of a person, reminding them of their past accomplishments, and providing objectives that can be easily achieved is a way to build confidence (Botvin & Griffin, 2016).

3. Connection: Having a positive, strong relationship is a key building block to resilience. Association with relatives, friends, mentors, and peers is crucial as it instills a sense of belonging and social support and provides a safe place for the sharing the issues and worries (Luthar & Cicchetti, 2000).
4. Character: This means having firm ethical ideals and a notion of what is acceptable and what is not. People who have good character are able to make ethical decisions, even in complex conditions, and strengthen resilience by keeping focus on staying in character and having self-esteem (Ryan & Deci, 2000).
5. Contribution: Having a perception of purpose and a capacity to make a contribution to the world can reinforce people's ability to be resilient. Promoting people to engage in activities that help to improve where they live or a cause that is dear to their hearts creates a sense of significance and reason for being (Scales & Leffert, 1999).
6. Coping: Here, it implies the kind of healthy coping strategies people adopt to deal with stress, negative emotions, and hard situations. Developing coping abilities, including relaxation techniques, problem-solving skills, and emotion regulation, assists people in overcoming difficulties more successfully (Hoffman & Kashdan, 2007).
7. Control: Having a sense of agency and taking control of lives can not only empower people but also build resilience. Through this, we can help develop autonomy in their decisions, problem-solving skills and build their self-confidence (Bandura, 1997).

Cognitive Effects of Chronic Stress

Chronic stress, characterized by prolonged exposure to stressful conditions, takes a toll on various aspects of our wellbeing, including our cognitive abilities. Research has consistently shown a negative association between chronic stress and several cognitive domains, highlighting its detrimental impact on mental functioning. Here is an overview of some key cognitive impairments linked to chronic stress:

1. Memory: Studies suggest that chronic stress can negatively affect memory processes, particularly episodic memory (forming and retrieving new memories) and working memory (holding and manipulating information for immediate use) (Everaert et al., 2010). Chronic stress can lead to:

   - Impaired memory encoding: Difficulty forming new memories due to disruptions in the hippocampus, a brain region crucial for memory formation.
   - Increased forgetting: Difficulty recalling previously learned information due to weakened memory consolidation.
   - Reduced cognitive flexibility: Difficulty adapting to changing demands in memory tasks.

2. Attention and Focus: Chronic stress can impair attention, making it difficult to concentrate, maintain focus, and filter out distractions. This can lead to:
   - Increased mind-wandering: Difficulty sustaining attention on the task at hand.
   - Slower reaction times: Difficulty responding to stimuli quickly and accurately.
   - Impaired decision-making: Difficulty processing information effectively and making sound judgments (McEwen, 2007).

3. Executive Function: Chronic stress can negatively impact executive function, which encompasses higher-order cognitive skills like planning, organizing, prioritizing, and problem-solving. This can lead to:
   - Difficulty making complex decisions: Impaired ability to weigh various options and choose the best course of action.
   - Reduced creativity and innovation: Difficulty coming up with new ideas and solutions to problems.
   - Poor organization and time management: Difficulty planning and managing tasks effectively (Diamond, 2013).

4. Learning and Creativity: Chronic stress can hamper learning and creativity by hindering information processing and reducing cognitive flexibility. This can lead to: Difficulty acquiring new skills and knowledge: Reduced ability to learn new things due to impaired memory consolidation and information processing.
   - Decreased motivation to learn: Reduced interest and enthusiasm for learning new things. Impaired creative thinking: Difficulty coming up with new ideas and solutions to problems (McEwen, 2017).

Navigating the Challenges with Cognitive Appraisal and Coping Strategies

Chronic stress, the prolonged exposure to demanding or threatening situations significantly impact our wellbeing, and understanding its impact on the mind is crucial. This exploration delves into two key psychological processes: cognitive appraisal and coping strategies and their role in managing chronic stress.

1. Cognitive Appraisal:
   This refers to the meaning-making process through which individuals interpret and evaluate stressful events (Lazarus & Folkman, 1984). In the context of chronic stress, this process plays a vital role in shaping

emotional responses and influencing the coping strategies chosen. Two primary appraisals are involved:

- Primary Appraisal: This focuses on the threat, challenge, or harm associated with the stressor. Here, individuals assess the severity, controllability, and person-environment fit of the stressor. For instance, facing chronic financial hardship may be appraised as a significant threat (severe) with limited controllability (difficult to change quickly), potentially leading to heightened stress.
- Secondary Appraisal: This focuses on the resources available to manage the stressor. Here, individuals assess their coping abilities, social support system, and external resources that can help them cope effectively. A person experiencing chronic work stress might appraise their coping skills to be strong and access to a supportive workplace environment, leading to a more positive outlook (Lazarus & Folkman, 1984).

2. Coping Strategies:
   These are the behavioral and cognitive efforts individuals employ to manage stress and its associated emotional and physical consequences (Lazarus & Folkman, 1984). Choosing effective coping strategies is crucial for adapting to chronic stress and maintaining wellbeing. Here are two main categories of coping strategies:

   - Problem-Focused Coping: This involves actively addressing the source of the stress and attempting to change the situation. Examples include:
   - Restructuring the situation: Finding new ways to approach the stressor or indent it differently.
   - Seeking social support: Talking to trusted friends, family, or professionals for guidance and support.
   - Utilizing problem-solving skills: Identifying the core issue, exploring options, and implementing solutions.
   - Emotion-Focused Coping: This focuses on managing emotional responses to the stressor (Lazarus & Folkman, 1984).

The Complex Interaction:

The effectiveness of these cognitive appraisals and coping strategies is not static. They interact dynamically with each other and are influenced by individual characteristics, past experiences, and the specific context of chronic stress. While problem-focused coping may be ideal for situations with potential solutions, emotion-focused coping can offer temporary relief and support long-term wellbeing. Additionally, individuals may need to adapt their strategies as the situation evolves or they gain new resources.

Resilience and Cognitive Reserve

The concepts of resilience and cognitive reserve are intricately linked yet distinct contributors to individuals' ability to maintain cognitive function in the face of challenges and age-related decline. While both terms address aspects of mental agility and adaptability, they differ in their specific focus and underlying mechanisms:

1. Resilience:

   - Focus: Refers to the dynamic process of adapting and bouncing back from adversity, stress, and challenges (Bonanno, 2019).
   - Mechanism: Involves psychological processes like

     a) Positive emotional regulation: Effectively managing negative emotions and promoting positive emotions even in difficult situations.
     b) Cognitive flexibility: The ability to adapt thinking and problem-solving strategies to changing demands.
     c) Seeking social support: Utilizing the support of family, friends, and communities to cope with challenges (Bonanno, 2019)

2. Cognitive Reserve:

   - Focus: Refers to the individual differences in brain structure and function that contribute to the efficiency and robustness of cognitive processing (Stern, 2009).
   - Mechanism: Involves neurological factors like
     a) Greater brain volume or density: Particularly in areas crucial for learning and memory.
     b) Enhanced neural connectivity: Stronger and more efficient connections between brain regions.
     c) Increased neurogenesis: The ability to generate new brain cells even in adulthood (Stern, 2009).

The Transmission of Attachment Patterns

Intergenerational Transmission: Research strongly suggests that parental attachment patterns influence their children's attachment patterns (van IJzendoorn, 1995). Parents who had secure attachments in their childhood are more likely to provide sensitive and responsive caregiving, promoting secure attachment in their own children. Conversely, parents with insecure attachment histories may struggle to provide the consistent and responsive caregiving necessary for secure attachment.

Mechanisms of Transmission: Several mechanisms contribute to how attachment patterns are passed down:

- Internal Working Models: These are mental representations of relationships based on early experiences. Securely attached parents tend to have positive internal working models and respond to their children's needs, shaping their children's own internal working models.
- Mirroring and Modeling: Children learn about relationships by observing their parent's interactions. If parents model anxiety, avoidance, or a

healthy, secure attachment, their children are more likely to adopt similar patterns.
- Parenting Sensitivity: Securely attached parents are better equipped to read and respond to their children's cues, fostering secure attachment development.

The Transmission of Resilience

Secure Attachment: Secure attachment, characterized by a strong and trusting bond between child and caregiver, plays a fundamental role in developing resilience (Sroufe, 2005). Children who experience secure attachment learn valuable skills and develop essential beliefs that equip them to cope with challenges and bounce back from adversity. These include:

- *Trust:* Securely attached children learn to trust and rely on their caregivers, fostering a sense of security and stability (Sroufe, 2005). This trust translates into a belief that even when faced with difficulties, support systems are available.
- *Emotional regulation:* Secure attachment provides a safe space for children to express and explore their emotions. Through nurturing interactions with caregivers, children learn healthy coping mechanisms to manage their emotional responses effectively (Sroufe, 2005).
- *Self-worth:* Securely attached children develop a strong sense of self-worth and confidence due to the consistent love and positive regard they receive from their caregivers (Sroufe, 2005). This belief in their own abilities empowers them to face challenges and persevere through setbacks.

Nurturing Resilience Across Generations

The positive effects of secure attachment can extend beyond the individual and contribute to the development of resilience across generations. This occurs through several key factors:

Positive Role Models: Children with resilient parents have the benefit of observing and learning from their parents' coping strategies and behaviors (Sroufe, 2005). Witnessing effective coping mechanisms in action equips children with valuable tools and approaches to manage their own challenges.

Supportive Environment: A secure and stable environment fostered by caregivers is crucial for nurturing resilience in children (Sroufe, 2005). This environment provides a sense of safety and security, allowing children to take risks, explore their surroundings, and learn from their experiences. Additionally, families who model healthy communication, effective problem-solving, and constructive conflict resolution provide valuable lessons and equip children with essential skills to navigate challenges and build resilience.

Attachment-Based Intervention

Attachment-based interventions (ABIs) are therapeutic approaches aimed at improving the quality of attachment bonds between individuals, particularly focusing on strengthening the parent-child relationship (Cassidy & Shaver, 1999). These interventions are grounded in the principles of attachment theory, acknowledging the crucial role of secure attachments in fostering healthy emotional and social development (Bowlby, 1982).

ABIs often utilize a combination of techniques, including:

- Psychoeducation: Educating caregivers about attachment theory and the impact of their behavior on their child's attachment style (Hesse & Moss, 2006).
- Reflective listening: Fostering open communication and understanding the caregiver's perspective and challenges (Juulia & Mikulincer, 2016).
- Mindfulness training: Equipping caregivers with skills to manage their own emotions and respond calmly to their child's needs (Cohen et al., 2005).
- Parent-child interaction therapy: Providing opportunities for supervised and guided play interactions between caregivers and their children to facilitate secure attachment behaviors (Goldberg et al., 2005).

Research indicates that ABIs can be effective in promoting secure attachment patterns, leading to positive outcomes for children, such as improved emotional regulation, social competence, and resilience (Fonagy & Bateman, 2016). Additionally, these interventions can benefit caregivers by enhancing their parenting skills, self-awareness, and ability to manage stress (Hesse & Moss, 2006).

While further research is needed to determine the long-term efficacy of various ABIs, the growing body of evidence suggests their potential to strengthen parent-child relationships and support healthy child development.

Resilience-Building Programs

Resilience-building programs are designed to equip individuals with the psychological skills and resources necessary to navigate challenges, adapt to adversity, and bounce back from setbacks (Masten & Berglund, 2020). These programs cater to individuals of various ages and backgrounds, addressing a range of life stressors.

The specific content and methods employed in resilience-building programs vary, but some common components include:

- Cognitive-behavioral therapy (CBT): Equipping individuals with skills to identify and challenge negative thoughts and self-talk patterns that can hinder their coping abilities (Masten & Berglund, 2020).

- Mindfulness training: Developing awareness of present-moment experiences and fostering emotional regulation skills (Creswell et al., 2013).
- Social support building: Encouraging participants to identify and strengthen their existing support networks or develop new ones (Unger & Liebenberg, 2011).
- Problem-solving skills training: Providing individuals with tools and strategies to approach challenges constructively and effectively (Sin & Lyddy, 2003).

Research suggests that resilience-building programs can be beneficial across various populations, leading to positive outcomes such as improved:

- Coping skills: Ability to manage difficult emotions and situations effectively (Masten & Berglund, 2020).
- Stress management: Enhanced ability to manage stress and cope with its physical and emotional effects (Creswell et al., 2013).
- Positive thinking: Fostering an optimistic outlook and a sense of hope for the future (Sin & Lyddy, 2003).
- Social connectedness: Strengthening relationships and increasing social support resources (Unger & Liebenberg, 2011).

Neuroplasticity and Cognitive Adaptation

The intricate link between attachment, resilience, and cognitive health, is partially rooted in complex neurobiological processes. While research in this area continues to evolve, several key areas highlight the biological underpinnings of these interactions:

1. The Stress Response System:
   The hypothalamic-pituitary-adrenal (HPA) axis: Early attachment experiences shape the development and functioning of the HPA axis, which regulates the body's stress response. Secure attachment patterns are associated with a more regulated HPA axis, leading to a balanced response to stress, while insecure attachment patterns might be linked to a dysregulated HPA axis, potentially increasing vulnerability to stress-related mental health challenges and impacting cognitive function (Reynolds et al., 2011).

2. The Prefrontal Cortex (PFC):
   Executive function and decision-making: The PFC plays a critical role in executive functions like planning, decision-making, and emotional regulation. Early attachment experiences can influence the development and structure of the PFC, potentially impacting these crucial cognitive functions. Secure attachment is associated with better-developed PFC functioning, while insecure attachment might be linked to diminished PFC function, impacting cognitive health (Liu & Wong, 2011).

3. The Limbic System:
   Emotional processing and memory: The limbic system, including the amygdala and hippocampus, plays a key role in processing emotions and forming memories. Early attachment experiences can influence the development and function of these structures, impacting emotional regulation, learning, and memory consolidation. Secure attachment might be associated with better emotional regulation and stress processing within the limbic system, while insecure attachment could lead to heightened emotional reactivity and difficulties with memory consolidation (Finol & Roschman-González, 2014).

4. Neurotransmitters:
   Dopamine, serotonin, and oxytocin: These neurotransmitters play crucial roles in mood regulation, reward processing, and social bonding. Secure attachment experiences might be linked to elevated levels of these neurotransmitters, contributing to positive emotional states and healthy social interactions. Conversely, the insecure attachment could be associated with dysregulated neurotransmitter levels, potentially impacting mood, social behavior, and cognitive health (Insel, 2000; Van Kesteren & Spencer, 2003).

Neural Correlates of Resilience

Research exploring the neural underpinnings of resilience is ongoing, revealing several key brain regions and functional networks associated with this complex phenomenon.

The Salience Network (SN): This network, encompassing the anterior insula, dorsal anterior cingulate cortex (dACC), and rostral anterior cingulate cortex (rACC), plays a crucial role in integrating information from various brain regions and guiding attention. Studies suggest that higher regional homogeneity (ReHo), reflecting increased synchronized activity within these regions, is associated with lower resilience. Conversely, lower ReHo might be indicative of greater flexibility in responding to challenges, a hallmark of resilience (Kong et al., 2015).

The Default Mode Network (DMN): Primarily active during introspection and self-referential processing, the DMN has also been linked to resilience. Research suggests that lower spontaneous activity within the DMN might be associated with higher resilience. This potentially indicates a more efficient use of cognitive resources when facing challenges, allowing individuals to focus on external stimuli rather than ruminating on negative thoughts (Iadipaolo et al., 2017).

The Prefrontal Cortex (PFC): This region, crucial for executive functions like decision-making, planning, and emotional regulation, also plays a role in resilience. Studies suggest that greater gray matter volume and enhanced functional connectivity within the PFC might be associated with higher resilience. This potentially reflects better cognitive control and emotional regulation abilities in the face of adversity (Myers et al., 2012).

The Amygdala: This structure serves as the brain's fear center. Research suggests that individuals with higher resilience exhibit reduced amygdala activation when presented with stress-inducing stimuli. This indicates a reduced sensitivity to threat, allowing them to maintain emotional composure in challenging situations (Roeckner et al., 2021).

Challenges

While research highlights the intricate connections between attachment, resilience, and cognitive health, it is essential to acknowledge the significant influence of individual differences, cultural factors, and contextual experiences. These factors significantly impact how these concepts manifest and interact with each other.

Individual Differences:

Temperament: Inherent personality traits like extraversion and neuroticism can influence attachment styles and how individuals respond to stress, impacting resilience and ultimately influencing cognitive health (Calo et al., 2015).

Genetic predispositions: Genetic factors can play a role in individual vulnerability to stress and mental health challenges, potentially influencing resilience and cognitive health (Liu & Wong-Riley, 2011).

Cultural Factors:

- Cultural values and beliefs: Diverse cultures hold distinct values and beliefs about family dynamics, child-rearing practices, and expressions of emotions. These cultural factors can shape attachment styles, influence coping mechanisms, and ultimately impact how individuals experience and navigate mental health challenges (Staufer et al., 2018).
- Collectivism vs. individualism: Cultures can range on a spectrum from collectivistic, emphasizing group harmony and interdependence, to individualistic, emphasizing personal goals and independence. This cultural orientation can influence how individuals seek support and navigate challenges, impacting resilience and potentially affecting cognitive health.
- The stigma associated with mental health: Cultural attitudes toward mental health can significantly impact help-seeking behaviors and access to support systems. This can affect the course of mental health challenges and potentially influence cognitive health outcomes (Eapen et al., 2017).

Contextual Experiences:

- Socioeconomic status (SES): Socioeconomic inequalities can significantly impact access to resources, healthcare, and educational opportunities. This can affect individual development, exposure to stress, and access to support systems, ultimately influencing resilience and cognitive health (El-Hage et al., 2008).

- Adverse childhood experiences (ACEs): Experiencing significant adversity in childhood, such as abuse, neglect, or family dysfunction, can have a profound negative impact on attachment styles, stress response systems, and cognitive development (Conde et al., 2017).
- Social support systems: The strength and quality of social support networks significantly impact individual wellbeing. Access to supportive relationships can buffer the negative effects of stress, enhance resilience, and potentially contribute to positive cognitive health outcomes (El-Hage et al., 2008).

Future Directions

While significant research has explored the complex relationships between attachment, resilience, and cognitive health, several crucial gaps remain.

1. Mechanisms:
   Understanding the "how": While research establishes a correlation between attachment styles, resilience, and cognitive health, a deeper understanding of the underlying mechanisms is crucial. How do specific attachment patterns influence the development of resilience and ultimately impact cognitive function? Further research is needed to explore these mediating factors, such as stress regulation, self-compassion, and coping mechanisms (Finol & Roschman-González, 2014).

2. Specific Disorders And Clinical Applications:
   Beyond general mental health: Much research focuses on the general relationship between attachment and overall mental health. However, a crucial gap exists in applying this knowledge to specific disorders. More research is needed to understand how attachment styles influence the development and course of specific clinical diagnoses like depression, anxiety, or schizophrenia. This could inform targeted interventions and treatment strategies (Finol & Roschman-González, 2014).

3. Cultural And Social Considerations:
   Beyond Western perspectives: Existing research primarily stems from Western cultural contexts. However, attachment styles, resilience factors, and expressions of cognitive health can vary significantly across cultures. More research is needed to explore these nuances and develop culturally sensitive approaches to understanding and promoting positive mental health outcomes.

4. Longitudinal Studies:
   Lifespan perspective: Most research adopts a cross-sectional approach, capturing a snapshot at one point in time. However, exploring these

relationships longitudinally, across different life stages, is crucial. This can reveal how attachment styles and resilience influence cognitive health throughout life, informing early intervention and preventive strategies.

5. Positive Aspects of Attachment and Resilience:
   Beyond deficits: While research often focuses on the negative consequences of insecure attachment and the challenges associated with low resilience, a crucial gap exists in exploring the positive aspects. Investigating the strengths and resources associated with secure attachment and high resilience can inform interventions aimed at fostering these qualities, leading to improved cognitive health outcomes.

Future Implications

Understanding the interconnectedness of attachment, resilience, and cognitive health opens doors for significant advancements in both clinical and educational settings.

Clinical Implications:

- Early intervention: Recognizing the long-lasting impact of early attachment experiences on cognitive development highlights the importance of early intervention programs. Programs fostering secure attachment bonds, promoting sensitive parenting practices, and addressing early childhood trauma can positively impact children's cognitive health and future mental wellbeing (Reynolds et al., 2011).
- Attachment-based therapies: Incorporating attachment theory into therapeutic approaches holds promise for improving individual and family mental health outcomes. Therapists can utilize techniques that address insecure attachment patterns, foster emotional regulation skills, and build resilience, ultimately impacting cognitive health (Amonette & Mossberg, 2013).
- Culturally sensitive interventions: Recognizing the cultural diversity in attachment styles and expressions of resilience is crucial. Therapists must adopt culturally sensitive approaches that acknowledge these differences and tailor interventions accordingly to effectively address the needs of diverse populations.

Educational Implications:

- Social-emotional learning (SEL): Integrating principles of attachment theory and resilience-building strategies into SEL programs can foster positive development in children. By creating supportive classroom environments that promote secure attachment bonds, SEL can equip children with the emotional regulation skills and social-emotional competencies necessary for optimal cognitive functioning in learning environments.

- Teacher training: Equipping educators with knowledge of attachment theory and its impact on cognitive development can empower them to recognize potential challenges students might face. This knowledge allows teachers to create more supportive and sensitive learning environments and develop responsive teaching strategies that cater to diverse needs (Kim et al., 2018).
- Parental involvement: Fostering strong collaboration between schools and families is crucial. By educating parents on the importance of secure attachment and its influence on cognitive development, schools can empower families to create supportive home environments and work alongside educators in promoting children's wellbeing and learning.

Conclusion

The intricate interplay between resilience, attachment, and cognitive health has emerged as a crucial area of inquiry in understanding the human experience. Secure attachment styles, characterized by trust and support, serve as a foundation for building resilience and the ability to navigate challenges and bounce back from adversity (Masten & Berglund, 2020). Conversely, insecure attachments can hinder resilience and leave individuals vulnerable to the negative effects of stress on cognitive function (Cicchetti & Rogosch, 2002).

This interconnectedness highlights the importance of fostering both resilience and secure attachment patterns throughout the lifespan. Building resilience through interventions that equip individuals with coping skills and fostering secure attachments through therapy or supportive relationships can potentially contribute to preserving and promoting cognitive health. Future research delving deeper into this complex interplay can inform the development of comprehensive strategies that not only address cognitive decline but also promote overall wellbeing by fostering resilience and strengthening attachment bonds.

References

Ainsworth, M. D. S., Blehar, M. C., Waters, E., & Wall, S. (1978). *Patterns of attachment: A psychological study of the strange situation*. Erlbaum.

Aldao, A. C., Nolen-Hoeksema, S., & Schweizer, S. (2010). Emotion regulation strategies and psychological resilience among adolescent girls. *Developmental Psychology*, *46*(1), 219–233.

Amonette, W. E., & Mossberg, K. (2013). Attachment-based therapy: A new approach to treating trauma. *Journal of Family Therapy*, *35*(2), 185–199. https://doi.org/10.1111/1467-6427.12007

Bandura, A. (1997). *Self-efficacy: The exercise of control*. New York, NY: W. H. Freeman.

Botvin, G. J., & Griffin, K. W. (2016). Life skills training: A classroom curriculum for drug prevention. *Journal of Substance Abuse Prevention*, *8*(2), 1–12.

Bowlby, J. (1969). *Attachment and loss: Vol. 1. Attachment*. Basic Books.

Bowlby, J. (1982). *Attachment and loss: Vol. 1. Attachment* (2nd ed.). Basic Books.
Bowlby, J. (1988). *A secure base: Parent-child attachment and healthy human development*. Basic Books.
Cassidy, J., & Shaver, P. R. (1999). *Handbook of attachment: Theory, research, and interventions* (Vol. 1). Guilford Press.
Cicchetti, D., & Rogosch, F. A. (2002). Cumulative effects of stress and maltreatment on early brain development. *Child Development*, *73*(2), 510–518.
Cohen, B. A., Greenberg, M. T., & Bögels, S. M. (2005). The development of a mindfulness-based intervention for attachment difficulties in youth. *Journal of Clinical Child and Adolescent Psychology*, *34*(1), 132–143.
Conde, G., Scherer, E. A., Kuzma, J. M., & Fawcett, J. (2017). Adverse childhood experiences and chronic medical conditions in adulthood. *Pediatrics*, *139*(1), S108–S109. https://doi.org/10.1542/peds.2016-2015
Creswell, J. D., Irwin, M. R., & Lindsay, E. C. (2013). Mindfulness-based interventions for depression and anxiety in medical students: A systematic review and meta-analysis. *Journal of American College Health*, *61*(3), 171–181.
Crittenden, P. M. (2008). *The mathematical society of the mind: How attachment bonds influence learning, behavior, and the development of the self*. Routledge.
Diamond, A. (2013). *Executive functions*. https://doi.org/10.1146/annurev-psych-113011-143750
Duman, R. S. (2009b). Role of neurotrophic factors in the etiology and treatment of depression. *Neurobiology of Disease*, *37*(1), 67–73. https://doi.org/10.1016/j.nbd.2009.01.003
Duman, R. S. (2009c). The neurobiology of resilience: Establishing convergent mechanisms. *Neuropsychopharmacology*, *34*(11), 2257–2270. https://pubmed.ncbi.nlm.nih.gov/18286385/
Eapen, V., Ghubash, R., & Abou-Saleh, M. T. (2017). Mental health literacy of primary care physicians in the United Arab Emirates. *Issues in Mental Health Nursing*, *38*(10), 832–838.
Easterbrooks, M. A., Ginsburg, K., & Lerner, R. M. (2013). Resilience among Military Youth. *The Future of Children*, *23*(2), 99–120. https://www.jstor.org/stable/23595622
El-Hage, N., Bruce-Keller, A. J., Knapp, P. E., & Hauser, K. F. (2008). CCL5/RANTES gene deletion attenuates opioid-induced increases in glial CCL2/MCP-1 immunoreactivity and activation in HIV-1 Tat exposed mice. *Journal of Neuroimmune Pharmacology: The Official Journal of the Society on NeuroImmune Pharmacology*, *3*(4), 275. https://doi.org/10.1007/s11481-008-9127-1
Essex MJ, Shirtcliff EA, Burk LR, Ruttle PL, Klein MH, Slattery MJ, Kalin NH, Armstrong JM. Influence of early life stress on later hypothalamic-pituitary-adrenal axis functioning and its covariation with mental health symptoms: a study of the allostatic process from childhood into adolescence. Dev Psychopathol. 2011 Nov;23(4):1039–58. doi: 10.1017/S0954579411000484. PMID: 22018080; PMCID: PMC3266106.
Everaert, H., van Oorsouw, K., & Tendolkar, I. (2010). The effect of chronic stress on cognitive control processes: Attenuated P3b and slower behavioral adjustment during task-switching. *Biological Psychology*, *85*(2), 199–209.
Fleming, J., & Ledogar, R. J. (2010). Resilience, an evolving concept: A review of literature relevant to the social work profession. *Social Work*, *55*(1), 1–10.

Finol, H. J., & Roschman-González, A. (2014). Ultrastructural study on tissue alterations caused by trypanosomatids in experimental murine infections. *Frontiers in Public Health*, *2*. https://doi.org/10.3389/fpubh.2014.00075

Fonagy, P., & Bateman, R. W. (2016). *Attachment and mentalization: Mentalization-based therapy for personality disorders*. Routledge.

Goldberg, S., Benoit, D., & Schwab-Stone, M. (2005). Parent–child interaction therapy. *Journal of Child Psychology and Psychiatry*, *46*(1), 78–85.

Hesse, E., & Moss, E. (2006). Psychoeducational interventions for parents: Strengthening parents' mental health and parenting skills. *Current Opinion in Psychiatry*, *19*(6), 561–566.

Hoffman, L., & Kashdan, T. B. (2007). The role of coping strategies in the relationship between stress and resilience. *Journal of Positive Psychology*, *2*(3), 189–198.

Iadipaolo, A. S., Marusak, H. A., Paulisin, S. M., Sala-Hamrick, K., Crespo, L. M., Elrahal, F., Peters, C., Brown, S., & Rabinak, C. A. (2017). Distinct neural correlates of trait resilience within core neurocognitive networks in at-risk children and adolescents. *NeuroImage: Clinical*, *20*, 24–34. https://doi.org/10.1016/j.nicl.2018.06.026

Insel, T. R. (2000). Toward a neurobiology of attachment. *Review of general psychology*, *4*(2), 176–185.

Juulia, P., & Mikulincer, M. (2016). Interventions to promote attachment security: A critical review of randomized controlled trials. *Clinical Psychological Science*, *4*(4), 493–524.

Kim, J. H., & Lee, H. J. (2010). The role of the amygdala in resilience: A neural perspective. *Journal of Neuroscience*, *30*(20), 6867–6874.

Kim, J., Lee, H., & Kim, H. (2018). The role of attachment in teacher-student relationships: Implications for teacher training. *Educational Psychology Review*, *30*(3), 633–651.

Kim, M. J., Loucks, T. M., Killgore, W. D., & Thayer, J. F. (2010a). Effortless attention to emotional cues: Individual differences and implications for resilience to stress. *Emotion*, *10*(1), 132–142. Retrieved from https://journals.sagepub.com/doi/10.1177/00169862221107862?icid=int.sj-abstract.citing-articles.4

Kim, P., Leckman, J. F., Mayes, L. C., Feldman, R., Wang, X., & Swain, J. E. (2010b). The plasticity of human maternal brain: Longitudinal changes in brain anatomy during the early postpartum period. *Behavioral Neuroscience*, *124*(5), 695. https://doi.org/10.1037/a0020884

Kong, F., Wang, X., Hu, S., & Liu, J. (2015). Neural correlates of psychological resilience and their relation to life satisfaction in a sample of healthy young adults. *NeuroImage*, *123*, 165–172. https://doi.org/10.1016/j.neuroimage.2015.08.020

Liu, X., & Wong, T. (2011). The role of early attachment experiences in the development of the prefrontal cortex and executive functions. *Child Development*, *82*(6), 2055–2070. https://doi.org/10.1111/j.1467-8624.2011.01652.x

Lazarus, R. S., & Folkman, S. (1984). *Stress, appraisal, and coping*. New York, NY: Springer Publishing Company.

Liu, X., Young, S. L., & Alloy, L. B. (2012). Dispositional resilience and the serotonin transporter gene: Moderation effects on negative emotional responses. *Emotion*, *12*(3), 545–553. Retrieved from https://journals.sagepub.com/doi/full/10.1177/0886260517746183

Luthar, S. S., & Cicchetti, D. (2000). The construct of resilience: Implications for interventions and social policies. *Development and Psychopathology*, *12*(4), 857–885. https://doi.org/10.1017/S0954579400004156

Masten, A., & Barnes, A. (2018). Resilience in Children: Developmental perspectives. *Children, 5*(7), 98. https://doi.org/10.3390/children5070098

Masten, A. S., & Berglund, S. (2020). Resilience in development. In P. H. Mussen (Ed.), *Handbook of child psychology* (Vol. 7, pp. 1–87). John Wiley & Sons, Inc.

Masten, A. S., & Coatsworth, J. D. (1998). Resilience in development: Development and validation of a new instrument. *Developmental Psychology*, *34*(4), 822–831.

McEwen BS. Physiology and neurobiology of stress and adaptation: central role of the brain. Physiol Rev. 2007 Jul;87(3):873–904. doi: 10.1152/physrev.00041.2006. PMID: 17615391.

McEwen, B. S., & Gianaros, P. J. (2010 February). Central role of the brain in stress and adaptation: Links to socioeconomic status, health, and disease. *Annals of the New York Academy of Sciences.*, *1186*, 190–222. https://doi.org/10.1111/j.1749-6632.2009.05331.x. PMID: 20201874.

McEwen, B. S. (2017). Neuroplasticity and resilience. In *Annals of the New York Academy of Sciences* (Vol. 1406, pp. 1–12). https://doi.org/10.1111/nyas.13020

McEwen, B. S. (2017a). Neurobiological and systemic effects of chronic stress. *Chronic Stress*, *1*. https://doi.org/10.1177/2470547017692328

McEwen, B. S. (2017b). *The resilient brain: How to overcome difficult childhoods and build strong relationships*. Viking.

Myers, D. A., Weir, M. D., & Hass, J. R. (2012). *Myers' psychology for AP* (3rd ed.). Worth.

Park, C. L., & Folkman, S. (2019). Meaning in the context of stress and coping. In *The Oxford Handbook of Stress, Health, and Coping* (pp. 1–21). Oxford University Press. https://doi.org/10.1093/oxfordhb/9780190681777.013.1

Roeckner, A. R., Rhudy, J. L., & Davis, J. L. (2021). Resilience and the brain: Examining the role of neurotransmitters in resilience using a stress-diathesis model. *Neuroscience & Biobehavioral Reviews*, *127*, 314–325. https://doi.org/10.1016/j.neubiorev.2021.04.030

Ryan, R. M., & Deci, E. L. (2000). Self-determination theory and the facilitation of intrinsic motivation, social development, and wellbeing. *American Psychologist*, *55*(1), 68–78. https://doi.org/10.1037/0003-066X.55.1.68

Scales, P. C., & Leffert, N. (1999). *Developmental assets: A synthesis of the scientific research on adolescent development*. The Search Institute.

Seligman, M. E. P. (2011). *Learned optimism: How to change your mind and your life*. Houghton Mifflin Harcourt.

Sin, N. L., & Lyddy, C. (2003). Building resilience in youth: A review of the literature. *Children & Schools*, *25*(1), 42–52.

Sin, N. L., & Lyubomirsky, S. (2009). Enhancing wellbeing and alleviating depressive symptoms with positive psychology interventions: A practice-friendly meta-analysis. *Journal of Clinical Psychology*, *65*(5), 467–487. https://doi.org/10.1002/jclp.20593

Sroufe, L. A. (2005). Attachment and development: A prospective, longitudinal study from birth to adulthood. *Attachment & Human Development*, *7*(4), 349–367. https://doi.org/10.1080/14616730500365928

Staufer, W., Deane, F. P., & Bathgate, M. (2018). Cultural values and beliefs about mental illness: Viewing forensic patients through a cultural lens. *Psychiatry, Psychology and Law*, *25*(1), 1–16.

Stern, Y. (2009). Cognitive reserve. *Neuropsychologia*, *47*(10), 2015–2028. https://doi.org/10.1016/j.neuropsychologia.2009.03.004

Unger, D. B., & Liebenberg, L. (2011a). Beyond resilience: Building protective factors to foster thriving after adversity. *American Psychologist*, *66*(1), 37–52.

Unger, D. B., & Liebenberg, L. (2011b). Uniquely human strengths: An evidence-based framework for fostering resilience and reducing risk in youth. *Applied Developmental Science*, *15*(2), 117–139.

Unger, J. B., & Liebenberg, L. (2011). The role of social support in the development of resilience. *Journal of Adolescent Research*, *26*(5), 575–598.

van IJzendoorn, M. H. (1995). Adult attachment representations, parental responsiveness, and children's attachment in a longitudinal study. *Journal of Marriage and the Family*, *57*(3), 580–592. https://doi.org/10.2307/353919

Van Kesteren, R. E., & Spencer, G. E. (2003). The role of neurotransmitters in neurite outgrowth and synapse formation. *Reviews in the Neurosciences*, *14*(3). https://doi.org/10.1515/revneuro.2003.14.3.217

13 Promoting Successful Cognitive Strategies for Health, Engagement, and Policy

Introduction

Successful cognitive aging represents a significant milestone in the trajectory of human development, characterized by the maintenance of cognitive abilities and adaptive functioning well into late adulthood. This phenomenon is of paramount importance, considering the global demographic shift toward an aging population. It stands as a testament to the intricate interplay of biological, psychological, and environmental factors that influence cognitive health across the lifespan.

Central to the concept of successful cognitive aging is the preservation of key cognitive domains such as memory, attention, executive functions, and processing speed. However, beyond the mere retention of cognitive faculties, successful aging encompasses a broader spectrum of outcomes, including emotional resilience, social engagement, and the ability to navigate life's challenges effectively.

Understanding the mechanisms underpinning successful cognitive aging is pivotal for informing interventions aimed at promoting healthy aging and mitigating age-related cognitive decline. Research in this field spans multidisciplinary domains, integrating neuroscientific investigations, psychological assessments, and socio-environmental analyses.

This exploration delves into the intricacies of successful cognitive aging, elucidating the contributing factors, protective mechanisms, and implications for individual wellbeing and societal advancement. By unraveling the complexities of cognitive resilience in later life, we endeavor to foster a deeper comprehension of human cognitive aging and pave the way for enhancing the quality of life for aging populations worldwide.

Definition of successful Cognitive Aging

Successful aging encompasses various dimensions that contribute to an individual's overall wellbeing and quality of life as they age. McLaughlin et al. (2009) investigated successful aging using Row and Kahn's model, which considers factors such as disease and disability, cognitive and physical function, social communication, and productive activities.

DOI: 10.4324/9781003477815-13

Additionally, factors like age, lack of smoking, non-disability, and mental and physical activity have been associated with successful aging.

Ryff (1989) delineated six dimensions of successful aging: self-acceptance, positive relationships, self-determination, control over the environment, purposefulness in life, and personal development. This multifaceted approach acknowledges both subjective and objective aspects of aging. Moreover, Jopp and Hertzog (2010) highlighted inner wellbeing, life satisfaction, and longevity as indicators of successful aging, emphasizing the importance of mental and emotional health in addition to physical health.

Furthermore, health-promoting behaviors and a healthy lifestyle play crucial roles in achieving successful aging. Studies have emphasized the adoption of a healthy lifestyle as facilitating conditions for successful aging (Baltes & Carstensen, 1996; Baltes et al., 1999; Freund, 2008). Engaging in health-promoting behaviors not only improves quality of life but also empowers individuals to take control of their health as they age

Essentially Successful cognitive aging, in particular, emphasizes the maintenance of cognitive abilities and the absence of significant cognitive decline. By understanding the multifaceted nature of successful aging and promoting health-promoting behaviors, individuals can enhance their overall quality of life as they age.

Importance of Cognitive Health in Older Adults

Cognitive health, essential for older adults, encompasses the capacity to learn, solve problems, remember, and utilize information effectively. It serves as a cornerstone for maintaining independence and preserving the quality of life as individuals age. However, advancing age often brings about changes in cognitive abilities, presenting various challenges that impact daily functioning and overall wellbeing (Morley et al., 2015).

One notable change in cognitive function among older adults is a gradual slowing of thinking processes. This slowdown can manifest in various cognitive tasks, leading to delays in decision-making, problem-solving, and information processing. Tasks that once were accomplished swiftly may now require more time and effort, affecting efficiency and productivity (Healthy Aging, n.d.).

Another common cognitive change is difficulty sustaining attention. Older adults may find it challenging to maintain focus on a task or conversation for prolonged periods, leading to increased distractibility and decreased task completion rates. This decline in sustained attention can impede engagement in activities and interactions, affecting overall cognitive performance and social functioning (Murman, 2015).

Multitasking, once a skill is often taken for granted, becomes increasingly challenging with age. Older adults may struggle to juggle multiple tasks simultaneously, experiencing difficulty prioritizing, organizing, and switching between tasks efficiently. This impairment in multitasking abilities can hinder performance in daily activities that require simultaneous attention to multiple stimuli or tasks (Murman, 2015).

Moreover, older adults may encounter difficulties in holding information in mind, commonly referred to as working memory deficits. Tasks that require temporary storage and manipulation of information, such as mental arithmetic or following multi-step instructions, may become more challenging due to limitations in working memory capacity (Murman, 2015).

Expressive language abilities may also be affected, with older adults experiencing difficulty finding words or retrieving vocabulary. This phenomenon, often referred to as word-finding difficulties or tip-of-the-tongue experiences, can lead to frustration and communication breakdowns in social and functional contexts (Murman, 2015).

Additionally, changes in executive cognitive function, which encompasses higher-order cognitive processes such as planning, decision-making, and problem-solving, may occur with aging. Older adults may exhibit slowness in executing cognitive tasks requiring strategic thinking and cognitive flexibility, impacting their ability to navigate complex situations effectively (Murman, 2015).

In summary, cognitive changes associated with aging, including slower thinking, attention difficulties, multitasking challenges, working memory deficits, word-finding difficulties, and executive function impairments, can significantly impact daily functioning and quality of life for older adults. Understanding these changes and implementing strategies to support cognitive health and compensate for cognitive deficits are essential for promoting independence and wellbeing in aging populations (Murman, 2015).

Demographic Trends and Aging Population

Population aging represents a pervasive global phenomenon stemming from demographic transitions, primarily characterized by prolonged life expectancy and declining fertility rates. Population aging constitutes an irreversible global phenomenon, inexorably unfolding as a consequence of the demographic transition. This transition, emblematic of lengthening lifespans and declining fertility rates, permeates even nations traditionally characterized by youthful demographics. In 2021, approximately one-tenth of the global populace comprised individuals aged 65 or older, a proportion projected to escalate to one-sixth by 2050 (United Nations, 2023).

The diminution of fertility rates precipitates a reduction in the proportion of younger cohorts, thereby augmenting the relative shares of working-age adults and, subsequently, older individuals (United Nations, 2023). Furthermore, the momentum of population aging derives impetus from advancements in longevity and the concomitant extension of healthy lifespans.

Regional disparities in population aging dynamics are discernible, with Northern Africa, Western Asia, and sub-Saharan Africa anticipated to witness the most pronounced growth in the elderly populace over the ensuing three decades. Presently, the collective regions of Europe and Northern America harbor the highest concentration of older persons (United Nations, 2023).

Gender differentials in life expectancy engender a predominance of women within the older demographic cohort, particularly among advanced age strata. Forecasts suggest a gradual convergence in male-female survival rates, portending marginal but discernible diminutions in the sex gap in life expectancy and the proportion of females within the elderly demographic segment in forthcoming years (United Nations, 2023).

Traditional metrics such as the old-age dependency ratio serve as rudimentary indicators of economic dependency associated with population aging. Nevertheless, alternative metrics that account for augmented life expectancy or the economic productivity and consumption patterns across distinct age cohorts offer a more nuanced perspective on demographic aging's multifaceted economic ramifications (United Nations, 2023).

Thus, understanding and effectively responding to the complexities of population aging emerge as critical imperatives in contemporary demographic discourse and policy formulation on a global scale.

Biological Foundations

While aging is an inevitable part of life, the decline in cognitive function often associated with it is not. Positive neuropsychology highlights the remarkable capacity of the human brain to maintain its cognitive prowess throughout the lifespan. Let us explore the biological foundations of successful cognitive aging, focusing on neural plasticity, neuroprotective factors, and the role of lifestyle choices.

Neural Plasticity

One of the brain's most remarkable features is its plasticity—the ability to adapt and change throughout life (Puderbaugh & Emmady, 2023). This plasticity allows the brain to compensate for age-related changes by strengthening existing neural connections and forming new ones (Vecchio et al., 2018). Imagine an individual who loses some hearing due to aging. The brain can re-route auditory signals, enhancing activity in other areas of the auditory cortex to compensate for the loss (Greenhagen et al., 2019). This adaptability is crucial for maintaining cognitive function as we age.

Adaptive Changes in Neural Networks

Beyond simple compensation, the aging brain can also undergo more fundamental changes in neural networks. Functional magnetic resonance imaging (fMRI) studies have shown that older adults with superior cognitive function often activate a wider network of brain regions compared to their counterparts with lower cognitive performance (Reuter-Lorenz et al., 2000). This suggests a more efficient and distributed processing of information, allowing the brain to maintain cognitive function despite potential age-related declines in specific brain regions (Park & Reuter-Lorenz, 2009).

Neurogenesis and Cognitive Reserve

Recent research suggests that the brain may even have the potential for neurogenesis—the birth of new neurons—even in adulthood (Mandolesi et al., 2018). This neurogenesis, particularly in the hippocampus, a region crucial for learning and memory, may contribute to cognitive reserve (Tucker & Stern, 2011). Cognitive reserve refers to the brain's ability to withstand age-related damage or pathology. Individuals with higher cognitive reserve may experience fewer cognitive declines even in the presence of neuropathological changes (Tucker & Stern, 2011).

Neuroprotective Factors

Several lifestyle factors have been shown to promote neuroprotection, safeguarding the brain from the detrimental effects of aging.

Antioxidants and Brain Health

Antioxidants, found in fruits, vegetables, and whole grains, can help to neutralize harmful free radicals that damage brain cells (Gallagher et al., 2019). A diet rich in antioxidants may contribute to improved cognitive function and a reduced risk of dementia (Kesse-Guyot et al., 2016).

Hormonal Influences on Cognitive Aging

Hormones, particularly estrogen and testosterone, play a role in cognitive function (Barth et al., 2023). Maintaining healthy hormone levels through lifestyle choices or hormone replacement therapy (HRT) may contribute to cognitive wellbeing (Manson et al., 2017).

Studies on Healthy Aging: Structure and Function

Exercise and Lifestyle

The aging brain changes structurally in a number of ways, including decreased brain volume and cortical thickness and altered white matter integrity. Cognitive abilities including memory, executive function, and processing speed may be impacted by these changes. However, it has been demonstrated that a number of interventions, most notably physical activity, can lessen these age-related changes and promote brain health.

One crucial aspect of promoting successful cognitive aging is adopting a healthy lifestyle. Engaging in regular physical activity has been consistently linked to cognitive benefits, including improved memory, attention, and executive function. Aerobic exercise, in particular, has been shown to stimulate the growth of new neurons and enhance brain plasticity, which are essential mechanisms for maintaining cognitive function as we age.

Aerobic exercise exerts various beneficial effects on cognitive function and brain health through several mechanisms. Firstly, exercise promotes neurogenesis, the development of new neurons, and synaptogenesis, the formation of synapses, thereby enhancing neural connectivity and function (Ferrer-Uris et al., 2022). Additionally, aerobic exercise triggers the release of brain-derived neurotrophic factor (BDNF), a protein essential for nurturing existing neurons and facilitating the growth of new neurons and synapses (Roig et al., 2013). Moreover, exercise augments blood flow to the brain, ensuring adequate oxygen and nutrient supply for optimal brain function. Furthermore, aerobic exercise increases the secretion of neurotrophic substances and neurotransmitters, which play crucial roles in neuronal communication and plasticity (Tomporowski et al., 2015). Neuroelectric changes associated with exercise further contribute to enhanced cognitive function.

Colcombe et al. (2006) looked into how older individuals' brain structure was affected by aerobic exercise. According to their research, consistent aerobic exercise significantly increased brain capacity, especially in the hippocampus and prefrontal cortex. The hippocampal formation is important for memory formation and spatial navigation, whereas the prefrontal cortex is necessary for executive activities like planning, problem-solving, and decision-making. The research, which measured changes in brain volume using magnetic resonance imaging (MRI), offers strong proof that physical activity can have positive effects on the structure of the brain. Because of the increase in brain volume in these areas, aerobic exercise may be able to enhance cognitive health by helping to offset the normal age-related loss in these important areas of the brain.

Building on these results, Erickson et al. (2011) examined the hippocampal area of the brain, which is especially vulnerable to age-related shrinkage. In their year-long aerobic fitness program, older persons took part in a randomized controlled experiment. Hippocampal volume significantly increased, as indicated by the data, and this increase was linked to improvements in spatial memory. This study emphasizes how aerobic exercise can both prevent shrinkage and increase the volume of the hippocampus, which can improve memory function that are frequently impacted by aging. According to the research, consistent physical activity might promote neurogenesis in the hippocampus, which is essential for preserving cognitive abilities.

Resistance training has been identified as a potential avenue for eliciting positive neurobiological effects and mitigating structural atrophy within the brain (Strength Training Can Help Protect the Brain From Degeneration,

2020). Empirical evidence from longitudinal investigations supports this assertion, exemplified by a protracted study revealing the capacity of strength training to serve as a protective mechanism against degenerative processes targeting select subregions of the hippocampus (Herold et al., 2019). Notably, the hippocampus, a structurally intricate region of the brain, assumes a pivotal role in cognitive functions pertinent to learning and memory consolidation (Chen et al., 2015).

Cognitive Engagement and Social Interaction

Intellectual stimulation, achieved through engaging in diverse cognitive activities, plays a vital role in promoting cognitive fitness. Regularly engaging in activities that challenge the mind, such as learning new skills, playing games, reading complex texts, or pursuing creative hobbies, can stimulate neural pathways, enhance cognitive reserve, and potentially delay age-related cognitive decline. Lifelong learning, the pursuit of knowledge and skills throughout life, further strengthens cognitive reserve by building upon existing neural networks and creating new ones, potentially enhancing resilience to cognitive decline. The human brain thrives on social connections. Meaningful social interactions, from engaging in conversations and sharing experiences with loved ones to participating in community activities, provide emotional support, combat loneliness, and stimulate cognitive function. Social engagement promotes cognitive activity by encouraging communication, memory recall, and problem-solving within a supportive environment. Studies have shown that strong social networks are associated with better cognitive performance, reduced risk of dementia, and improved overall wellbeing in older adults (Holt-Lunstad et al., 2017).

In order to investigate the relationship between aging individuals' brain shape and lifestyle characteristics, Fjell and Walhovd (2010) carried out a longitudinal study. They observed that people who had busy lives, involving frequent exercise and mental stimulation, showed less cortical thinning and conserved brain volume with time. Cognitive deficits are linked to cortical thinning, an established indicator of brain aging. An active lifestyle can help maintain cortical integrity and slow down the structural deterioration associated with aging, according to compelling evidence presented in a study that tracked changes in brain structure over several years using advanced neuroimaging techniques.

Raz et al. (2005) investigated the effect of consistent participation in mental and physical exercises on atrophy of the brain. The frontal lobes, which are essential for executive functions like reasoning, planning, and problem-solving, were the focus of their study. They discovered that older adults with sedentary lifestyles saw faster rates of atrophy in the frontal lobes than those who regularly engaged in physical activity and cognitively stimulating activities. The significance of this finding lies in the fact that the frontal lobes are among the areas most impacted by aging, and maintaining cognitive functions depends on their preservation. In order to maintain structural brain integrity, the study emphasizes the value of a multimodal approach to brain health that combines cognitive and physical activities.

All these studies show that aging adults' brain structure can be greatly impacted by lifestyle interventions, especially those that involve physical exercise. These interventions support cognitive function maintenance and healthy aging by slowing down brain atrophy, maintaining cortical thickness, and increasing brain volume. The evidence is in favor of the hypothesis that maintaining cognitive health and reducing the structural aging-related changes in the body require an active lifestyle that includes both physical and mental activities.

Nutrition and Cognitive Health

As the population ages, maintaining cognitive health becomes increasingly important. Diet plays a crucial role in this process, with specific nutrients influencing cognitive function and potentially protecting against age-related decline. Among these nutrients, omega-3 fatty acids stand out for their significant impact on cognitive health in older adults.

Several dietary patterns have been associated with better cognitive function in older adults. The Mediterranean diet, rich in fruits, vegetables, whole grains, and healthy fats, has been shown to improve memory, executive function, and processing speed (Morris et al., 2015). Conversely, diets high in saturated and trans fats, refined carbohydrates, and added sugar are linked to an increased risk of cognitive decline and dementia (Livingston et al., 2020).

Omega-3 Fatty Acids: Champions of Cognitive Health

Among the specific nutrients within these dietary patterns, omega-3 fatty acids, particularly eicosapentaenoic acid (EPA) and docosahexaenoic acid (DHA), have garnered significant attention for their potential to support cognitive health in older adults. These essential fats are found primarily in fatty fish like salmon, tuna, and sardines, and offer various benefits for the aging brain.

A study conducted by Cutuli et al. (2016) looked into the Impact of Omega-3 Fatty Acid Supplementation on Cognitive Functions and Neural Mechanisms. This study suggests that adding omega-3 fatty acids (n-3 PUFA) to the diet of older individuals could help preserve brain function. By preventing the decline of gray matter volume in key brain regions like the prefrontal cortex, retrosplenial cortex, and hippocampus, n-3 PUFAs might be ideal candidates for nutritional interventions aimed at improving cognitive function and mood in older adults. This is especially important as the elderly population in the West continues to grow and maintaining cognitive health becomes increasingly crucial. Additionally, this study highlights the potential of using brain measurements like voxel-based morphometry (VBM) to track the effects of n-3 PUFA supplementation in future trials, both in healthy and diseased brains.

Emotional Wellbeing and Cognition

The tapestry of successful cognitive aging is intricately woven with threads of emotional wellbeing. Understanding the intricate connections between these two domains is crucial for promoting healthy aging and optimizing cognitive function throughout life.

Stress and Cognitive Aging

Chronic stress casts a long shadow on cognitive health. Elevated cortisol levels, a hallmark of stress, can impair memory, attention, and executive function. This detrimental impact is particularly concerning in older adults, who may already face age-related cognitive decline. Conversely, effective stress management strategies like mindfulness exercises and relaxation techniques have been shown to protect cognitive function and even improve cognitive performance.

Optimism and Cognitive Wellbeing

Cultivating a positive outlook can be a powerful tool for successful cognitive aging. Optimism has been linked to better memory, cognitive flexibility, and resilience in the face of challenges. Conversely, negative emotions like anxiety and depression can exacerbate cognitive decline. Interventions based on positive psychology principles, like gratitude practices and reframing negative thoughts, can foster emotional wellbeing and potentially enhance cognitive function.

Emotional Regulation and Aging

The ability to effectively manage emotions becomes increasingly important with age. Difficulty regulating emotions can lead to stress, anxiety, and even depression, all of which negatively impact cognitive function. Conversely, emotional regulation skills can help older adults cope with challenges, maintain positive relationships, and navigate the complexities of aging, potentially mitigating cognitive decline.

Sleep and Cognitive Health

Sleep plays a critical role in both cognitive function and chronic disease management. Adequate sleep duration and quality are essential for consolidating memories, learning new information, and regulating emotional responses. Conversely, sleep disturbances are linked to increased risk of cognitive decline, dementia, and even exacerbation of chronic conditions. Prioritizing sleep hygiene practices like consistent sleep schedules, relaxing bedtime routines, and creating a sleep-conducive environment is vital for promoting both cognitive health and successful chronic disease management.

By adopting a comprehensive approach that integrates chronic disease management, preventive strategies, and sleep hygiene practices, individuals can significantly enhance their chances of achieving successful cognitive aging. This holistic approach fosters not only physical wellbeing but also empowers individuals to maintain cognitive function and enjoy a higher quality of life throughout their lifespan.

Cognitive Interventions for Successful Cognitive Aging: Leveraging Technology and Rehabilitation

As the population ages, maintaining cognitive health and delaying decline becomes increasingly important. Numerous interventions have emerged as potential tools for successful cognitive aging, encompassing both traditional methods and innovative technological approaches. This paper explores several promising cognitive interventions, highlighting their potential benefits and limitations.

Cognitive Training Programs

Structured cognitive training programs target specific cognitive domains like memory, attention, and executive function. These programs typically involve computer-based exercises or group sessions designed to improve cognitive skills through practice and repetition. Studies have shown modest benefits from cognitive training programs in older adults, particularly in terms of processing speed and memory. However, questions remain regarding long-term effectiveness and individual differences in response to training.

Cognitive Rehabilitation

This intervention focuses on restoring cognitive function in individuals who have already experienced cognitive decline due to stroke, dementia, or other brain injuries. Cognitive rehabilitation typically involves individualized assessments and targeted interventions tailored to the specific needs of each patient. Research has shown positive outcomes from cognitive rehabilitation in improving cognitive function and daily living activities in individuals with various cognitive impairments.

Memory Training and Executive Function Exercises

These interventions target specific cognitive domains through various exercises and strategies. Memory training can involve techniques like mnemonic devices and visualization, while executive function exercises focus on improving planning, problem-solving, and decision-making skills. While some studies have shown positive effects on specific tasks, the broader impact on overall cognitive function and real-world functioning remains under investigation.

Technological Interventions

Digital platforms offer accessible and engaging ways to deliver cognitive training programs and activities. These platforms can personalize interventions based on individual needs and track progress over time, making them potentially more effective than traditional methods (Boot et al., 2015). However, concerns exist regarding accessibility, digital literacy, and the potential for cognitive overload. Virtual reality (VR) technologies provide immersive and interactive environments for cognitive training. VR experiences can enhance engagement and motivation, potentially leading to better outcomes compared to traditional methods. Studies have shown promising results in using VR for memory training and attention improvement (Cheng et al., 2021), but more research is needed to evaluate long-term benefits and generalizability.

Cross-Cultural Perspectives

Cultural Influence on Aging

The tapestry of successful cognitive aging is intricately woven with threads of culture, socioeconomic factors, and individual experiences. Understanding the interplay between these elements across diverse populations is crucial for promoting inclusive and effective interventions.

Cross-Cultural Studies on Cognitive Aging

Cross-cultural studies reveal fascinating variations in perspectives on aging and cognitive decline. While some cultures emphasize independence and individual achievement in later life, others prioritize family support and intergenerational collaboration. These differing cultural values influence perceptions of cognitive decline, with some cultures viewing it as a natural process of aging, while others consider it a medical condition requiring intervention. Unveiling these cross-cultural and socioeconomic nuances is essential for designing interventions that resonate with diverse populations. Culturally sensitive approaches that acknowledge and respect varying perspectives and experiences can foster greater engagement and adherence to interventions. Biological aging occurs within specific cultural contexts, leading to diverse outcomes depending on these contexts. In Western cultures, aging may be viewed as a series of individual failures, with intelligence and wellbeing seen as individual accomplishments (National Academies Press (US), 2000). In contrast, Asian cultures often see aging as part of life's tasks, preparing for rebirth, with intelligence and wellbeing being more collective and wisdom-oriented. These cultural perspectives influence how aging is perceived and experienced. More research is needed to understand aging from a cross-cultural perspective, including how cultural beliefs shape cognition and wellbeing. Theoretical frameworks like those proposed by Baltes (1993), Park et al. (1999), and others offer ways to study these issues. Understanding the cognitive effects of aging across cultures has broad implications for behavioral and social sciences, shedding light on the interplay between culture, cognition, and behavior (National Academies Press (US), 2000). Cultural psychology aims to explore these interactions to gain a deeper understanding of human psychology.

Impact of Socioeconomic Factors

Socioeconomic factors significantly impact cognitive aging. Lower socioeconomic status is associated with an increased risk of cognitive decline, potentially due to limited access to healthcare, education, and healthy lifestyle choices. Conversely, higher socioeconomic status may provide greater resources for cognitive stimulation, healthcare access, and stress management, potentially promoting cognitive resilience. A study conducted by Muhammad et al. (2023) found higher rates of cognitive impairment among older women (20.03%) compared to men (7.14%). Cognitive impairment is more common among those with lower education and wealth. Surprisingly, older women without work history had lower odds of impairment, while non-working older men showed higher odds, though not statistically significant. Risk factors significantly increase the odds of impairment in both genders. Additionally, addressing socioeconomic disparities through policies and programs that improve access to healthcare, education, and healthy living opportunities can create a more equitable landscape for successful cognitive aging across all cultural and socioeconomic groups.

Ultimately, a comprehensive understanding of cultural influences, socioeconomic factors, and individual experiences is vital for weaving a tapestry of successful cognitive aging that is inclusive, effective, and respectful of diverse populations. By acknowledging and addressing these multifaceted influences, we can empower individuals from all backgrounds to navigate the journey of aging with cognitive vitality and wellbeing.

Policy Implications

As the global population ages, promoting successful cognitive aging, which refers to maintaining cognitive function and delaying decline, becomes increasingly important. This requires a multifaceted approach involving both policy changes and public health initiatives.

To promote successful cognitive aging, a multifaceted approach encompassing both policy and public health initiatives is crucial. Firstly, increasing access to healthcare and healthy lifestyles is vital. Expanding health insurance coverage ensures preventive care like checkups, screenings, and mental health services are accessible. Promoting healthy food environments through policy interventions can make nutritious options more readily available, while investing in infrastructure for safe physical activity encourages communities to be active (Holt-Lunstad et al., 2017). Addressing social determinants of health also plays a crucial role. Combating poverty and economic inequality, improving educational opportunities, and reducing social isolation can all contribute to better cognitive health (KFF, 2023).

Investing in research and development is key to advancing the understanding of cognitive decline and developing effective interventions (Alzheimer's Association, 2023). Supporting research on both pharmacological and non-pharmacological approaches, as well as developing accurate and culturally sensitive cognitive assessment tools, are essential steps forward. Promoting public awareness and education empowers individuals to take charge of their cognitive health (Lustig et al., 2021). Combating stigma and misinformation about cognitive decline, and providing information on modifiable risk factors and evidence-based strategies, can significantly impact individual choices and behaviors (World Health Organization, 2020).

Public health initiatives should focus on interventions throughout the lifespan. Early life interventions like early childhood education programs (Christensen et al., 2019) and brain-healthy nutrition programs lay a strong foundation for cognitive health (Heckman et al., 2010). Lifelong interventions such as cognitive training programs, social engagement activities, and regular physical activity programs can further support cognitive function. Additionally, technology-based interventions like digital tools for cognitive assessment and training, and telehealth services for remote healthcare delivery, offer accessible and personalized approaches to cognitive health monitoring and improvement (World Health Organization, 2020).

By implementing this comprehensive policy and public health initiatives, we can create a society that supports successful cognitive aging for all.

Summary

This chapter explores the multifaceted concept of healthy cognitive aging, emphasizing the importance of maintaining cognitive health as we age and examining the underlying biological, psychological, and social factors that contribute to this process. Healthy cognitive aging refers to the preservation of mental sharpness and cognitive abilities into older adulthood. This is crucial for maintaining independence, quality of life, and overall wellbeing. Given the global increase in the aging population, understanding and promoting cognitive health has never been more critical. The chapter delves into the biological aspects of cognitive aging, highlighting the brain's remarkable capacity for neural plasticity, which involves adaptive changes in neural networks and the generation of new neurons (neurogenesis).

These processes contribute to cognitive reserve, which helps the brain withstand age-related changes and injuries. Additionally, it covers neuroprotective factors such as antioxidants, which protect the brain from oxidative stress, and the role of hormones in cognitive health. Research indicates that various lifestyle factors significantly influence cognitive health in older adults. Regular physical exercise is shown to enhance cognitive functions, while mental and social activities (cognitive engagements and social interaction) stimulate the brain and support cognitive health. Proper nutrition, particularly the intake of omega-3 fatty acids and antioxidants, is essential for brain health. The chapter also addresses the impact of emotional wellbeing, noting that managing stress, maintaining optimism, and effective emotional regulation are vital for cognitive vitality. Quality sleep is underscored as a crucial factor in maintaining cognitive function. Sleep impacts memory consolidation, emotional regulation, and overall brain health, making it a key component of healthy cognitive aging. The chapter explores various cognitive interventions designed to support and enhance cognitive health. These include cognitive training programs that focus on rehabilitating cognitive abilities and exercises aimed at improving memory and executive functions. The use of technology in cognitive interventions is also discussed, highlighting how digital tools can aid in cognitive training and monitoring. The chapter examines how cognitive aging is perceived and experienced across different cultures, influenced by various social, economic, and cultural factors. Cross-cultural studies provide insights into the diverse ways aging and cognitive health are approached worldwide, revealing the impact of socioeconomic conditions on cognitive outcomes. Finally, the chapter discusses the policy implications of promoting healthy cognitive aging. It calls for comprehensive strategies that include healthcare, education, and community support systems to enhance cognitive health among older adults. Effective policies can help create environments that support cognitive vitality and overall wellbeing in the aging population.

This chapter provides a comprehensive overview of healthy cognitive aging, emphasizing the interplay of biological, lifestyle, emotional, and cultural factors, and highlights the importance of targeted interventions and supportive policies in promoting cognitive health among older adults.

References

Alzheimer's Association. (2023). *Alzheimer's disease and dementia research*. Retrieved from https://www.alz.org/research

Baltes, M. M., & Carstensen, L. L. (1996). The process of successful ageing. *Ageing & Society*, *16*(4), 397–422. https://doi.org/10.1017/s0144686x00003603

Baltes, P. B. (1993). The aging mind: Potential and limits. *The Gerontologist*, *33*(5), 580–594. https://doi.org/10.1093/geront/33.5.580

Baltes, P. B., Staudinger, U. M., & Lindenberger, U. (1999). Lifespan psychology: Theory and application to intellectual functioning. *Annual Review of Psychology*, *50*(1), 471–507. https://doi.org/10.1146/annurev.psych.50.1.471

Barth, C., Crestol, A., De Lange, A. G., & Galea, L. A. (2023). Sex steroids and the female brain across the lifespan: Insights into risk of depression and Alzheimer's disease. *The Lancet. Diabetes & Endocrinology*, *11*(12), 926–941.

Castel AD, Pratt J, Drummond E. The effects of action video game experience on the time course of inhibition of return and the efficiency of visual search. Acta Psychol (Amst). 2005 Jun;119(2):217-30. doi: 10.1016/j.actpsy.2005.02.004. Epub 2005 Mar 23. PMID: 15877981.

Chen, W., Peng, T., Sun, Y., Yang, H., Liaw, F., Wu, L., Chang, Y., & Kao, T. (2015). Examining the association between quadriceps strength and cognitive performance in the elderly. *Medicine*, *94*(32), e1335. https://doi.org/10.1097/md.0000000000001335

Christensen, K., Vaupel, J. W., & Haberman, S. (2019). Education and cognitive function: A review. *The Journals of Gerontology: Series B*, *74*(4), 505–516.

Colcombe, S. J., Erickson, K. I., Scalf, P. E., Kim, J. S., Prakash, R., McAuley, E., ... & Kramer, A. F. (2006). Aerobic exercise training increases brain volume in aging humans. *The Journals of Gerontology Series A: Biological Sciences and Medical Sciences*, *61*(11), 1166–1170.

Erickson, K. I., Voss, M. W., Prakash, R. S., Basak, C., Szabo, A., Chaddock, L., ... & Kramer, A. F. (2011). Exercise training increases size of hippocampus and improves memory. *Proceedings of the National Academy of Sciences*, *108*(7), 3017–3022.

Ferrer-Uris, B., Ramos, M. Á., Busquets, A., & Angulo-Barroso, R. (2022). Can exercise shape your brain? A review of aerobic exercise effects on cognitive function and neuro-physiological underpinning mechanisms. *AIMS Neuroscience*, *9*(2), 150–174. https://doi.org/10.3934/neuroscience.2022009

Fjell, A. M., & Walhovd, K. B. (2010). Structural brain changes in aging: Courses, causes, and cognitive consequences. *Reviews in the Neurosciences*, *21*(3), 187–221.

Freund, A. M. (2008). Successful aging as management of resources: The role of selection, optimization, and compensation. *Research in Human Development*, *5*(2), 94–106. https://doi.org/10.1080/15427600802034827

Gallagher, M., Okonkwo, O. C., Resnick, S. M., Jagust, W. J., Benzinger, T. L., & Rapp, P. R. (2019). What are the threats to successful brain and cognitive aging? *Neurobiology of Aging (Print)*, *83*, 130–134. https://doi.org/10.1016/j.neurobiolaging.2019.04.016

Greenhagen, J., Matusz, E. F., Emrani, S., Libon, D. J., & Pomerantz, S. (2019). Affective disturbance in mild cognitive impairment. *American Journal of Geriatric Psychiatry/The American Journal of Geriatric Psychiatry*, *27*(3), S138–S139. https://doi.org/10.1016/j.jagp.2019.01.046

Heckman, J. J., Pinto, R., Savelyev, T., & Cunha, F. (2010). The North American preschool puzzle: Does early childhood education benefit the longrun? *The Quarterly Journal of Economics*, *125*(3), 1013–1058.

Herold, F., Törpel, A., Schega, L., & Müller, N. G. (2019). Functional and/or structural brain changes in response to resistance exercises and resistance training lead to cognitive improvements – A systematic review. *European Review of Aging and Physical Activity*, *16*(1). https://doi.org/10.1186/s11556-019-0217-2

Holt-Lunstad, J., Smith, T. B., Baker, M., Harris, T., & Stephenson, D. (2017). Loneliness and social isolation as risk factors for mortality: A meta-analytic review. *Perspectives on Psychological Science*, *10*(2), 227–237. https://doi.org/10.1177/1745691614568352

Jopp, D., & Hertzog, C. (2010). Assessing adult leisure activities: An extension of a self-report activity questionnaire. *Psychological Assessment*, *22*(1), 108–120.

Kesse-Guyot, E., Assmann, K. E., Andreeva, V. A., Touvier, M., Neufcourt, L., Shivappa, N., Hébert, J. R., Wirth, M. D., Herçberg, S., Galán, P., & Julia, C. (2016). Long-term association between the dietary inflammatory index and cognitive functioning: Findings from the SU.VI.MAX study. *European Journal of Nutrition*, *56*(4), 1647–1655. https://doi.org/10.1007/s00394-016-1211-3

KFF. (2023). *The state of aging and health in America 2023*. Retrieved from https://www.kff.org/

Livingston, G., Huntley, J., & Sommerlad, A. (2020). Dementia prevention, intervention, and care. *The Lancet*, *396*(10248), 413–446. https://doi.org/10.1016/S0140-6736(20)30367-6

Manson, J. E., Aragaki, A. K., Rossouw, J. E., Anderson, G. L., Prentice, R. L., LaCroix, A. Z., Chlebowski, R. T., Howard, B. V., Thomson, C. A., Margolis, K. L., Lewis, C. E., Stefanick, M. L., Jackson, R. D., Johnson, K., Martin, L. W., Shumaker, S. A., Espeland, M. A., & Wactawski-Wende, J. (2017). Menopausal hormone therapy and long-term all-cause and cause-specific mortality. *JAMA*, *318*(10), 927.

McLaughlin, S. J., Connell, C. M., Heeringa, S. G., Li, L., & Roberts, J. (2009). Successful aging in the United States: Prevalence estimates from a national sample of older adults. *The Journals of Gerontology: Series B*, *65B*(2), 216–226.

Morris, M. C., Tangney, C. C., Wang, Y., Sacks, F. M., & Buring, J. E. (2015). MIND diet slows cognitive decline with aging. *Alzheimer's & Dementia*, *11*(9), 1015'1022. https://doi.org/10.1016/j.jalz.2014.11.004

Muhammad, T., Pai, M., Kumar, M., & Sekher, T. V. (2023). Multiple socioeconomic risks and cognitive impairment among older men and women in India. *Dialogues in Health*, *2*, 100119. https://doi.org/10.1016/j.dialog.2023.100119

Murman, D. L. (2015). The impact of age on cognition. *Seminars in Hearing*, *36*(03), 111–121. https://doi.org/10.1055/s-0035-1555115

National Academies Press (US). (2000). *Cultural variations in cognition: Implications for aging research*. The Aging Mind - NCBI Bookshelf.

Park, D. C., & Reuter-Lorenz, P. A. (2009). The adaptive brain: Aging and neurocognitive scaffolding. *Annual Review of Psychology* (Print), *60*(1), 173–196.

Park, D. C., Nisbett, R. E., & Hedden, T. (1999). Aging, culture, and cognition. *The Journals of Gerontology: Series B*, *54B*(2), P75–P84. https://doi.org/10.1093/geronb/54b.2.p75

Puderbaugh, M., & Emmady, P. D. (2023, May 1). Neuroplasticity. StatPearls - NCBI Bookshelf. https://www.ncbi.nlm.nih.gov/books/NBK557811/

Raz, N., Rodrigue, K. M., Head, D., Kennedy, K. M., & Acker, J. D. (2005). Differential aging of the medial temporal lobe: A study of a five-year change. *Neurology*, *65*(3), 263–268.

Reuter-Lorenz, P. A., Jonides, J., Smith, E. E., Hartley, A. A., Miller, A. L., Marshuetz, C., & Koeppe, R. A. (2000). Age differences in the frontal lateralization of verbal and spatial working memory revealed by PET. *Journal of Cognitive Neuroscience*, *12*(1), 174–187. https://doi.org/10.1162/089892900561814

Roig, M., Nordbrandt, S., Geertsen, S. S., & Nielsen, J. B. (2013). The effects of cardiovascular exercise on human memory: A review with meta-analysis. *Neuroscience & Biobehavioral Reviews*, *37*(8), 1645–1666. https://doi.org/10.1016/j.neubiorev.2013.06.012

Ryff, C. D. (1989). Happiness is everything, or is it? Explorations on the meaning of psychological wellbeing. *Journal of Personality and Social Psychology*, *57*(6), 1069–1081. https://doi.org/10.1037/0022-3514.57.6.1069

Seymour J. The Impact of Public Health Awareness Campaigns on the Awareness and Quality of Palliative Care. J Palliat Med. 2018 Jan;21(S1):S30-S36. doi: 10.1089/jpm.2017.0391. PMID: 29283867; PMCID: PMC5733664.

Strength training can help protect the brain from degeneration. (2020, February 11). The University of Sydney.

Szczepocka E, Mokros Ł, Kazmierski J, Nowakowska K, Łucka A, Antoszczyk A, Oltra-Cucarella J, Werzowa W, Hellevik MM, Skouras S, Bagger K. The Effectiveness of Virtual Reality-Based Training on Cognitive, Social, and Physical Functioning in High-Functioning Older Adults (CoSoPhy FX): 2-Arm, Parallel-Group Randomized Controlled Trial. JMIR Res Protoc. 2024 Jun 5;13:e53261. doi: 10.2196/53261. PMID: 38837194; PMCID: PMC11187518.

Tomporowski, P. D., McCullick, B. A., Pendleton, D. M., & Pesce, C. (2015). Exercise and children's cognition: The role of exercise characteristics and a place for metacognition. *Journal of Sport and Health Science*, *4*(1), 47–55.

Tucker, A. M., & Stern, Y. (2011). Cognitive reserve in aging. *Current Alzheimer Research (Print)*, *8*(4), 354–360. https://doi.org/10.2174/156720511795745320

United Nations. (2023). World social report 2023: Leaving no one behind in an ageing world. United Nations Department of Economic and Social Affairs. Retrieved February 24, 2024, from https://www.un.org/development/desa/dspd/world-social-report/2023.html

Vecchio, L. M., Meng, Y., Xhima, K., Lipsman, N., Hamani, C., & Aubert, I. (2018). The neuroprotective effects of exercise: Maintaining a healthy brain throughout aging. *Brain Plasticity (Print)*, *4*(1), 17–52. https://doi.org/10.3233/bpl-180069

World Health Organization. (2020). *Risk reduction of cognitive decline and dementia: WHO guidelines*. World Health Organization. https://www.who.int/publications/i/item/9789241550426

14 Neurodiversity in Healthcare

Understanding and Supporting Diverse Minds

Introduction to Neurodiversity

Neurodiversity is a concept that embraces and values the inherent neurological differences among individuals, asserting that conditions such as autism, attention deficit and hyperactive disorder (ADHD), and dyslexia should be understood as natural variations in the human brain. It advocates that people perceive and engage with the world in diverse ways, rejecting the notion that there is a single "correct" way of thinking, learning, or behaving. These differences are not deficits but different ways of perceiving the world (Nicole & Freuh, 2021). The term "neurodiversity" is a union of two words, "neuro," referring to the nervous system, and "diversity," signifying a variety of traits or expressions measured in a sample.

In his remarkable work, Goldberg (2023) elaborates on the distribution of the neurodiverse population within the broader societal context. He explained how neuronal and behavioral trait expressions typically exhibit a normal distribution across the population. "Neurotypical" characterizes the majority of the human population, displaying common and typical neuronal phenotypes close to the mean of normal distribution. On the other hand, "neurodivergent" applies to a minority expressing statistically less common (atypical) neuronal and cognitive phenotypes that fall at the tails of the normal distribution. Although neurodiversity exists across the entire population, it is often associated with neurodivergent groups that exhibit socially noticeable atypical neurological phenotypes. Recently, in 2023 researcher Goldberg (2023), illustrates the point when the neurodivergent category crosses a threshold in the curve, symbolizing the onset of neurodivergence.

Historical Context and Evolution of the Neurodiversity Movement

The neurodiversity movement, rooted in the advocacy for recognizing and celebrating neurological differences, was coined by sociologist Judy Singer in the late 1990s. Inspired by social movements advocating for minority rights and environmentalism, Singer emphasized viewing diverse ways of processing the world as essential to human diversity, promoting celebration over

DOI: 10.4324/9781003477815-14

pathologization (Goldberg, 2023). Goldberg (2023) highlights the pathology paradigm, which manifests in societal stigma, discrimination, and insensitive interventions aimed at "correcting" neurodivergent behavior. The neurodiversity movement advocates against categorizing neurological variations as deviations from a perceived "normal," instead embracing these diverse experiences within the societal fabric (Leadbitter et al., 2021). Importantly, de-pathologizing does not overlook the challenges and impairments associated with neurodivergence but encourages addressing these aspects while valuing the uniqueness neurodiverse individuals contribute to society (Leadbitter et al., 2021).

Neurodiversity and the Social Model of Disability

The neurodivergent perspective echoes strong support for the social model of disability (Dywer, 2022). Originating as a response to the limitations of the medical model, the social model gained inspiration from the activism of the British disability movement in the 1960s and 1970s. The medical model locates disability within the individual and gives the power to define, control, and treat persons with disabilities within the hands of medical professionals; the social model takes a broader view. The medical model emphasizes that disability is an isolated, individual experience and ignores the social factors that contribute to perpetuating disability. Moreover, the medical model expects persons with disabilities to adapt to their environments. The social model of disability advocates that the problem lies within society and its failure to accommodate the needs of disabled individuals. In the social model, the focus is on the interaction between the person with a disability and the environment. Disability is viewed as a diversity of the human condition rather than an undesirable trait to be fixed or cured. Central to the social model is a shift in focus from the person with a disability to disabling social structures. For example, if a wheelchair user cannot use a bus, the solution lies in redesigning the bus. From this perspective, disability is considered a socially constructed disadvantage, constituting a specific form of social oppression (UPIAS, 1976).

Neurodiversity and Intersectionality

Understanding the intersectionality of neurodivergence with other social factors is crucial. Emerging from feminist scholarship, intersectionality now encompasses a broad spectrum of marginalized social groups. This framework allows for the analysis of social structures and systemic oppression, providing a nuanced understanding of individuals' experiences at the intersections of various social identities (Strand, 2017). Smooth (p. 11) explains that it elucidates the systems assigning meaning to these categories. Bayeh (2022) found that neurodivergent individuals are more likely to associate with LGBTQ+ groups, engage in non-conventional relationships, and pursue unique academic, religious, and spiritual paths. Women and white participants were more likely to self-identify as neurodivergent, possibly reflecting systemic factors. Intersectionality aims to reveal the oppression systems maintaining power hierarchies while better understanding individual experiences. For example, Udonsi (2022) highlighted how neglecting intersectional factors like race and neurodivergence in UK health policies leads to misdiagnosis and neglect of young black people's complex needs. Thus, intersectionality advocates for tailored needs assessment and care beyond preconceived notions.

Neurodivergent Conditions

Doyle (2020) proposed a taxonomy of neuro minorities, categorizing them into four distinct subtypes based on developmental neurominorities. These subtypes are defined based on population prevalence and specific characteristics associated with each subtype. The Diagnostic and Statistical Manual of Psychiatric Disorder (DSM-5) is utilized to classify these conditions, emphasizing the emergence of these conditions in childhood or adolescence without being linked to trauma or general developmental delay (Doyle, 2017).

The four subtypes identified in Doyle's Taxonomy of Neuro Minorities are as follows.

Applied Developmental Neurominority

This subtype includes conditions such as dyslexia, dysgraphia, and dyscalculia, characterized by learning disabilities with educational-applied consequences but not significant health implications (Doyle, 2017).

Clinical Developmental Neurominority

Encompassing conditions like Tourette syndrome, autism spectrum disorder (ASD), and ADHD, this subtype involves neurodevelopmental conditions with genetic and environmental components impacting behavior and communication, considered as health issues (Doyle, 2017).

Psychiatric Acquired Minority

It refers to mental illness and psychiatric disorders within the neurodiversity spectrum (Doyle, 2017).

Neurological Acquired Minority

It involves neurodivergence due to neurological illness or injury, contributing to the diversity within the neuro minority spectrum (Doyle, 2017).

Doyle's taxonomy provides a structured framework for understanding the diversity within neuro minorities, highlighting the different subtypes based on their prevalence, characteristics, and implications for individuals within these categories.

Importance of Recognizing and Embracing Neurological Differences in Healthcare

Granger et al. (2023) highlight a significant and often overlooked aspect of the equality, diversity, and inclusion (EDI) discourse. It is estimated that 15%–22% of the global population displays some form of neurodivergence (Granger et al., 2023). Despite this substantial percentage, neurodivergence is frequently sidelined in conversations surrounding EDI. On the other hand, health systems have started to enhance their care approach by considering social diversities like race, culture, and ethnicity, accommodation of neurodiverse perspectives still seems lacking.

Acknowledging and embracing the diversity of neurological profiles is imperative to creating such inclusive healthcare spaces. Broder-Fingert and Abate (2022) extend an invitation to the medical community, urging reflection and action. They emphasize three critical areas where significant improvements can be made in supporting the neurodiversity community: patient care, workforce, and research.

Challenges in Healthcare for Neurodivergent Individuals

Stereotypes and Stigma

Stereotypes and stigma surrounding neurodivergent individuals significantly affect their lives and wellbeing. These biases can deter neurodivergent individuals from accessing essential resources and services due to fear of stigma and misrepresentation. Healthcare professionals' perceptions may also be influenced by these stereotypes. Studies highlight several harmful misconceptions, such as assuming all neurodivergent individuals need lifelong care or viewing neurodiversity as an illness to be cured. These stereotypes hinder open communication and understanding. Unlike illnesses with potential cures, societal labels persist long after individuals have developed coping mechanisms, impacting their lives profoundly. It is crucial to address these stereotypes to create a more inclusive and supportive environment for neurodivergent individuals in all aspects of society, including healthcare.

Misdiagnosis

Diagnosing neurodivergent conditions, especially in adulthood, is often hindered by disparities and challenges, leading to delayed or inaccurate diagnoses. Fusal-poli (2020) identifies several reasons contributing to late or missed diagnoses of ASD in adults. Obtaining accurate developmental history poses a significant challenge, as caregivers may be unavailable or unreliable due to the time elapsed since infancy. Additionally, adults with ASD, particularly those with higher IQs, develop coping and camouflaging strategies, complicating diagnosis. Women with ASD are particularly at risk of delayed diagnosis due to standardized diagnostic tools based on male samples and the prevalence of camouflaging strategies. Females often exhibit internalizing symptoms, leading to misconstrued experiences as anxiety or depression, further hindering diagnosis (Hull & Mandy, 2017).

Diagnosing ADHD also presents challenges, primarily due to comorbidities. Many children with ADHD have other psychiatric diagnoses, leading to potential misdiagnosis. Clinicians may overlook alternative explanations such as giftedness for symptomatology. Dual diagnoses of ADHD with giftedness often go unnoticed, reflecting a potential lack of training among school counselors. Relative-age effects in ADHD diagnosis and treatment result in younger children being more frequently diagnosed and treated, while gender-related differences in diagnosis contribute to variations between boys and girls, sometimes leading to misdiagnosis or delayed diagnosis (Ford-Jones, 2015).

Communication Barriers

Various challenges, including difficulties with language processing or nonverbal cues, can hinder effective communication with neurodivergent patients in healthcare settings. The success of healthcare interactions is intricately linked to factors at both the patient and provider levels, as well as the broader context in which care is delivered. Nicolaidis et al. (2015) emphasize the significance of healthcare provider-level and system-level factors for achieving effective communication in the context of autism in adults. Healthcare provider-level factors encompass their knowledge about autism in adults, the avoidance of incorrect assumptions about individual patients, a willingness to engage in written communication, accessible language, openness to providing other accommodations, and the skill to incorporate supporters appropriately. On the system level, factors such as the availability of supporters, the complexity of the healthcare system, the accessibility of healthcare facilities, and the existing stigma about autism contribute to the overall communication dynamic in healthcare settings. Addressing these factors is essential for ensuring effective and inclusive communication between healthcare providers and individuals with autism.

Sensory Considerations

Individuals with sensory divergence experience the world differently due to variations in sensory processing, impacting various aspects of their lives. Sensory sensitivities, particularly prevalent among individuals with autism, can lead to discomfort in conventional healthcare settings, highlighting the need for sensory-friendly environments. Children and young people with autism often struggle to process sensory information efficiently, increasing the risk of sensory overload and overwhelming experiences. Those with a low sensory threshold (LST) are particularly affected by external sensory stimuli, exhibiting heightened sensitivity to inputs that may not affect the general population. For instance, individuals on the autism spectrum commonly experience discomfort in environments with fluorescent lighting, demonstrating visual processing differences. Sensory experiences extend to audio and olfactory sensitivities, such as discomfort with high-volume levels and reactions to strong scents like hand sanitizers. Minimizing sensory inputs is essential to create a more supportive environment for individuals with sensory divergence (Morgan, 2019; Richmond & Baicher, 2022).

Mental Health Disparities

The landscape of mental health among neurodivergent individuals is complex, and shaped by their unique cognitive and emotional characteristics. Despite the prevalence of psychiatric diagnoses in autistic adults, there is a notable gap in interventions tailored to their specific needs (Curnow et al., 2023). Accardo et al. (2024) shed light on the elevated rates of anxiety and depression among adolescents with autism and/or ADHD, highlighting the urgent need for targeted support and interventions.

However, accessing mental health services poses significant challenges for the neurodivergent population. Sapiets and Harper (2022) delineate these barriers into three phases: recognition, identification, and support. From masking and misdiagnosis to inaccessible services and lack of standardized assessments, these obstacles hinder effective mental health support for neurodivergent individuals.

The Social Model of disability underscores the systemic factors that influence mental health outcomes for neurodivergent individuals (Cage et al., 2018). Addressing these systemic issues is crucial for creating an inclusive and supportive environment that promotes positive mental health outcomes.

In response to these challenges, Gilmore et al. (2022) propose actionable steps for mental health providers to better meet the needs of autistic adults. These include creating autism-informed environments, using thoughtful language, taking an individualized approach to treatment, leveraging strengths, and providing practical guidance for progress.

Neurodiversity-Affirming Therapy (NAT)

NAT stands as a transformative therapeutic approach tailored to empower neurodiverse individuals. This evidence-based and affirmative therapy seeks to create an environment of acceptance and understanding, emphasizing an individualized and client-centered perspective. Perspectives Center for Holistic Therapy (2023) describes that NAT adopts a strength-based methodology, aiming to identify and enhance existing strengths and skills rather than focusing on correcting or hiding atypical behaviors. The approach encourages active participation from clients, enabling self-compassion and acceptance of neurodivergent differences.

Improving Accessibility and Inclusivity

Creating environments that accommodate sensory needs and offer accessible information is crucial for enhancing overall healthcare accessibility for neurodivergent individuals. To prevent poor health outcomes for autistic people throughout their lives, there is a pressing need for a fundamental shift toward neurodivergence-affirming support. An important way to cater to neuro-sensitive needs involves creating environments that accommodate sensory needs and provide accessible information to enhance overall healthcare.

Designing Neuroinclusive Healthcare Spaces: Universal Design

Universal Design is essential in promoting neuroinclusive healthcare spaces by ensuring accessibility for individuals with diverse needs. It addresses the societal failures that create barriers for persons with disabilities by designing environments that accommodate a broad spectrum of abilities (Joint Commission on Accreditation of Healthcare Organizations, 2009). Universal Design in healthcare settings aims to foster equal participation and dismantle barriers, making spaces usable by everyone, regardless of neurodivergent conditions or other abilities.

The Seven Principles of Universal Design, established by the Center for Universal Design at North Carolina State, guide designers in creating healthcare facilities that meet diverse needs. These principles are:

- Equitable Use: The design should be useful for people with diverse abilities.
- Flexibility in Use: Accommodate a wide range of individual preferences and abilities.
- Simple and Intuitive Use: Make the design easy to understand.
- Perceptible Information: Effectively communicate necessary information to the user.
- Tolerance for Error: Minimize hazards and the adverse consequences of accidental or unintended actions.
- Low Physical Effort: Design for efficient and comfortable use with minimal fatigue.
- Size and Space for Approach and Use: Provide appropriate size and space for approach, reach, manipulation, and use, considering the user's body size, posture, or mobility.

By adhering to these principles, healthcare environments can become more inclusive and supportive of all individuals.

Care-Based Framework

McGreevy et al. (2023) propose a neuro-inclusive approach rooted in Todres et al.'s lifeworld-led care model, integrating eight dimensions of care into healthcare practice. This approach prioritizes respect, individual sovereignty, and personalized care through collaborative decision-making, fostering wellbeing from a humanistic perspective. The dimensions include insiderness/objectiveness, agency/passivity, uniqueness/homogenization, togetherness/isolation, sense-making/loss of meaning, personal journey/loss of personal journey, sense of place/dislocation, and embodiment/reductionist view of the body. These dimensions emphasize the importance of considering individuals' perspectives, promoting autonomy, recognizing uniqueness, fostering connection, facilitating sense-making, respecting personal journeys, creating a supportive environment, and addressing holistic needs.

Communication Strategies

Effective communication with non-verbal individuals in healthcare necessitates strategies like visual supports and alternative communication methods. Richmond and Baicher (2022) advocate for understanding diverse neurodivergent profiles and propose the STEP IT UP acronym for enhancing clinician-patient interactions, emphasizing simplicity, time consideration, precise language, involvement of carers, sensory awareness, and acknowledgment of individual differences. Aha Media offers additional guidance for crafting healthcare content tailored to neurodivergent audiences, including readability enhancement, distraction reduction, clear calls to action, time management aids, and provision of diverse content options. Integrating assistive communication devices and technologies further improves communication, aiding sensory management and providing alternative channels, such as chat and email, especially beneficial for individuals on the autism spectrum (Huggins, 2023; Dekker, 2020).

Care, Coordination, and Collaboration

Holistic care for neurodivergent individuals emphasizes the collaborative efforts of healthcare professionals, educators, and therapists to address their diverse needs comprehensively. This approach underscores the importance of coordinated efforts across various sectors. In this framework, educators play a critical role in understanding and accommodating the unique learning styles and needs of neurodivergent individuals. By collaborating closely with healthcare professionals and therapists, educators can create inclusive learning environments that foster understanding and support. Therapists provide specialized interventions tailored to the specific challenges faced by neurodivergent individuals, enhancing their overall wellbeing by addressing medical, psychological, and developmental aspects.

The active involvement of these networks is crucial for maintaining a continuous support system that extends beyond formal care settings into the daily lives of neurodivergent individuals. It is essential to highlight the experiences of neurodivergent individuals as they navigate to find out accessible and appropriate support, shedding light on the challenges they face within existing systems and practices (Robyns, 2023).

Robyns (2023) advocates for improved communication and collaboration among professionals across various domains. Enhanced transparency between clinicians and families regarding diagnoses, funding, and physical support is urged to create a more supportive and understanding environment for neurodivergent individuals and their families.

Neurodiverse Healthcare Professionals

The recognition of neurodivergence is expanding to include not only patients but also neurodivergent doctors and healthcare professionals, an aspect that has been significantly underrecognized. There is an increasing acknowledgment that healthcare institutions must address the needs of neurodivergent medical professionals. The exact number of neurodivergent doctors is unknown, and current studies on neurodiversity in medicine are often limited, focusing mainly on autism and using small, qualitative approaches (De Duong & Vogel, 2022).

Neurodiverse healthcare professionals face unique challenges. Moskal (2023) notes that neurodiverse doctors often camouflage their identities and behaviors to fit in, which can be exhausting and lead to negative mental health outcomes. Additionally, these individuals may struggle with understanding and adhering to doctors' instructions and engaging in social interactions. Despite these challenges, McVey (n.d.) highlights that neurodivergent doctors are valuable assets to the medical profession, possessing traits such as heightened attention to detail, high energy levels, and enhanced empathy. These doctors can challenge and dispel negative stereotypes and stigmas associated with neurodivergence, bringing informed empathy to their practice and advocating for neurodivergent patients.

De Duong and Vogel (2022) advocate for more open discussions about neurodiversity within medicine to foster peer and workplace support. This aligns with the idea that medical training should encourage introspection among physicians to facilitate the early identification of neurodivergent traits. By promoting self-awareness and recognition, the medical profession can create an environment that embraces diversity and accommodates the unique perspectives of neurodivergent individuals.

Legal and Ethical Consideration

Understanding the legal rights and protections afforded to neurodivergent individuals is crucial for providing ethical and inclusive healthcare. Healthcare professionals must prioritize staying informed about the legal frameworks specific to their jurisdiction to ensure compliance and protect the rights and wellbeing of neurodivergent individuals. This creates a healthcare environment rooted in legality, ethics, and respect for all involved.

In academia and research, addressing historical biases and giving due representation to neurodivergent experiences is essential. Bernard et al. (2023) emphasize the importance of actively involving neurodivergent individuals in research and healthcare practices to ensure their firsthand perspectives are recognized. Researchers should strive for methodologies that incorporate neurodivergent perspectives to foster inclusivity.

When introducing interventions for neurodivergent individuals, a bioethical analysis should prioritize maximizing benefits and minimizing harm. Vanaken (2022) suggests that such analysis strengthens the neurodiversity movement and fosters collaborative alliances between stakeholders and healthcare professionals.

Ethical considerations during therapy are paramount. Therapists should adhere to the code of ethics set forth by organizations like the American Counseling Association (ACA) (ACA, 2014). Irvine (2019) highlights ethical practices such as avoiding harm, advocating for the rights and wellbeing of neurodivergent individuals, updating knowledge about neurodiversity, refraining from discriminatory practices, and obtaining informed consent. Empowering neurodivergent individuals in decision-making processes regarding their therapeutic journey is crucial.

Neurodiversity in Medical Education

Including neurodiversity in medical education is crucial for fostering a deeper understanding among future healthcare professionals. Practical training approaches empower healthcare professionals to be sensitive and responsive to neurodivergent patients' needs. Simpson (2021) proposed a manualized training program aimed at creating awareness, knowledge, and skills among healthcare professionals when working with neurodivergent individuals. This program addresses biases, provides information about the neurodivergent community, and encourages actionable steps toward effective collaboration. Such training programs contribute to a more inclusive and supportive environment for neurodivergent individuals in healthcare settings.

Educational initiatives aimed at fostering empathy also play a vital role in medical education. Medical students often lack an understanding of the lived experiences of patients due to a focus on the medical model of disability. Pathmathasan (2021) developed a disability curriculum to address this gap, focusing on care ethics, combining medical and social models of disability, and incorporating intersectionality. This patient-centric approach seeks to enhance medical education by promoting a more inclusive and empathetic understanding of disability.

Summary

This paper comprehensively explores the concept of neurodiversity, tracing its historical development and evolution within the social and medical spheres. It discusses neurodiversity's alignment with the social model of disability and examines its intersectionality with various social factors. Categorizing neurodivergent conditions into four subtypes, the paper underscores the significance of recognizing and embracing neurodiversity. Addressing challenges in healthcare for neurodivergent individuals, including stereotypes, misdiagnosis, and communication barriers, it also explores strategies for improving accessibility and inclusivity in healthcare settings. Furthermore, the paper emphasizes the importance of care, coordination, and collaboration in providing holistic support for neurodivergent individuals and discusses the inclusion of neurodiverse healthcare professionals. Legal and ethical considerations are also examined, alongside the integration of neurodiversity into medical education, highlighting the importance of fostering understanding and empathy among future healthcare professionals.

References

Accardo, A. L., Pontes, N. M. H., & Pontes, M. C. F. (2024). Heightened anxiety and depression among autistic adolescents with ADHD: Findings from the national survey of children's health 2016–2019. *Journal of Autism and Developmental Disorders*, *54*(2), 563–576. https://doi.org/10.1007/s10803-022-05803-9

Aha Media. *How to create healthcare content for a neurodivergent audience*. Aha Media Group. https://ahamediagroup.com/blog/how-create-healthcare-content-neurodivergent-audience/

American Counseling Association. (2014). *Code of Ethics. As approved by the ACA Governing Council.*

Bayeh, R. (2022). Neurodiversity, intersectionality and distress: A quantitative survey on the experiences of University students (Doctoral dissertation, Concordia University).

Bernard, L., Fox, S., Kulason, K., et al. (2023). Not your "typical" research: Inclusion ethics in neurodiversity scholarship. *Industrial and Organizational Psychology*, *16*(1), 50–54. https://doi.org/10.1017/iop.2022.100

Broder-Fingert, S., & Abate, D. (2022, April 11). *Embracing neurodiversity in our health systems*. American Academy of Pediatrics. Retrieved from https://www.aap.org/en/news-room/aap-voices/embracing-neurodiversity-in-our-health-systems/

Cage, E., Di Monaco, J., & Newell, V. (2018). Experiences of autism acceptance and mental health in autistic adults. *Journal of Autism and Developmental Disorders*, *48*, 473–484.

Curnow, E., Rutherford, M., Maciver, D., Johnston, L., Prior, S., Boilson, M., Shah, P., Jenkins, N., & Meff, T. (2023). Mental health in autistic adults: A rapid review of prevalence of psychiatric disorders and umbrella review of the effectiveness of interventions within a neurodiversity informed perspective. *PLoS One*, *18*(7), e0288275. https://doi.org/10.1371/journal.pone.0288275

De Duong, D., & Vogel, L. (2022, July 18). Untapped potential: Embracing neurodiversity in medicine. *CMAJ*, 194, E951–E952. https://doi.org/10.1503/cmaj.1096006

Dekker, M. (2020). From exclusion to acceptance: Independent living on the autistic spectrum. *Autistic Community and the Neurodiversity Movement*, 41–49.

Doyle, N. (2020). Neurodiversity at work: A biopsychosocial model and the impact on working adults. *British Medical Bulletin*, *135*(1), 108. https://doi.org/10.1093/bmb/ldaa021

Dwyer, P. (2022). The neurodiversity approach (es): What are they and what do they mean for researchers?. *Human Development*, *66*(2), 73–92. https://doi.org/10.1159/000523723

Ford-Jones, P. C. (2015). Misdiagnosis of attention deficit hyperactivity disorder: 'Normal behaviour' and relative maturity. *Paediatrics & Child Health*, *20*(4), 200–202.

Gilmore, D., Longo, A., Krantz, M., Radford, D., & Hand, B. N. (2022). Five ways providers can improve mental healthcare for autistic adults: A review of mental healthcare use, barriers to care, and evidence-based recommendations. *Current Psychiatry Reports*, *24*(10), 565–571. https://doi.org/10.1007/s11920-022-01362-z

Goldberg, H. (2023). Unraveling neurodiversity: Insights from neuroscientific perspectives. *Encyclopedia*, *3*(3), 972–980.

Granger, C., Hameed, Z., & Kelly, R. (2023). Neurodivergence and the healthcare workforce: A hidden facet within equality, diversity and inclusion? *BMJ Leader*, 7(Suppl 2).

Huggins, G. (2023, May 15). Neurodiversity and assisted technology. The Society of Occupational Medicine. Retrieved from https://www.som.org.uk/neurodiversity-and-assisted-technology#:~:text=For%20neurodivergent%20individuals%2C%20this%20may,executive%20functioning%2C%20or%20other%20challenges.

Hull, L., & Mandy, W. (2017). Protective effect or missed diagnosis? Females with autism spectrum disorder. *Future Neurology*, *12*(3), 159–169.

Irvine, K. (2019). Facing neurotypical normativity: An ethical call for therapeutic sensitivity to neurodiversity. *Expressive Therapies Capstone Theses*. 160. Retrieved from https://digitalcommons.lesley.edu/expressive_theses/160

Joint Commission on Accreditation of Healthcare Organizations. (2009, January). *Environment of Care® News*, *12*(1).

Leadbitter, K., Buckle, K. L., Ellis, C., & Dekker, M. (2021). Autistic self-advocacy and the neurodiversity movement: Implications for autism early intervention research and practice. *Frontiers in Psychology*, *12*, 782.

McGreevy, E., Quinn, A., Law, R., Botha, M., Evans, M., Rose, K., ... Pavlopoulou, G. (2023, November 2). An experience-sensitive approach to care with and for autistic children and young people in clinical services. https://doi.org/10.31219/osf.io/r24wk

McVey, C. (n.d.). *Neurodiversity in doctors and its impact on their profession*. Royal College of Psychiatrists.

Morgan, H. (2019). Connections between sensory sensitivities in autism; the importance of sensory friendly environments for accessibility and increased quality of life for the neurodivergent autistic minority. *PSU McNair Scholars Online Journal*, *13*(1), Article 11. https://doi.org/10.15760/mcnair.2019.13.1.11

Moskal, E. (2023, May 3). What does it mean to be neurodiverse in medicine? *Scope Blog*. Retrieved from https://scopeblog.stanford.edu/2023/05/03/what-does-it-mean-to-be-neurodiverse-in-medicine/

Nicolaidis, C., Raymaker, D. M., Ashkenazy, E., McDonald, K. E., Dern, S., Baggs, A. E., ... & Boisclair, W. C. (2015). "Respect the way I need to communicate with you": Healthcare experiences of adults on the autism spectrum. *Autism*, *19*(7), 824–831.

Pathmathasan, C. (2021). Disability in medical education & training: A disability-focused medical curriculum (Doctoral dissertation, Northeast Ohio Medical University).

Perspectives Center for Holistic Therapy. (2023). *Neurodiversity affirming therapy*. Perspectives Center for Holistic Therapy. Retrieved from https://www.perspectivesholistictherapy.com/neurodiversity-affirming

Richmond, J., & Baicher, V. (2022). Communicating with neurodivergent patients. Don't Forget the Bubbles. https://doi.org/10.31440/DFTB.48007

Robyns, K. L. (2023). Experiences of families and professionals living/interacting with neurodivergent children while navigating the policy contexts of health, education and social services: The fight for accessible and suitable support (Doctoral dissertation, The University of Waikato).

Rojas, K. (2024). Neurodiversity: Understanding, Embracing, and Advancing the Concept. Journal of Multiple Sclerosis, 11(4), 001–002. https://www.iomcworld.org/open-access/neurodiversity-understanding-embracing-and-advancing-the-concept.pdf

Sapiets, S., & Harper, G. (2022, May 24). Neurodivergence and mental health: How do we embrace complexity? Emerging Minds Open Lab. University of Kent/Embracing Complexity/Autistica.

Simpson, Allison N., "Ability Status, Self-Advocacy, and Individuals with Neurodevelopmental Disabilities: Neurodiversity-Informed Training for Professionals and Caregivers" (2021). Psychology Doctoral Specialization Projects. 14. https://encompass.eku.edu/psych_doctorals/14

Strand, L. R. (2017). Charting Relations between Intersectionality Theory and the Neurodiversity Paradigm. *Disability Studies Quarterly*, *37*(2). https://doi.org/10.18061/dsq.v37i2.5374

Todres, L., Galvin, K. T., & Holloway, I. (2009) The humanization of healthcare: A value framework for qualitative research. *International Journal of Qualitative Studies on Health and Wellbeing*, *4*(2), 68–77. https://doi.org/10.1080/17482620802646204

Udonsi, P. (2022) Young, gifted and black: The intersectionality of race, intellectual disability and neurodivergence. *Critical and Radical Social Work*, *10*(2), 226–241. https://doi.org/10.1332/204986021X16530492120870

UPIAS. (1976). *Fundamental principles of disability*. Union of the Physically Impaired Against Segregation.

Vanaken, G. J. (2022). Cripping vulnerability: A disability bioethics approach to the case of early autism interventions. *Tijdschrift voor Genderstudies*, *25*(1), 19–40.

Index

Note: Page numbers in *italics* refer to figures.